GUNSLINGER
SPAWN
VOLUME 5

TODD MCFARLANE
DEXTER SOY
CARLO BARBERI
IVAN NUNES

GUNSLINGER

SPAWN

VOLUME 5

TODD McFARLANE

SCRIPT / PLOT

DEXTER SOY

ISSUES 25-28

CARLO BARBERI

ISSUES 29-30

ART

THOMAS HEALY	EDITOR-IN-CHIEF
YVETTE ARTEAGA	PUBLISHING COORDINATOR
RYAN KEIZER	PRODUCTION ARTIST
ZABRIEL KENNEDY	PRODUCTION ARTIST
IMANI DAVIS	INTERN
ERIC STEPHENSON	PUBLISHER FOR IMAGE COMICS

SPAWN CREATED BY TODD McFARLANE

Gunslinger Spawn Volume 5. November 2024. First Printing. Published by Image Comics, Inc. Office of publication: PO BOX 14457, Portland, OR 97293 USA. Originally published in single issue format as Gunslinger Spawn issues #25-30. PRINTED IN CANADA. ISBN: 978-1-5343-8264-0.

image

TODD McFARLANE PRODUCTIONS

McFARLANE.COM

IVAN NUNES
COLORIST

TOM ORZECHOWSKI
LETTERER

RAYMOND GAY
COLLECTED EDITION COVER

DAN PANOSIAN
ZÉ CARLOS
FEDERICO SABBATINI
PAUL RENAUD
VON RANDAL
MARCO FAILLA
KEVIN KEANE
GABRIEL GOMEZ
MARCIAL TOLEDANO
RAYMOND GAY
THADDEUS ROBECK
JAVIER FERNANDEZ
COVER ARTISTS

MARTINA FARI
ROBERT NUGENT
MARCELLO IOZZOLI
FCO PLASCENCIA
COVER COLORISTS

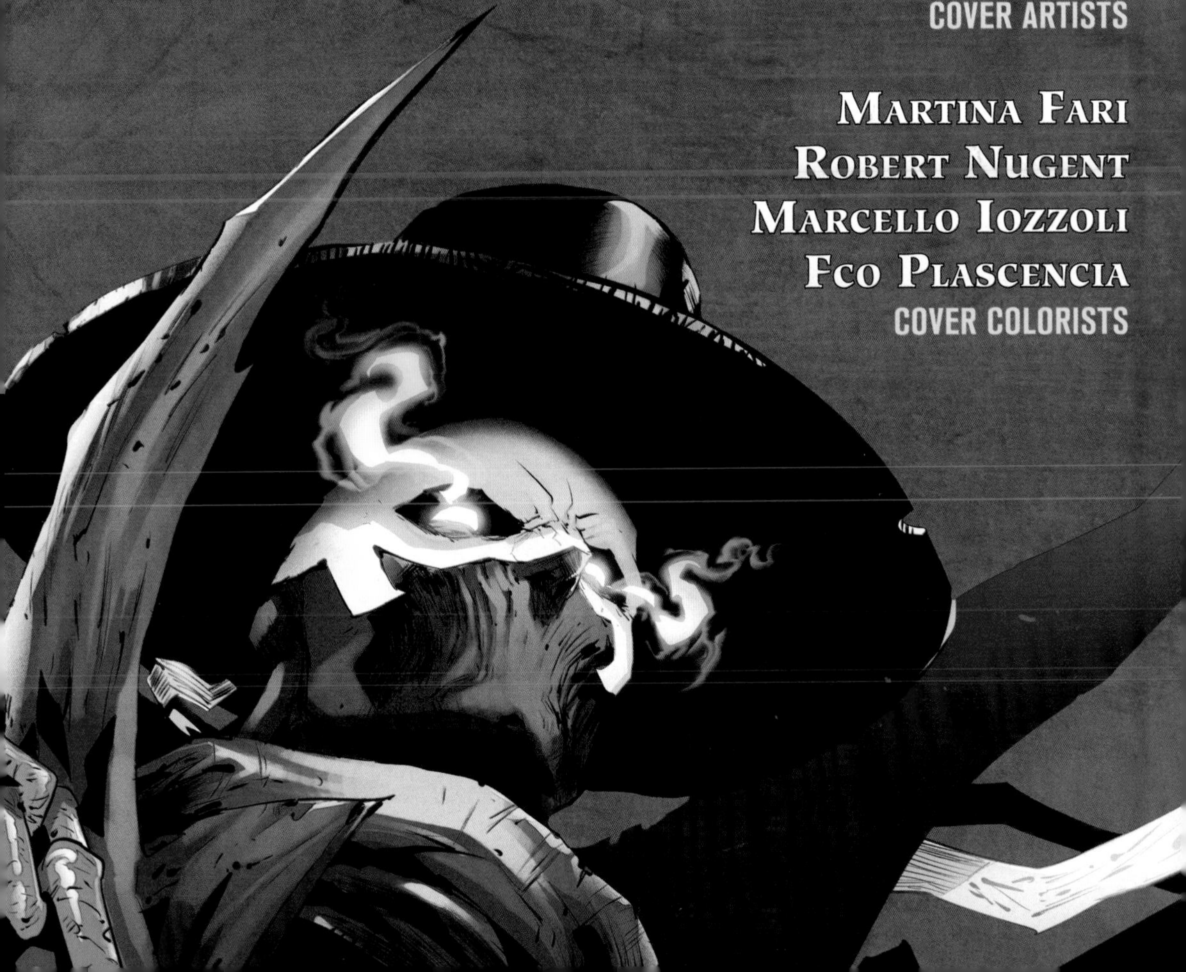

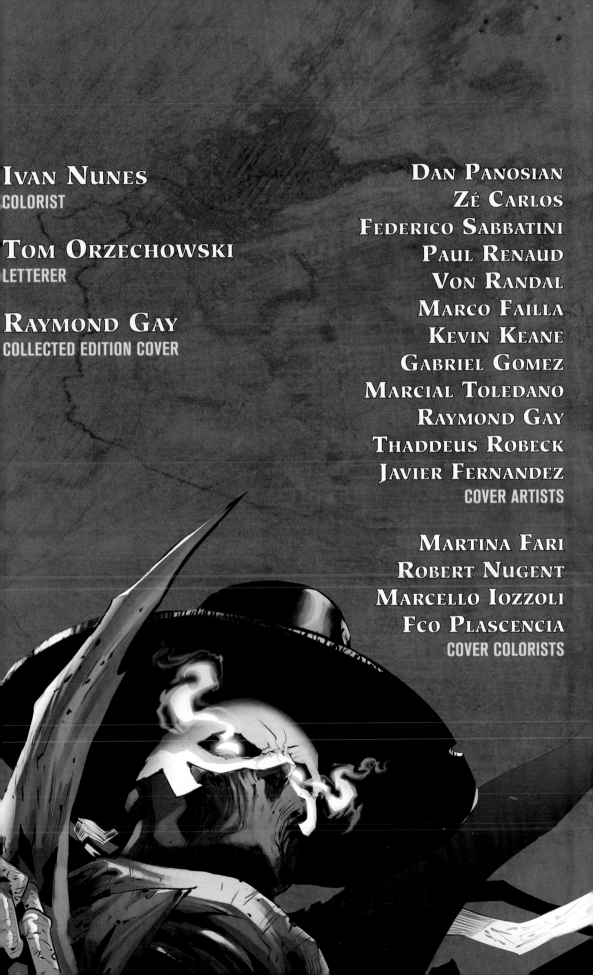

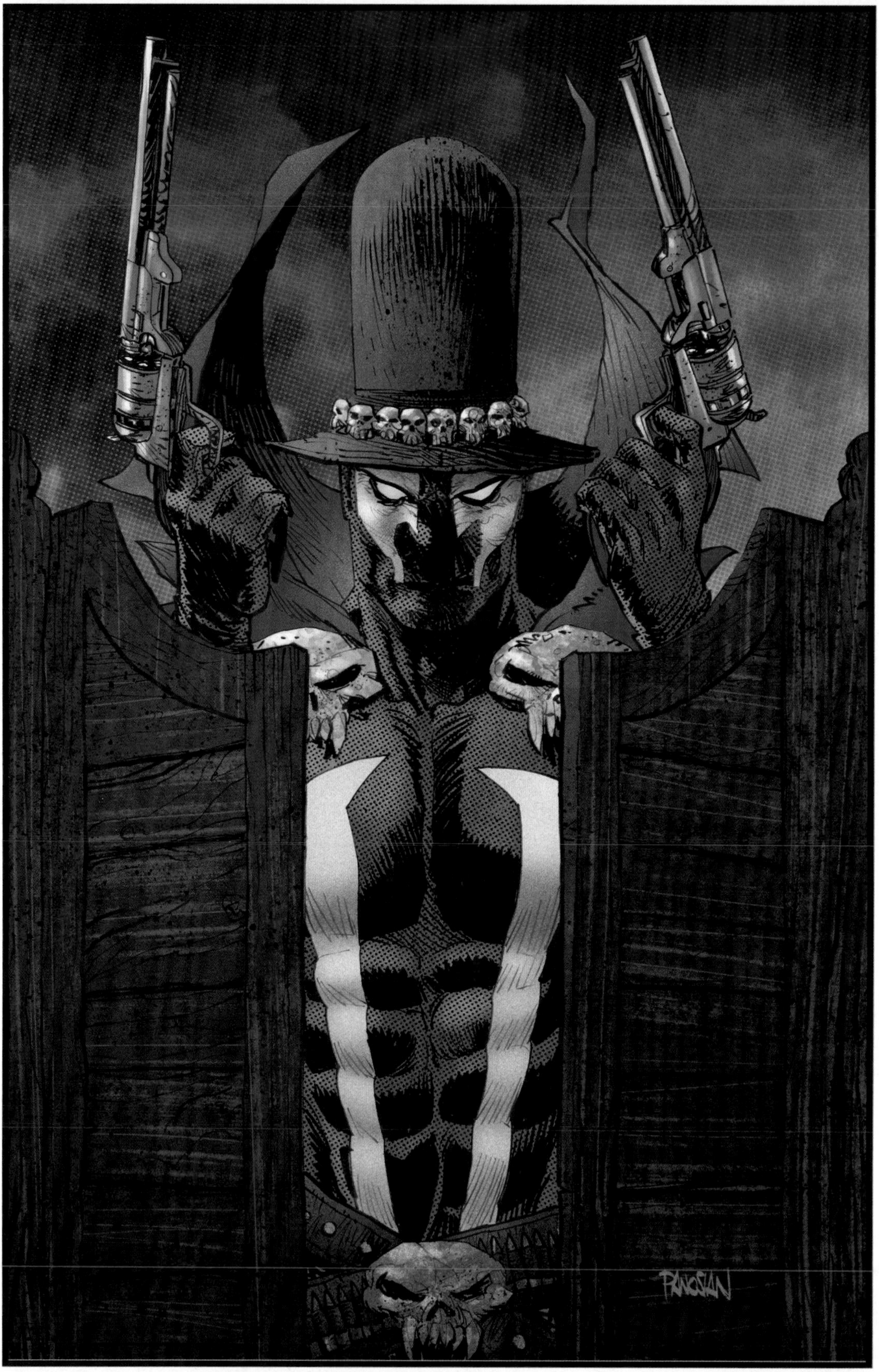
PANOSIAN
GUNSLINGER SPAWN #25 COVER 'A' BY DAN PANOSIAN

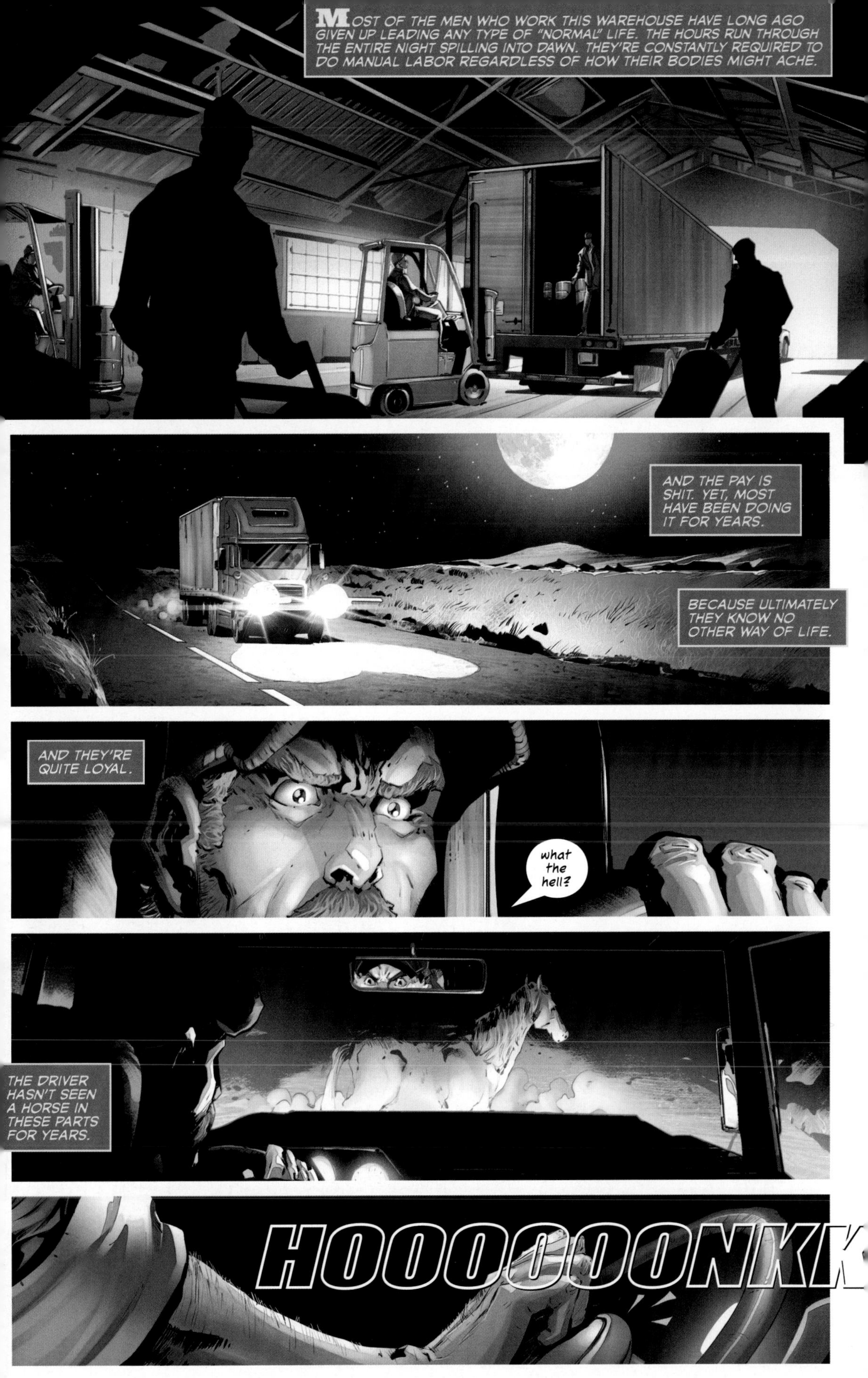
MOST OF THE MEN WHO WORK THIS WAREHOUSE HAVE LONG AGO GIVEN UP LEADING ANY TYPE OF "NORMAL" LIFE. THE HOURS RUN THROUGH THE ENTIRE NIGHT SPILLING INTO DAWN. THEY'RE CONSTANTLY REQUIRED TO DO MANUAL LABOR REGARDLESS OF HOW THEIR BODIES MIGHT ACHE.
AND THE PAY IS SHIT. YET, MOST HAVE BEEN DOING IT FOR YEARS.
BECAUSE ULTIMATELY THEY KNOW NO OTHER WAY OF LIFE.
AND THEY'RE QUITE LOYAL.
what the hell?
THE DRIVER HASN'T SEEN A HORSE IN THESE PARTS FOR YEARS.
HOOOOOOONKK

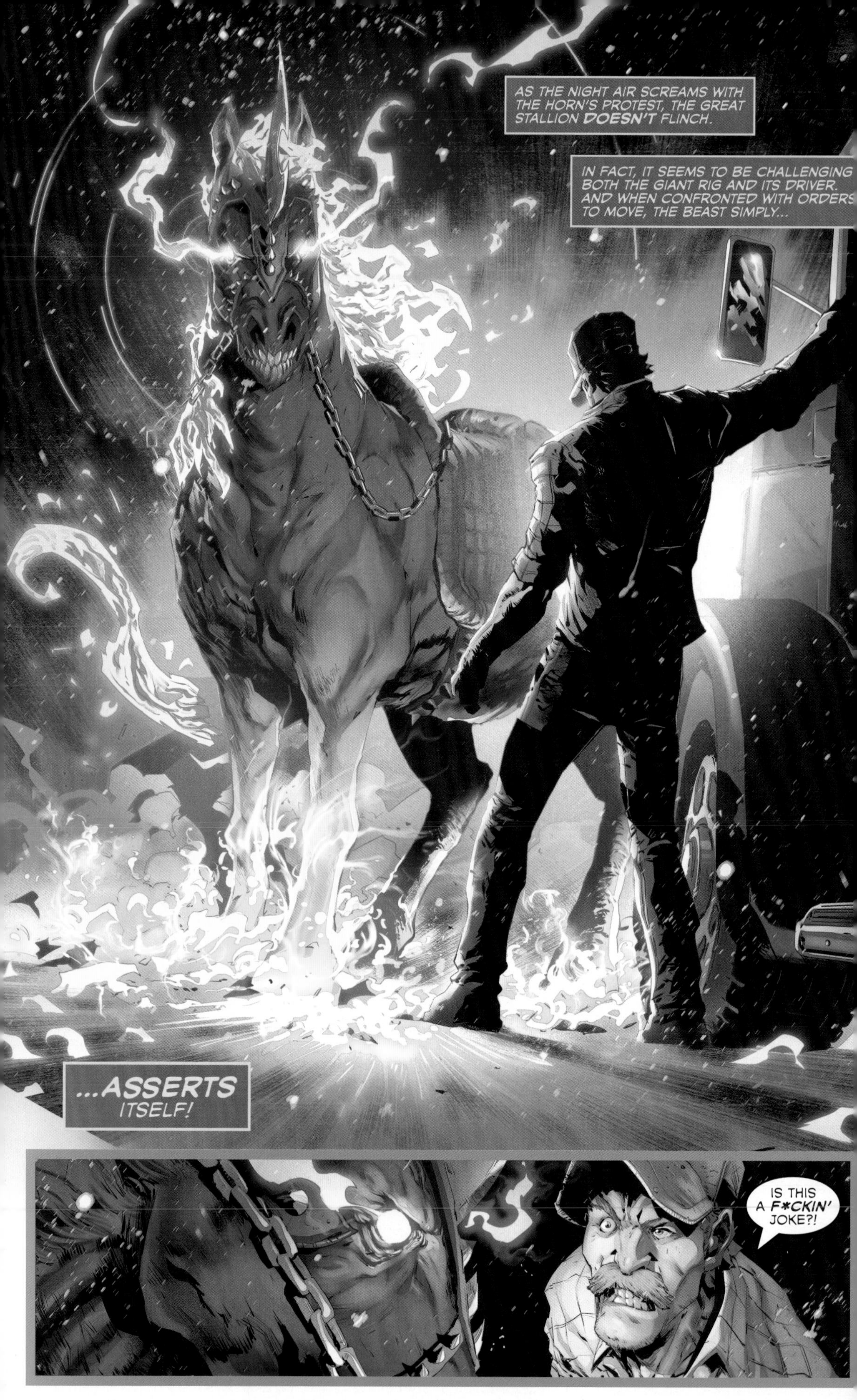
AS THE NIGHT AIR SCREAMS WITH THE HORN'S PROTEST, THE GREAT STALLION DOESN'T FLINCH.
IN FACT, IT SEEMS TO BE CHALLENGING BOTH THE GIANT RIG AND ITS DRIVER. AND WHEN CONFRONTED WITH ORDERS TO MOVE, THE BEAST SIMPLY...
...ASSERTS ITSELF!
IS THIS A F*CKIN' JOKE?!

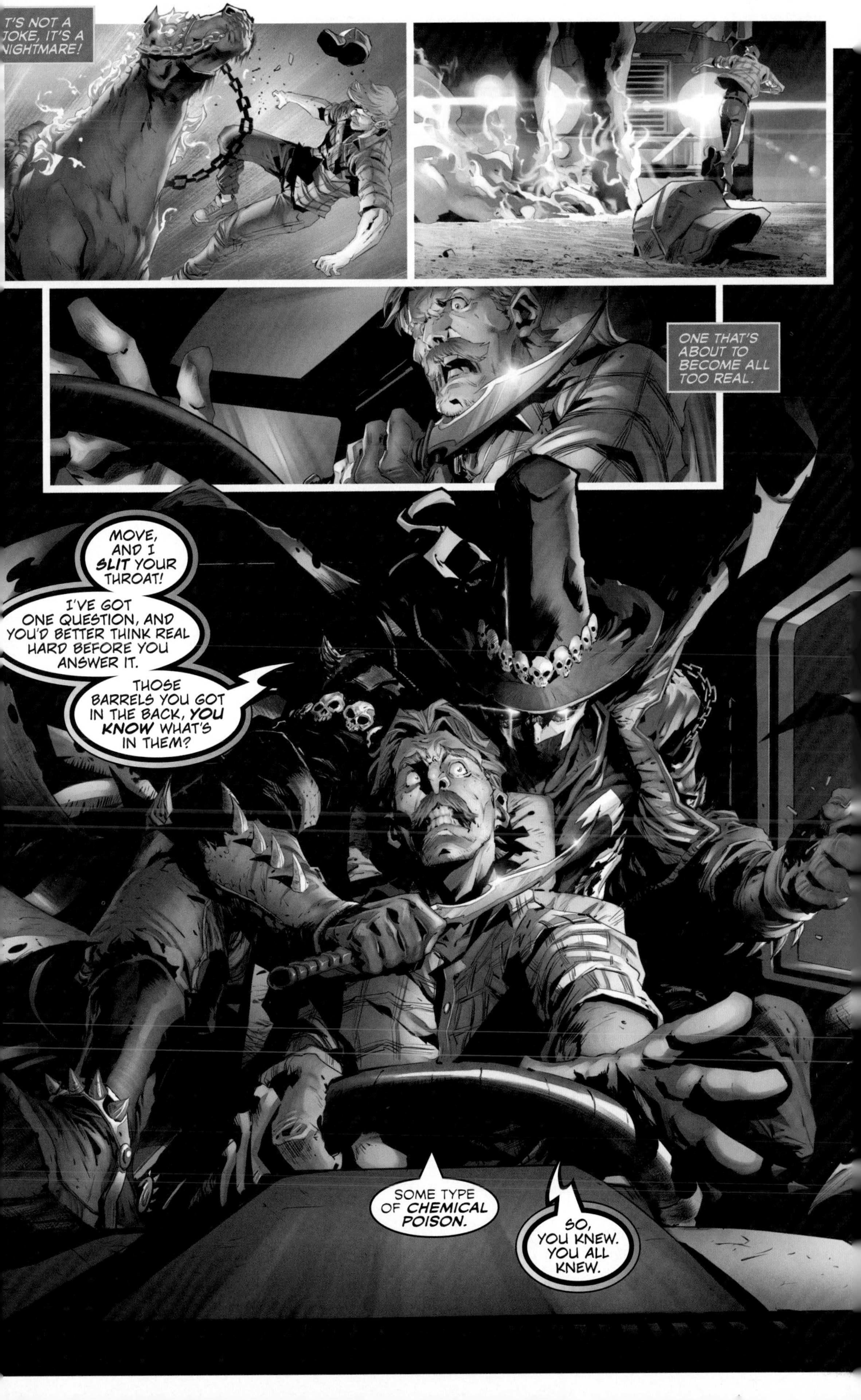
T'S NOT A JOKE, IT'S A NIGHTMARE!
ONE THAT'S ABOUT TO BECOME ALL TOO REAL.
MOVE, AND I SLIT YOUR THROAT!
I'VE GOT ONE QUESTION, AND YOU'D BETTER THINK REAL HARD BEFORE YOU ANSWER IT.
THOSE BARRELS YOU GOT IN THE BACK, YOU KNOW WHAT'S IN THEM?
SOME TYPE OF CHEMICAL POISON.
SO, YOU KNEW. YOU ALL KNEW.

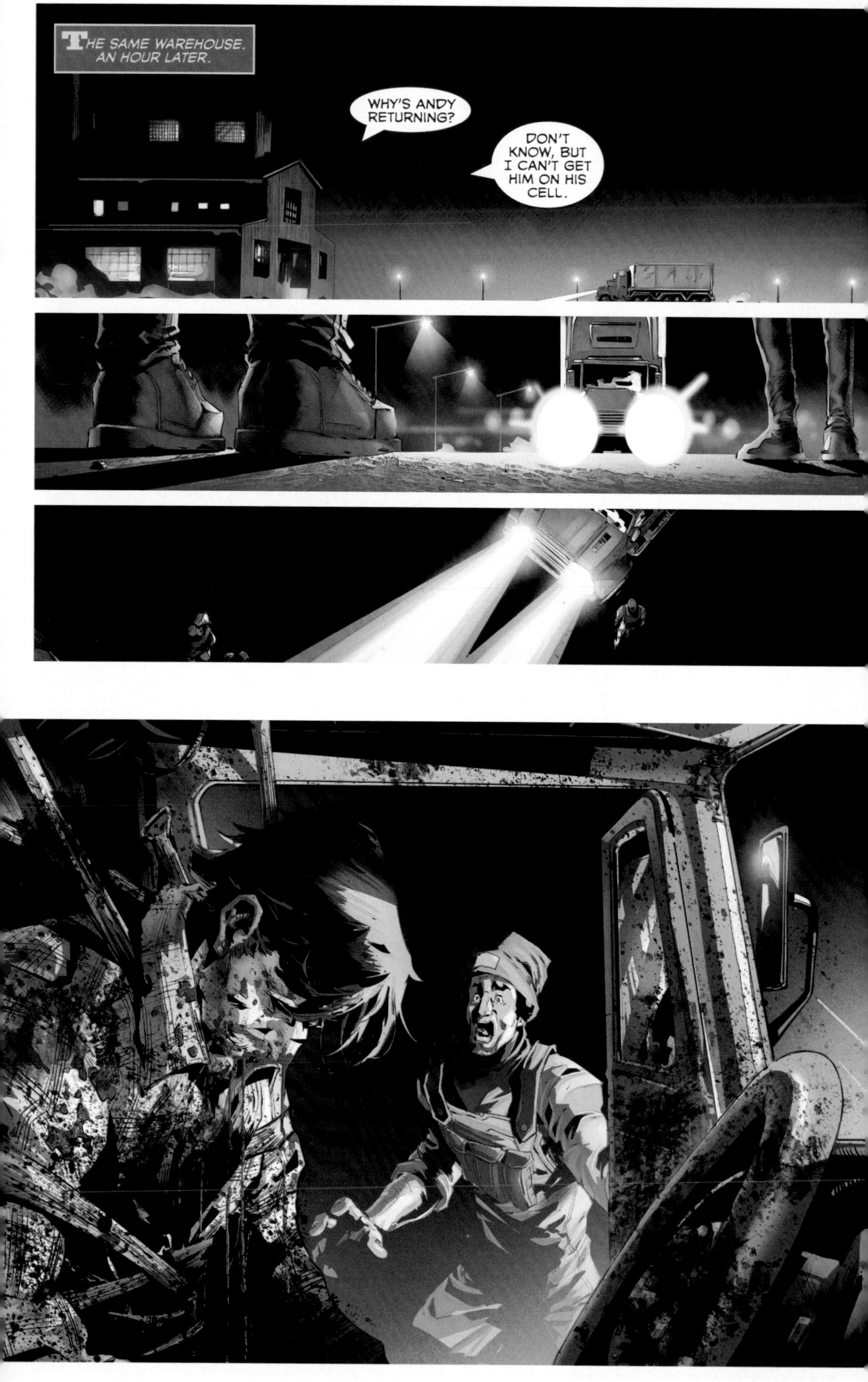
THE SAME WAREHOUSE. AN HOUR LATER.
WHY'S ANDY RETURNING?
DON'T KNOW, BUT I CAN'T GET HIM ON HIS CELL.

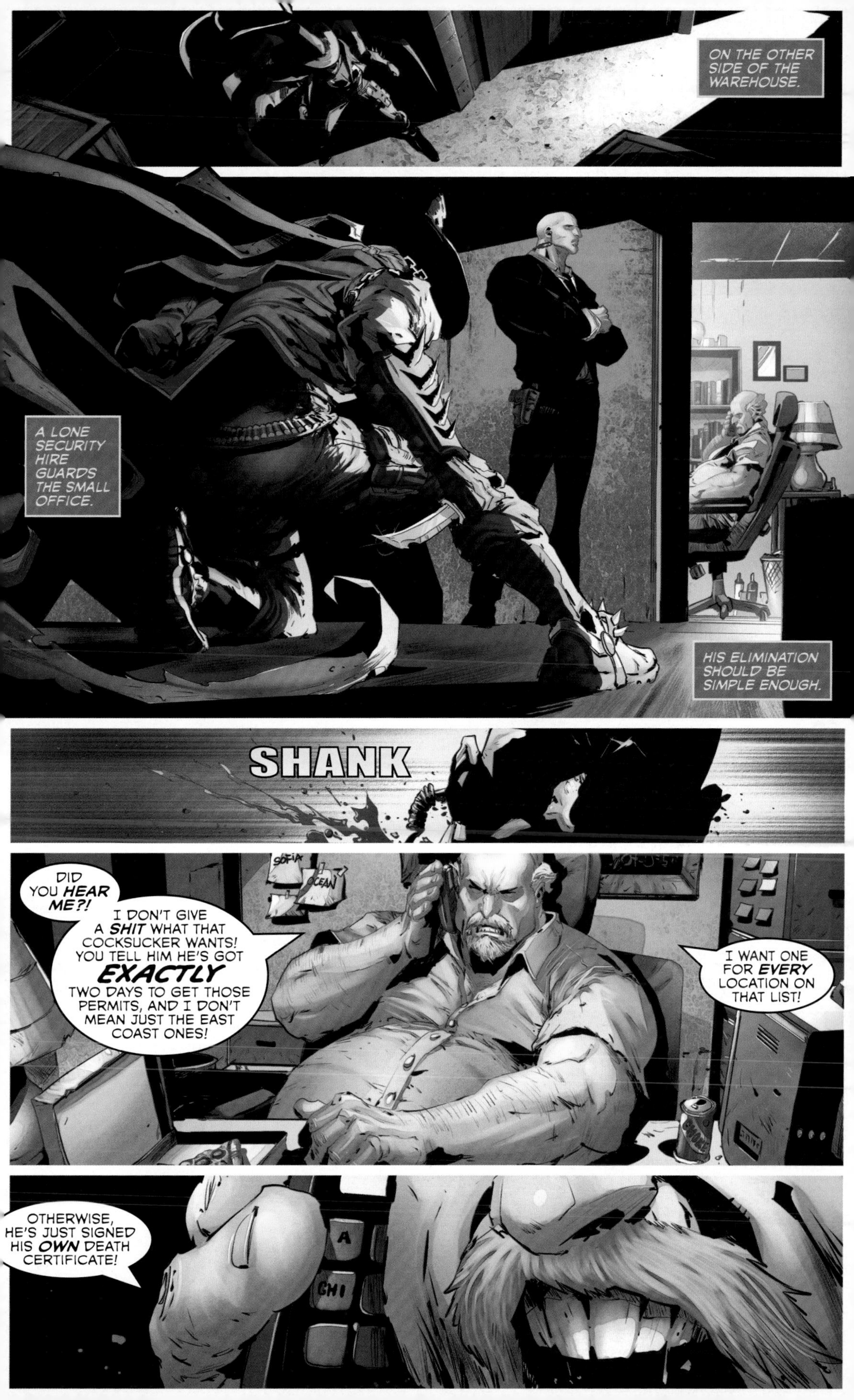
ON THE OTHER SIDE OF THE WAREHOUSE.
A LONE SECURITY HIRE GUARDS THE SMALL OFFICE.
HIS ELIMINATION SHOULD BE SIMPLE ENOUGH.
SHANK
DID YOU HEAR ME?!
I DON'T GIVE A SHIT WHAT THAT COCKSUCKER WANTS! YOU TELL HIM HE'S GOT EXACTLY TWO DAYS TO GET THOSE PERMITS, AND I DON'T MEAN JUST THE EAST COAST ONES!
I WANT ONE FOR EVERY LOCATION ON THAT LIST!
OTHERWISE, HE'S JUST SIGNED HIS OWN DEATH CERTIFICATE!

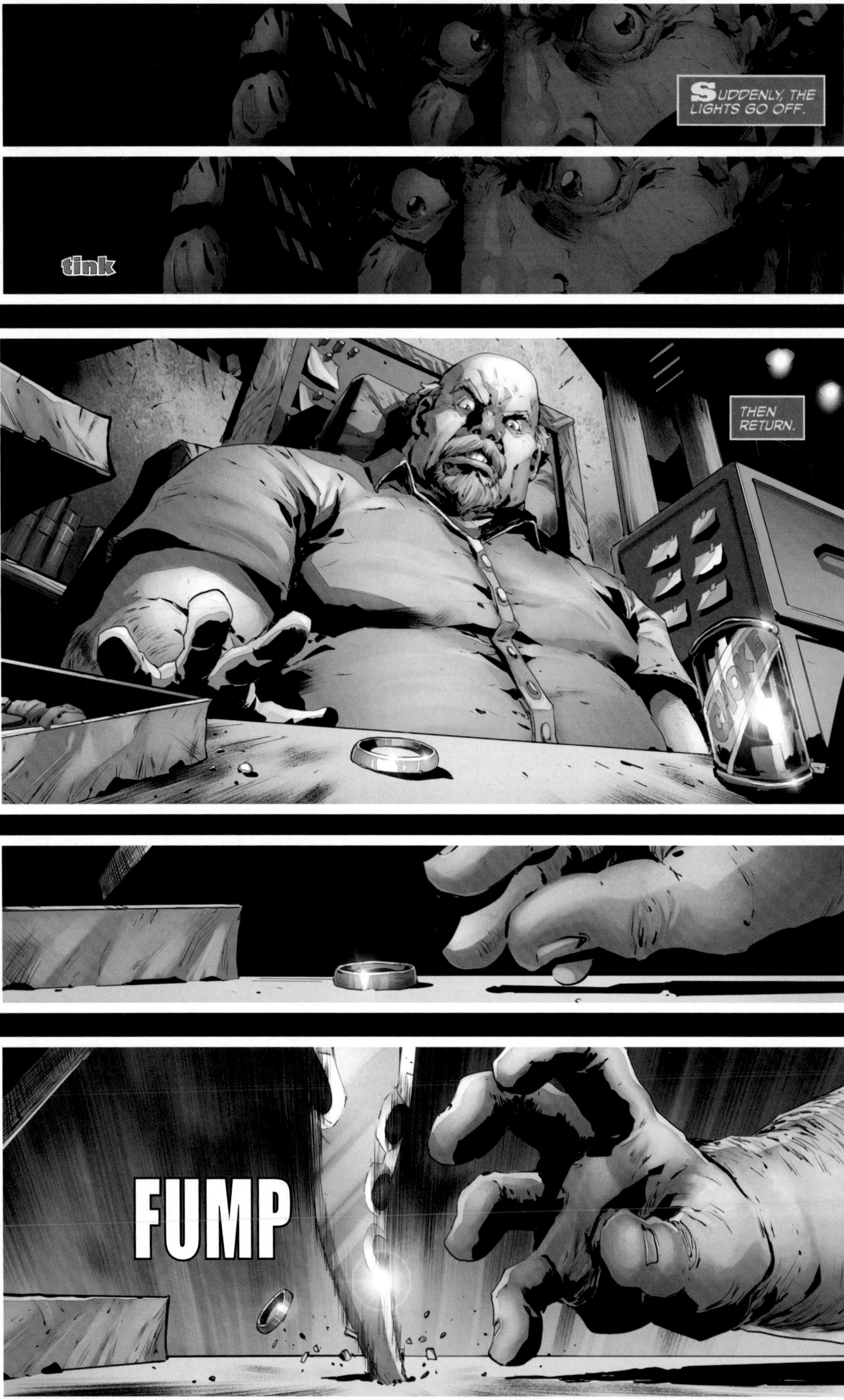
SUDDENLY, THE LIGHTS GO OFF.
tink
THEN RETURN.
FUMP

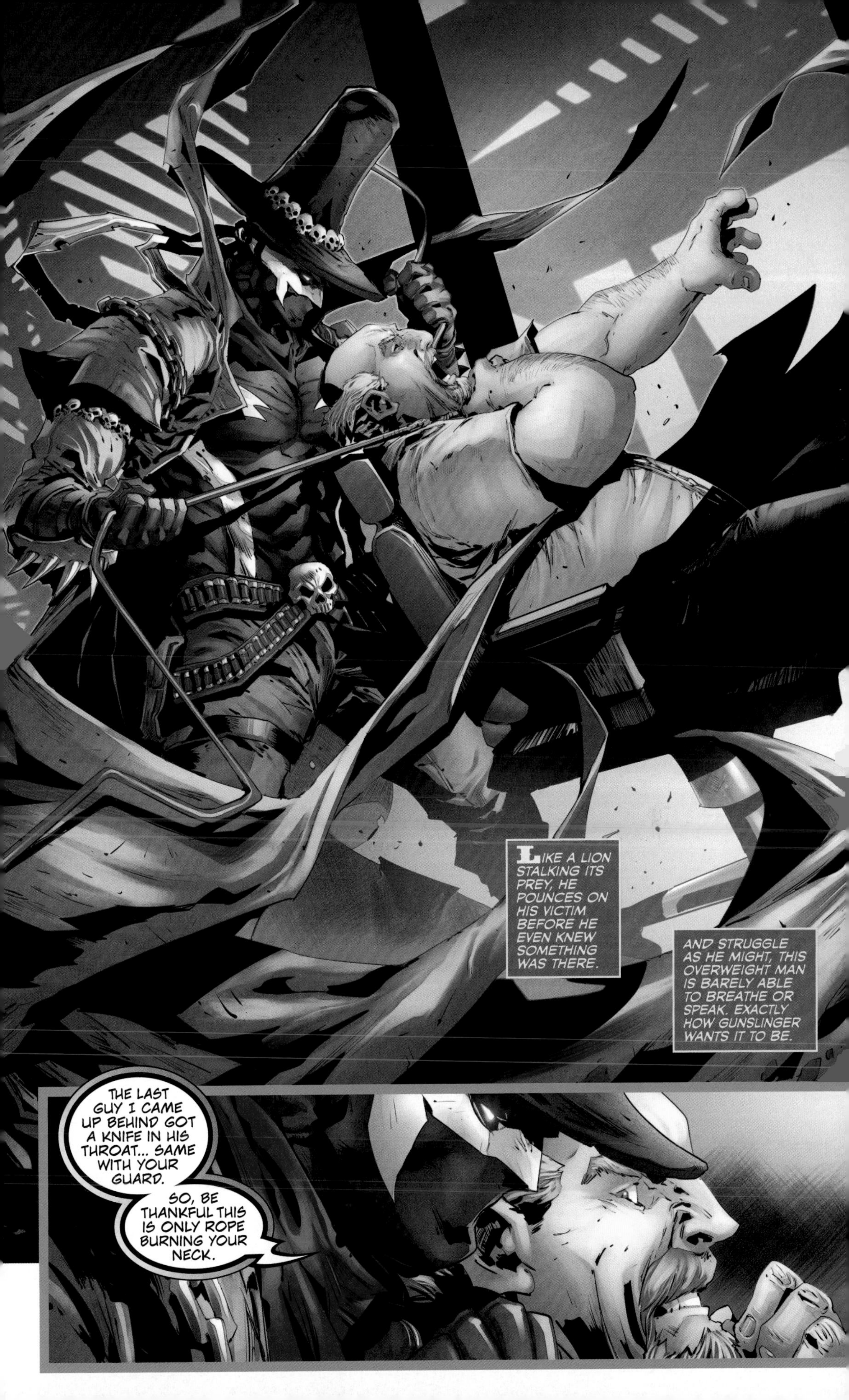
LIKE A LION STALKING ITS PREY, HE POUNCES ON HIS VICTIM BEFORE HE EVEN KNEW SOMETHING WAS THERE.
AND STRUGGLE AS HE MIGHT, THIS OVERWEIGHT MAN IS BARELY ABLE TO BREATHE OR SPEAK. EXACTLY HOW GUNSLINGER WANTS IT TO BE.
THE LAST GUY I CAME UP BEHIND GOT A KNIFE IN HIS THROAT... SAME WITH YOUR GUARD.
SO, BE THANKFUL THIS IS ONLY ROPE BURNING YOUR NECK.

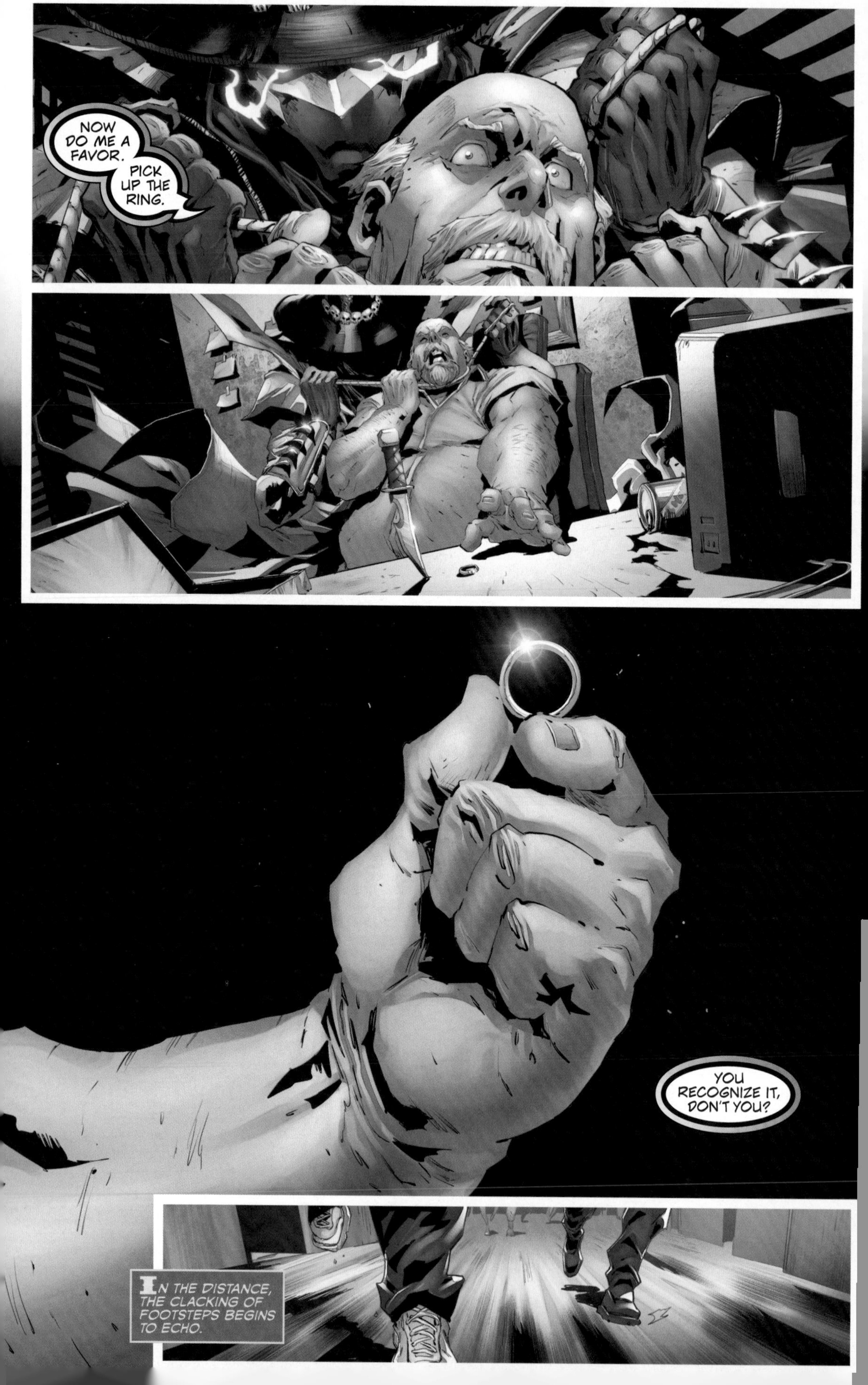
NOW DO ME A FAVOR.
PICK UP THE RING.
YOU RECOGNIZE IT, DON'T YOU?
IN THE DISTANCE, THE CLACKING OF FOOTSTEPS BEGINS TO ECHO.

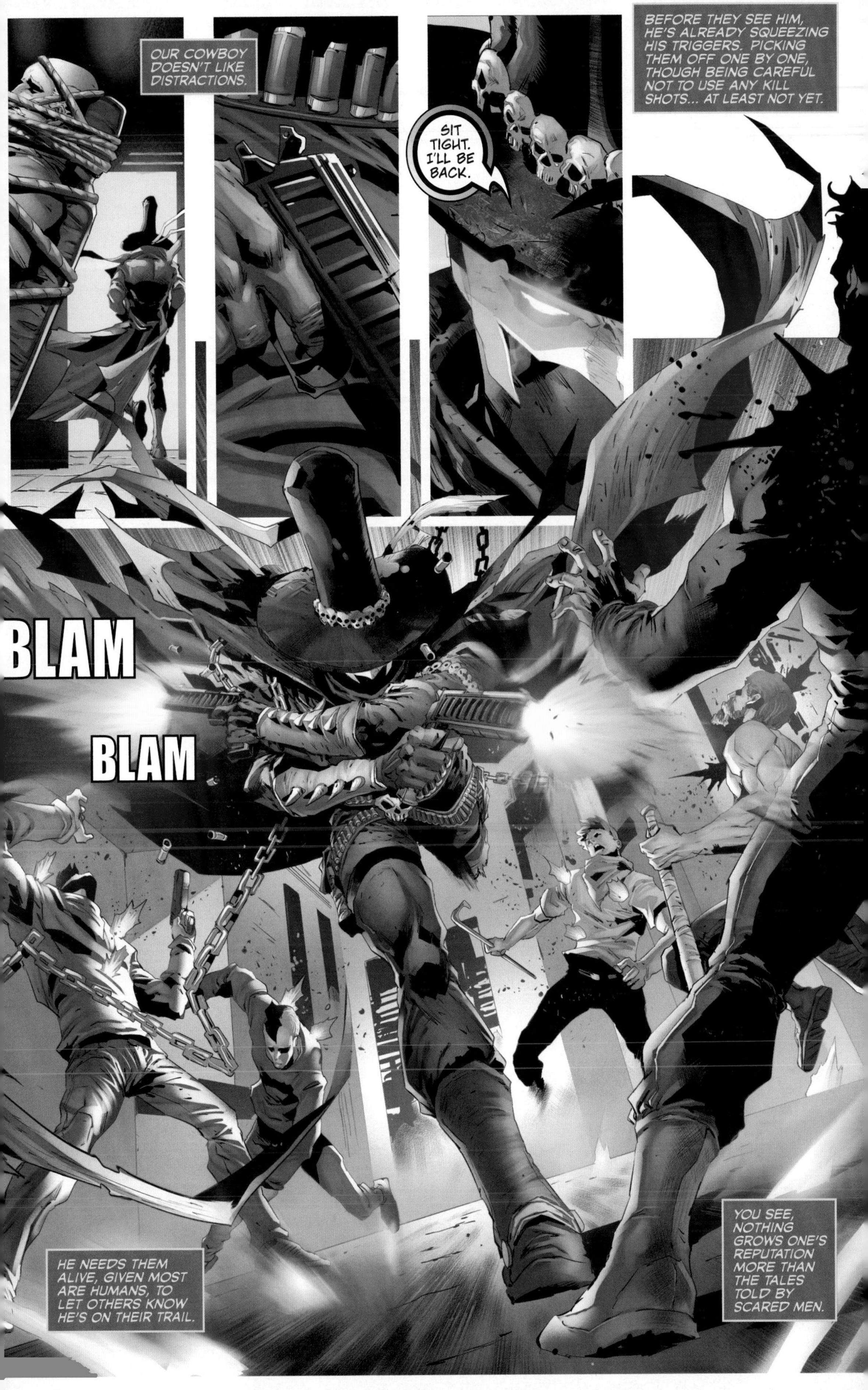
OUR COWBOY DOESN'T LIKE DISTRACTIONS.
SIT TIGHT. I'LL BE BACK.
BEFORE THEY SEE HIM, HE'S ALREADY SQUEEZING HIS TRIGGERS. PICKING THEM OFF ONE BY ONE, THOUGH BEING CAREFUL NOT TO USE ANY KILL SHOTS... AT LEAST NOT YET.
BLAM
BLAM
HE NEEDS THEM ALIVE, GIVEN MOST ARE HUMANS, TO LET OTHERS KNOW HE'S ON THEIR TRAIL.
YOU SEE, NOTHING GROWS ONE'S REPUTATION MORE THAN THE TALES TOLD BY SCARED MEN.

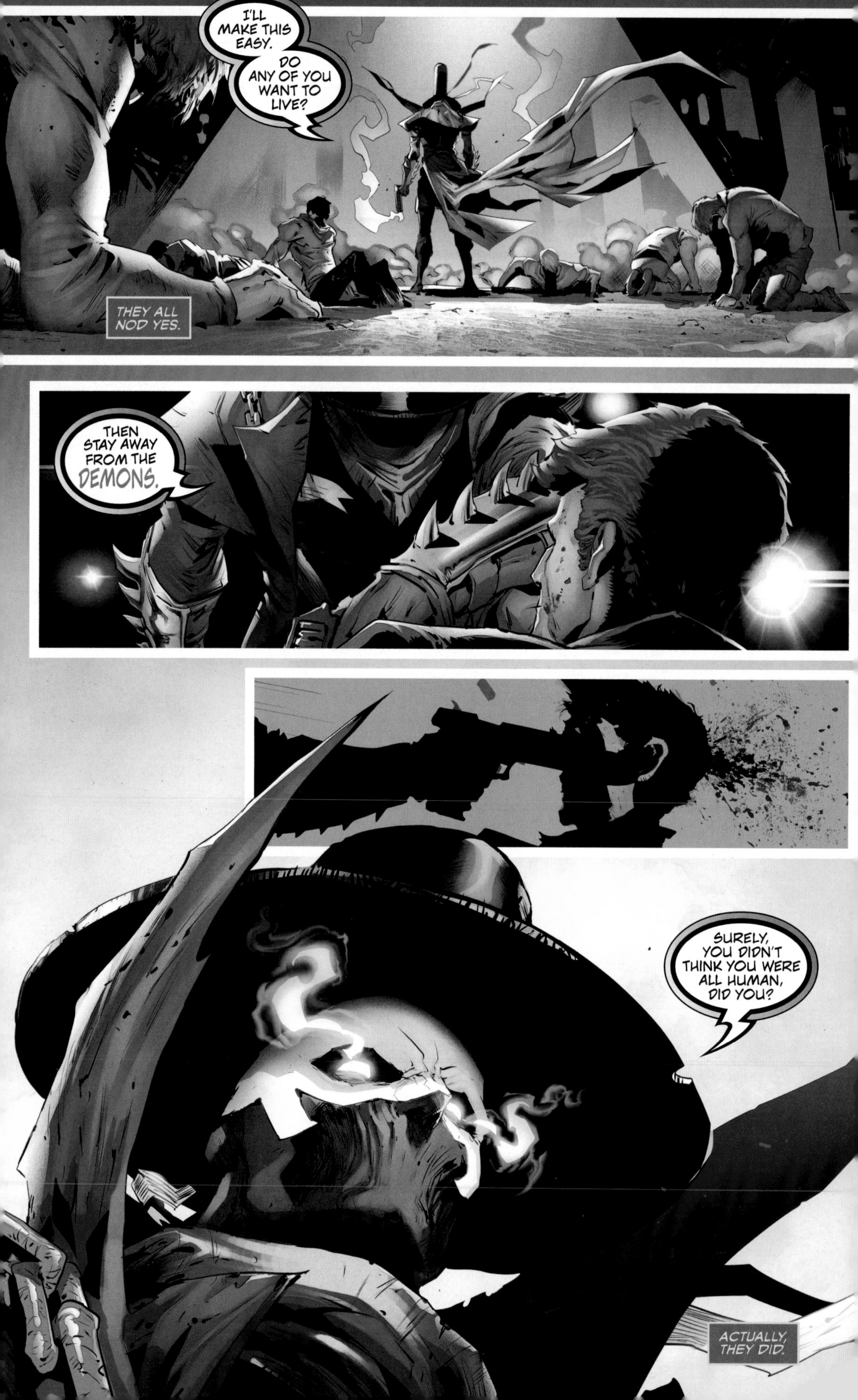
I'LL MAKE THIS EASY.
DO ANY OF YOU WANT TO LIVE?
THEY ALL NOD YES.
THEN STAY AWAY FROM THE DEMONS.
SURELY, YOU DIDN'T THINK YOU WERE ALL HUMAN, DID YOU?
ACTUALLY, THEY DID.

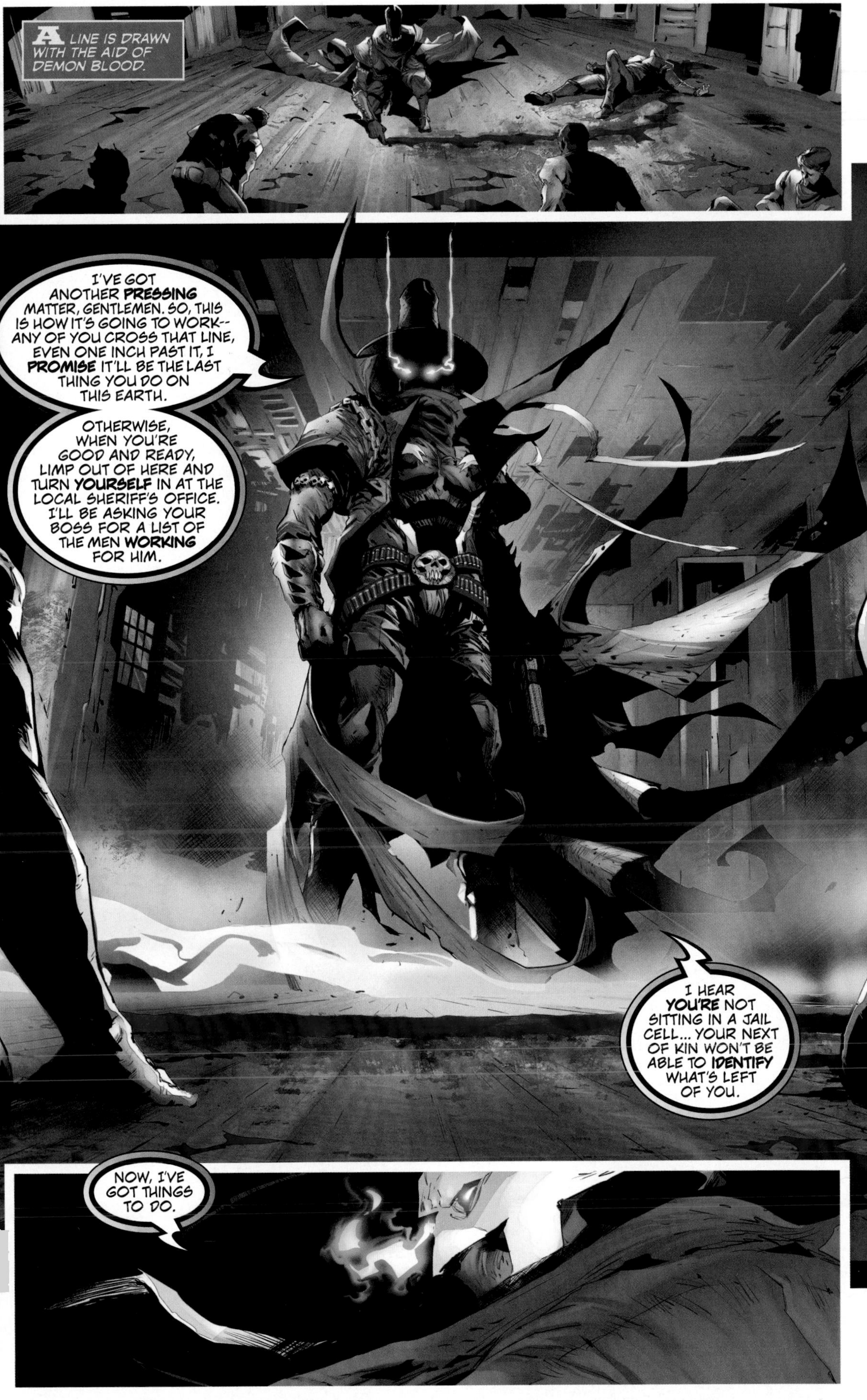A LINE IS DRAWN WITH THE AID OF DEMON BLOOD.
I'VE GOT ANOTHER PRESSING MATTER, GENTLEMEN. SO, THIS IS HOW IT'S GOING TO WORK-- ANY OF YOU CROSS THAT LINE, EVEN ONE INCH PAST IT, I PROMISE IT'LL BE THE LAST THING YOU DO ON THIS EARTH.
OTHERWISE, WHEN YOU'RE GOOD AND READY, LIMP OUT OF HERE AND TURN YOURSELF IN AT THE LOCAL SHERIFF'S OFFICE. I'LL BE ASKING YOUR BOSS FOR A LIST OF THE MEN WORKING FOR HIM.
I HEAR YOU'RE NOT SITTING IN A JAIL CELL... YOUR NEXT OF KIN WON'T BE ABLE TO IDENTIFY WHAT'S LEFT OF YOU.
NOW, I'VE GOT THINGS TO DO.

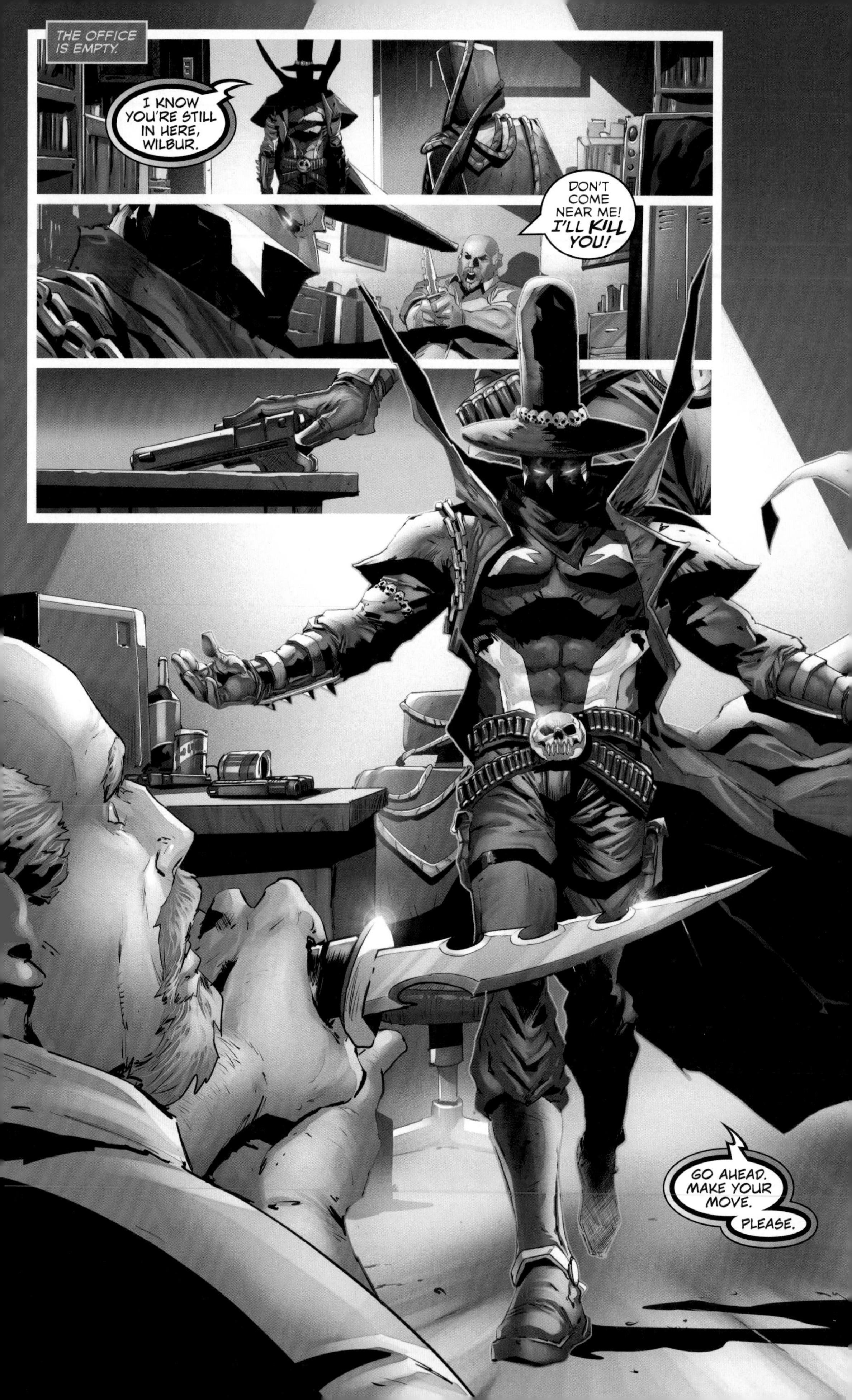
THE OFFICE IS EMPTY.
I KNOW YOU'RE STILL IN HERE, WILBUR.
DON'T COME NEAR ME! I'LL KILL YOU!
GO AHEAD. MAKE YOUR MOVE.
PLEASE.

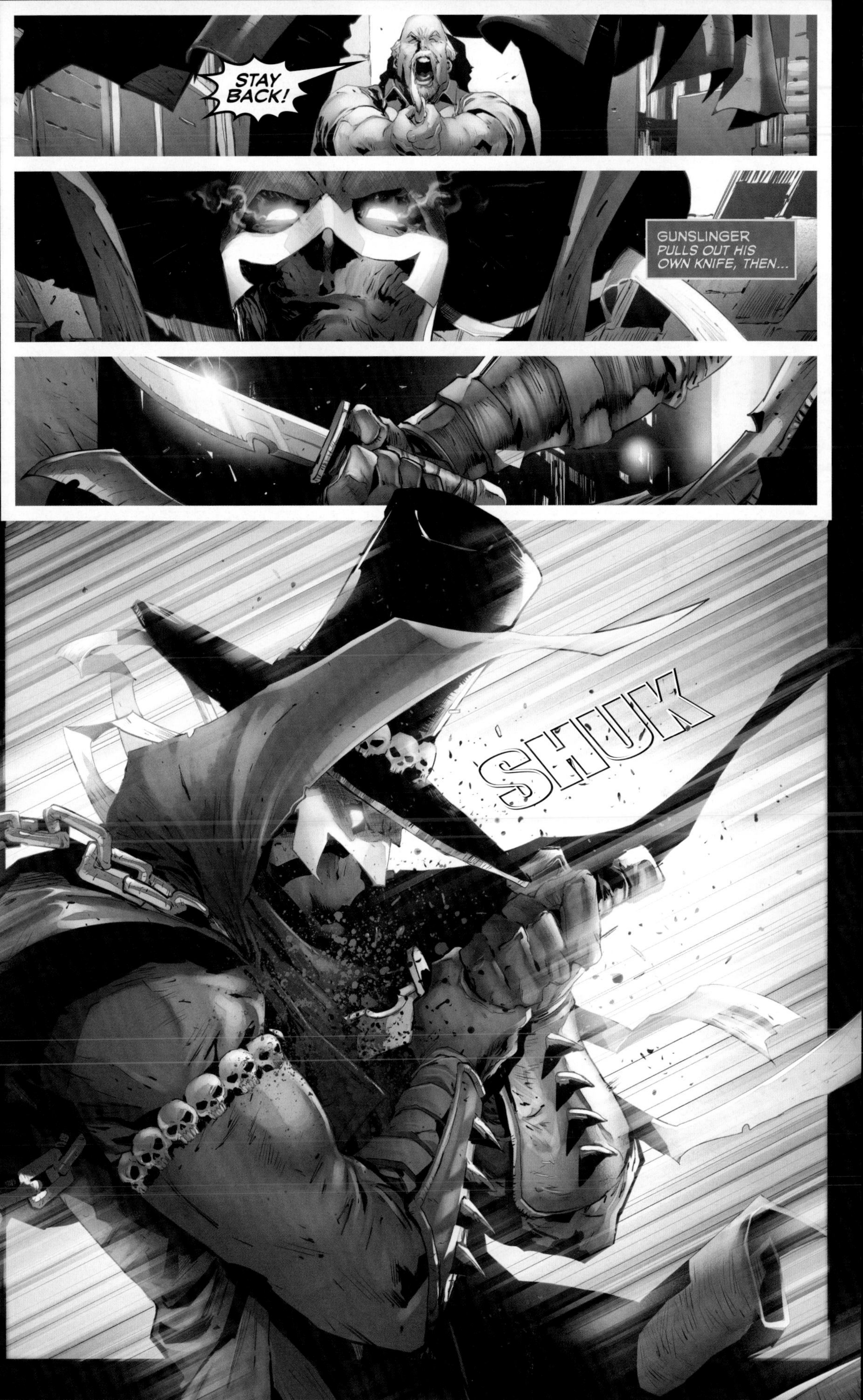
STAY BACK!
GUNSLINGER PULLS OUT HIS OWN KNIFE, THEN...
SHUK

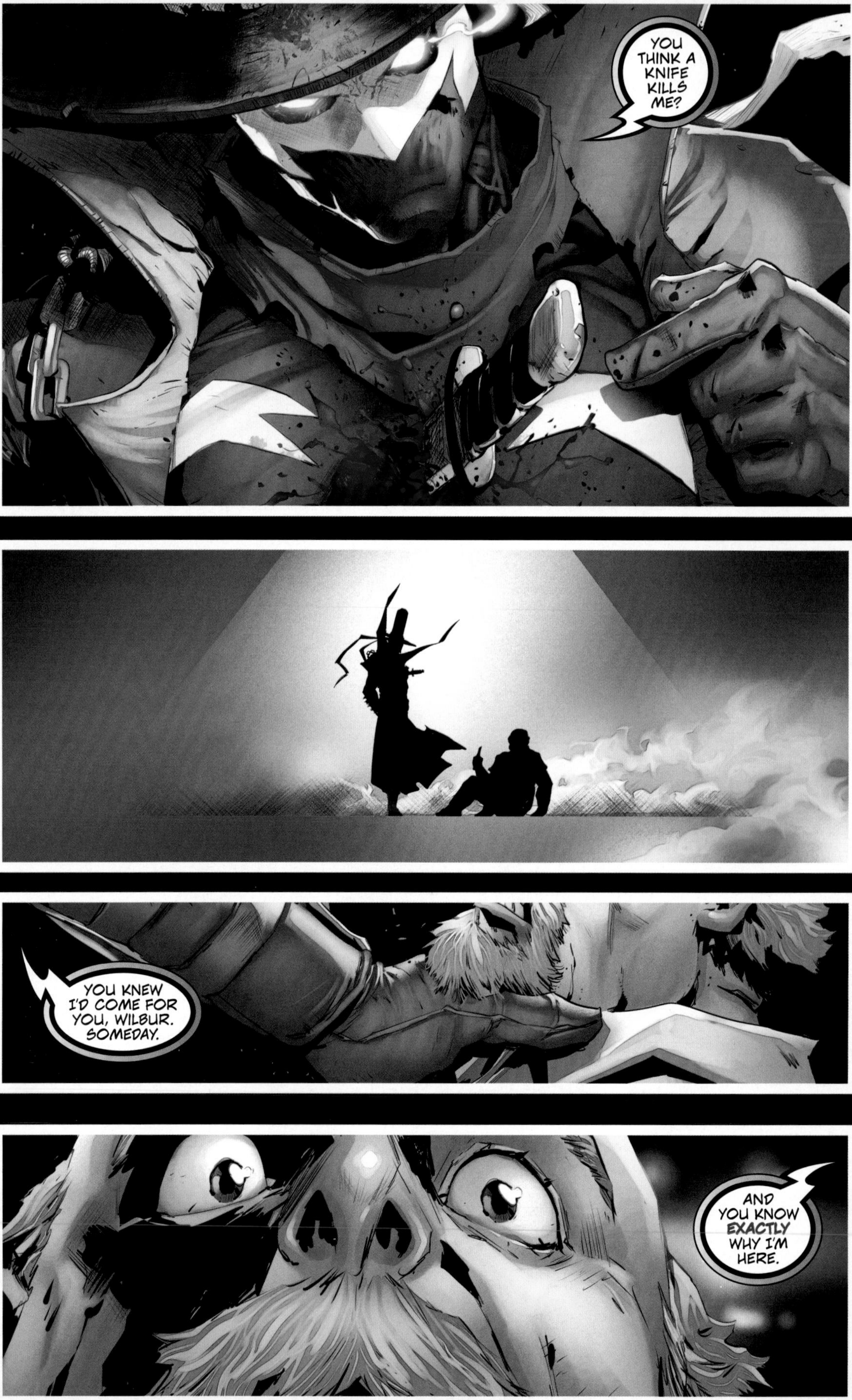
YOU THINK A KNIFE KILLS ME?
YOU KNEW I'D COME FOR YOU, WILBUR. SOMEDAY.
AND YOU KNOW EXACTLY WHY I'M HERE.

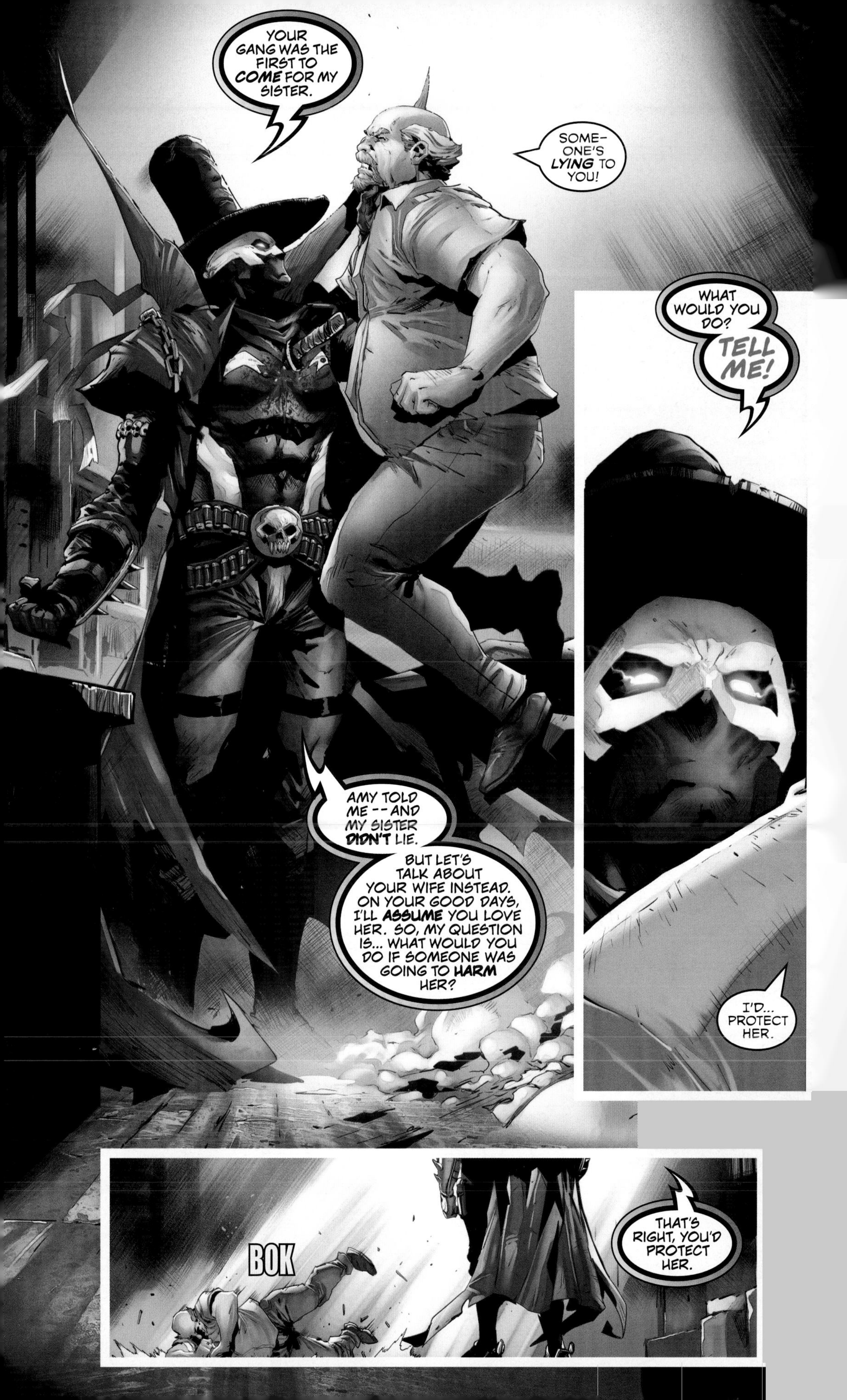
YOUR GANG WAS THE FIRST TO COME FOR MY SISTER.
SOME-ONE'S LYING TO YOU!
WHAT WOULD YOU DO?
TELL ME!
AMY TOLD ME -- AND MY SISTER DIDN'T LIE.
BUT LET'S TALK ABOUT YOUR WIFE INSTEAD. ON YOUR GOOD DAYS, I'LL ASSUME YOU LOVE HER. SO, MY QUESTION IS... WHAT WOULD YOU DO IF SOMEONE WAS GOING TO HARM HER?
I'D... PROTECT HER.
BOK
THAT'S RIGHT, YOU'D PROTECT HER.

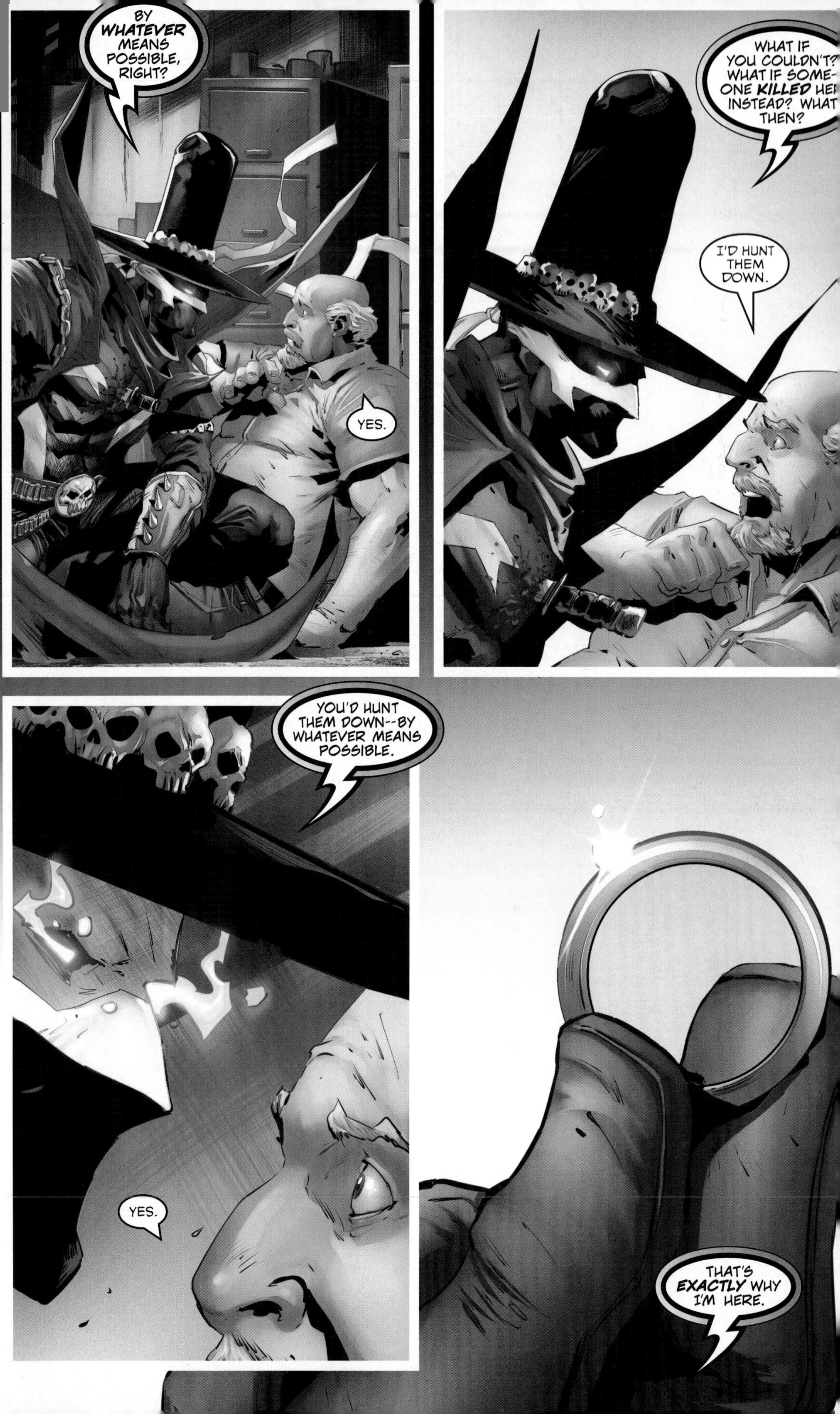
BY WHATEVER MEANS POSSIBLE, RIGHT?
YES.
WHAT IF YOU COULDN'T? WHAT IF SOME-ONE KILLED HER INSTEAD? WHAT THEN?
I'D HUNT THEM DOWN.
YOU'D HUNT THEM DOWN--BY WHATEVER MEANS POSSIBLE.
YES.
THAT'S EXACTLY WHY I'M HERE.

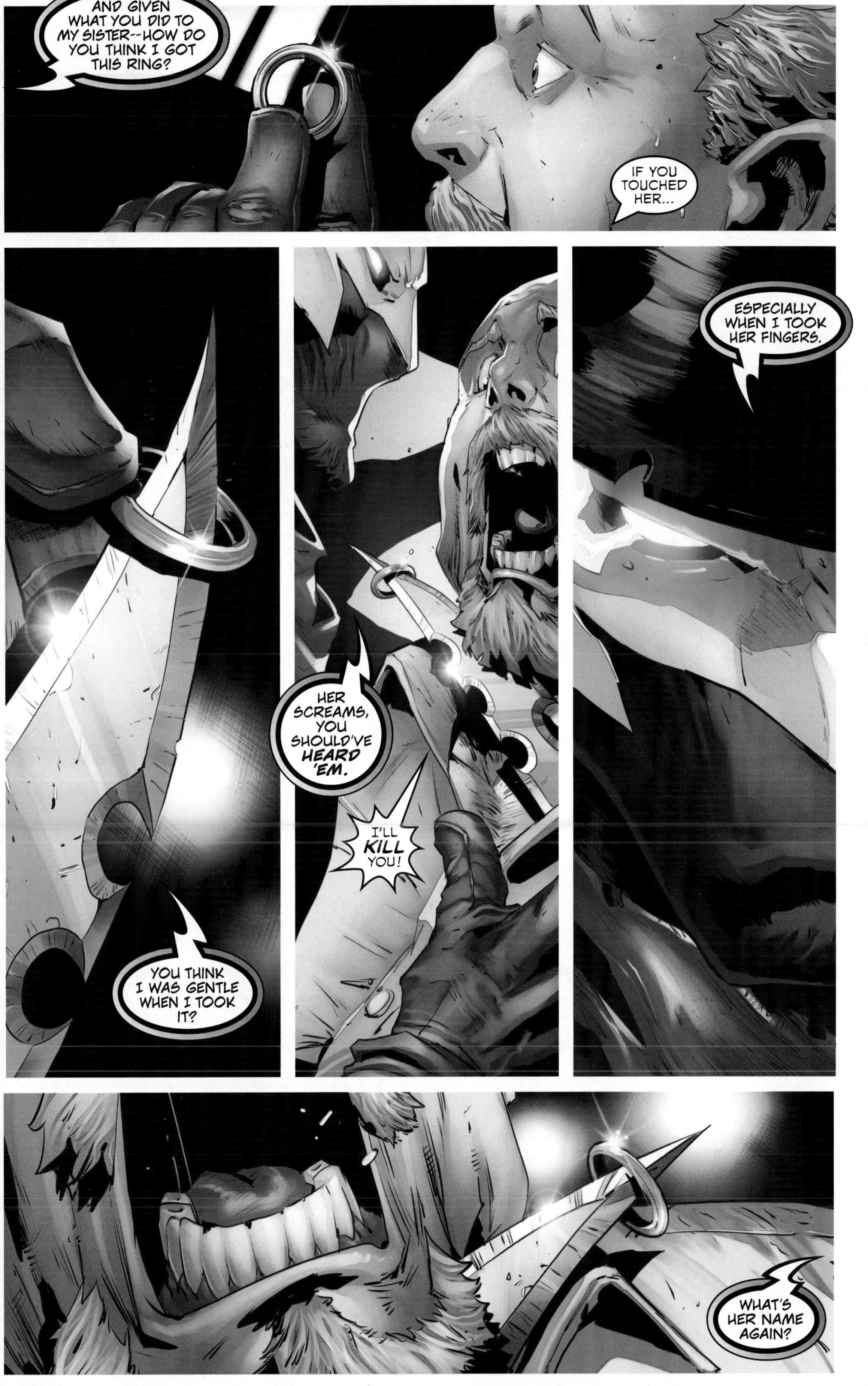
AND GIVEN WHAT YOU DID TO MY SISTER--HOW DO YOU THINK I GOT THIS RING?
IF YOU TOUCHED HER...
YOU THINK I WAS GENTLE WHEN I TOOK IT?
HER SCREAMS, YOU SHOULD'VE HEARD 'EM.
I'LL KILL YOU!
ESPECIALLY WHEN I TOOK HER FINGERS.
WHAT'S HER NAME AGAIN?

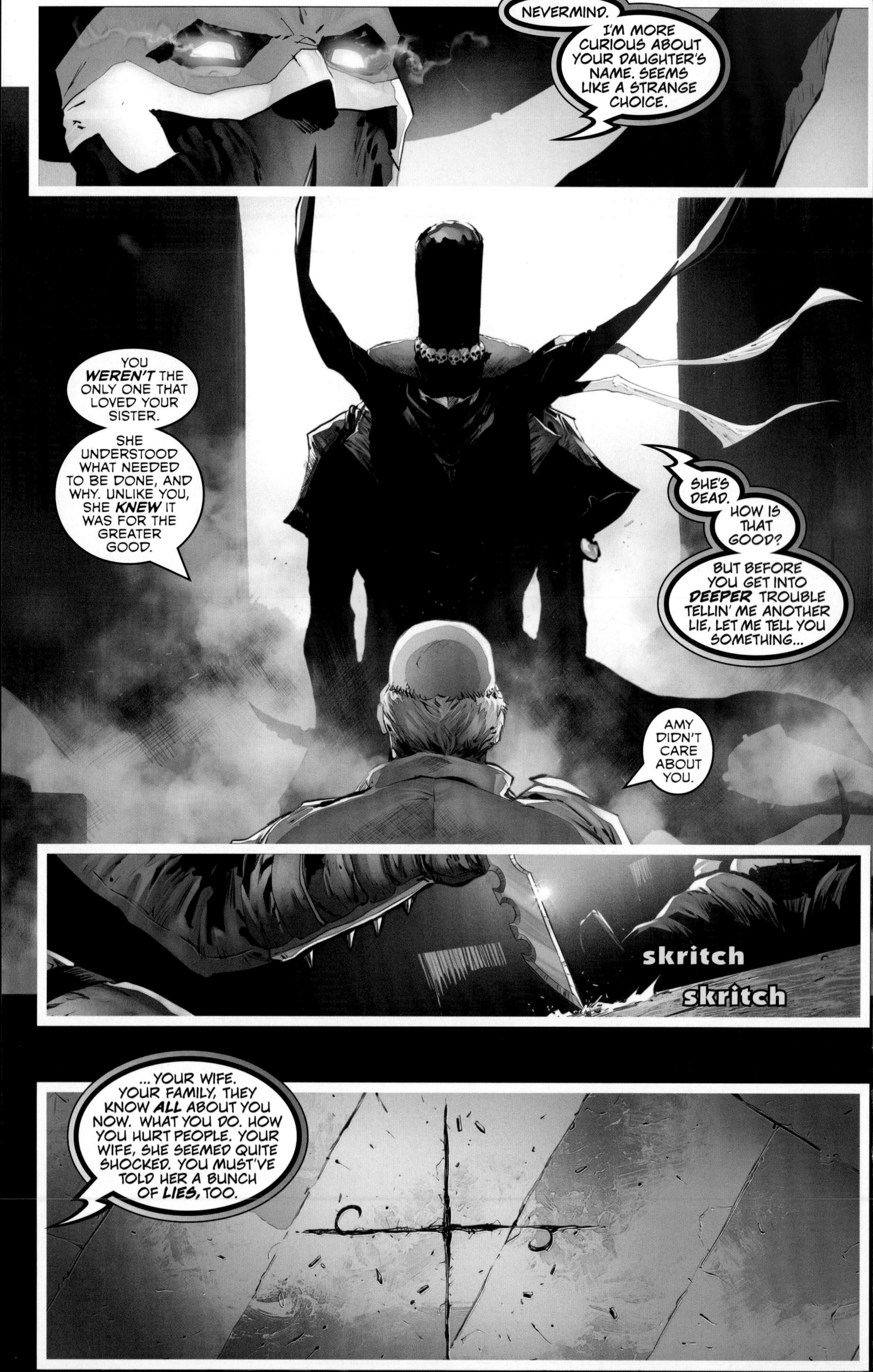
NEVERMIND. I'M MORE CURIOUS ABOUT YOUR DAUGHTER'S NAME. SEEMS LIKE A STRANGE CHOICE.
YOU **WEREN'T** THE ONLY ONE THAT LOVED YOUR SISTER.
SHE UNDERSTOOD WHAT NEEDED TO BE DONE, AND WHY. UNLIKE YOU, SHE **KNEW** IT WAS FOR THE GREATER GOOD.
SHE'S DEAD. HOW IS THAT GOOD?
BUT BEFORE YOU GET INTO **DEEPER** TROUBLE TELLIN' ME ANOTHER LIE, LET ME TELL YOU SOMETHING...
AMY DIDN'T CARE ABOUT YOU.
skritch
skritch
...YOUR WIFE. YOUR FAMILY, THEY KNOW **ALL** ABOUT YOU NOW. WHAT YOU DO. HOW YOU HURT PEOPLE. YOUR WIFE, SHE SEEMED QUITE SHOCKED. YOU MUST'VE TOLD HER A BUNCH OF **LIES**, TOO.

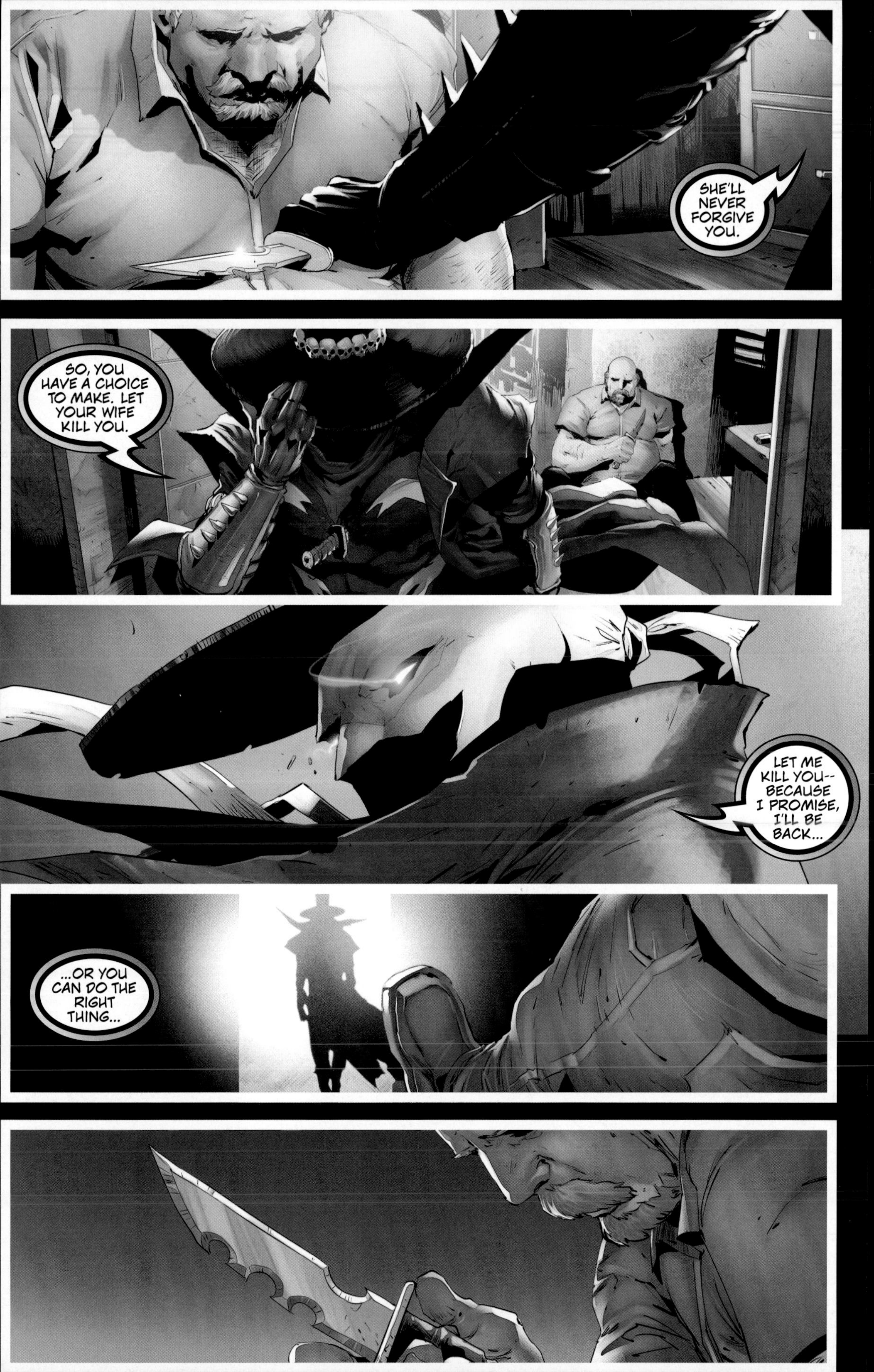

SHE'LL NEVER FORGIVE YOU.
SO, YOU HAVE A CHOICE TO MAKE. LET YOUR WIFE KILL YOU.
LET ME KILL YOU-- BECAUSE I PROMISE, I'LL BE BACK...
...OR YOU CAN DO THE RIGHT THING...

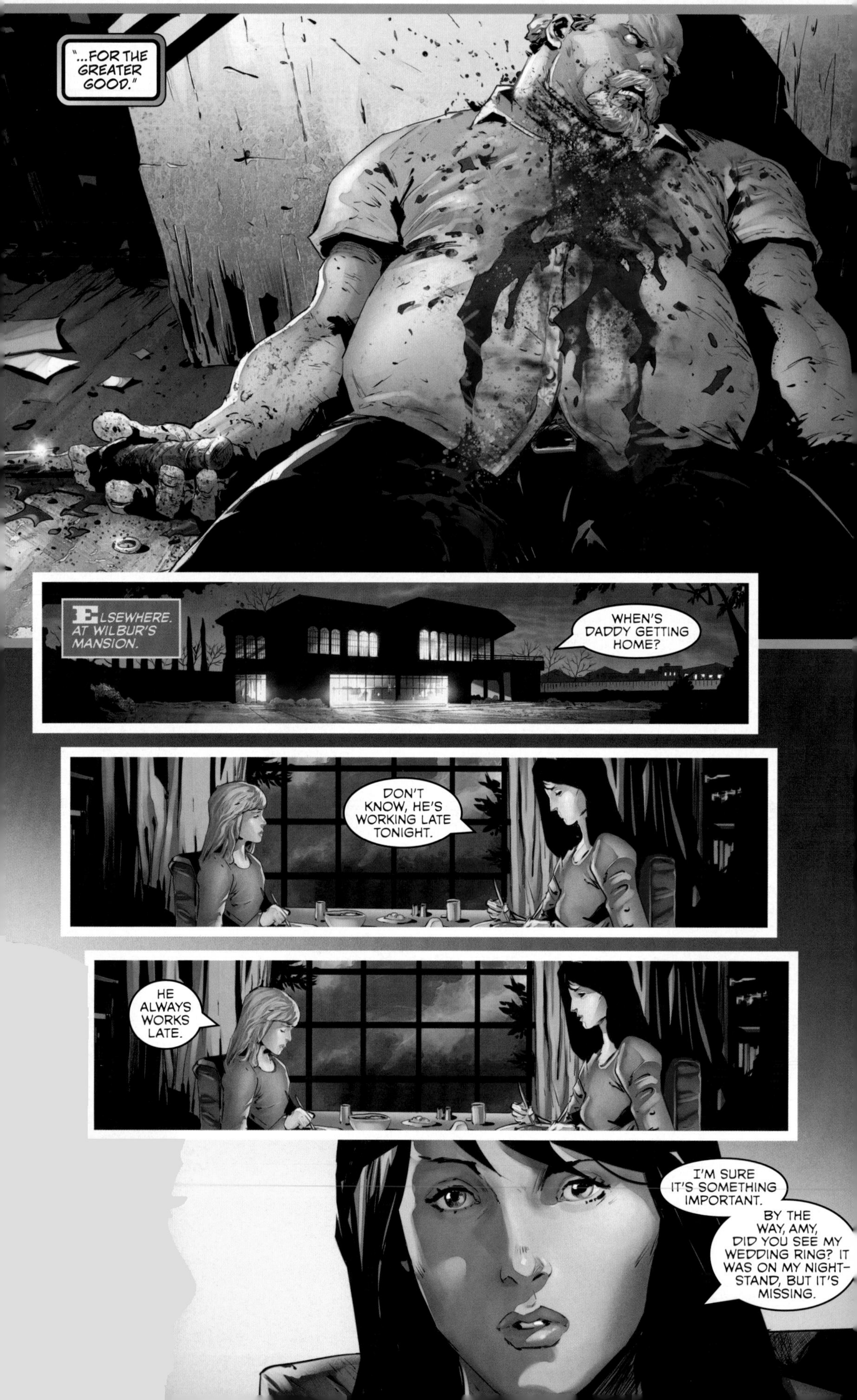
"...FOR THE GREATER GOOD."
ELSEWHERE. AT WILBUR'S MANSION.
WHEN'S DADDY GETTING HOME?
DON'T KNOW, HE'S WORKING LATE TONIGHT.
HE ALWAYS WORKS LATE.
I'M SURE IT'S SOMETHING IMPORTANT.
BY THE WAY, AMY, DID YOU SEE MY WEDDING RING? IT WAS ON MY NIGHT-STAND, BUT IT'S MISSING.

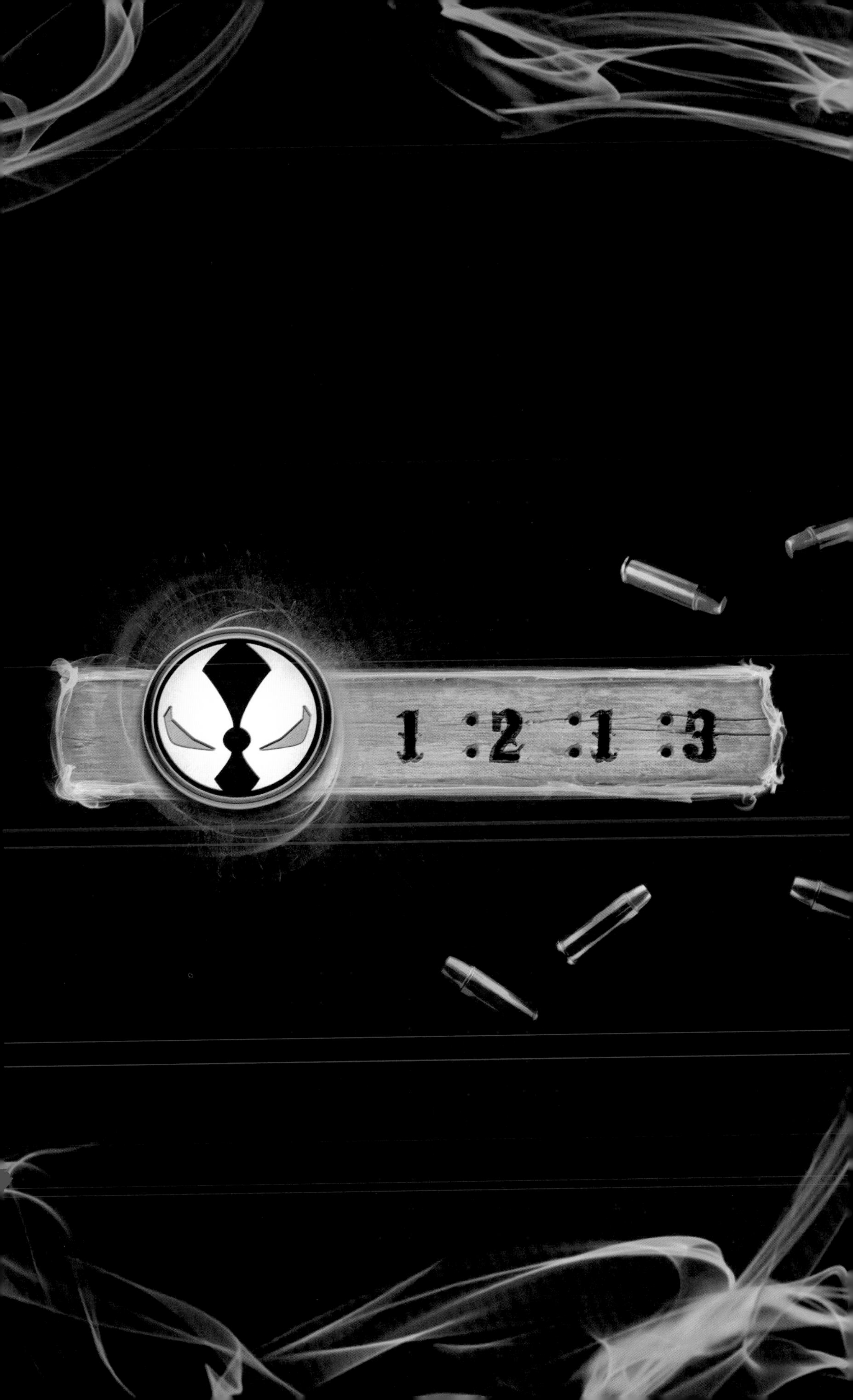
1 :2 :1 :3

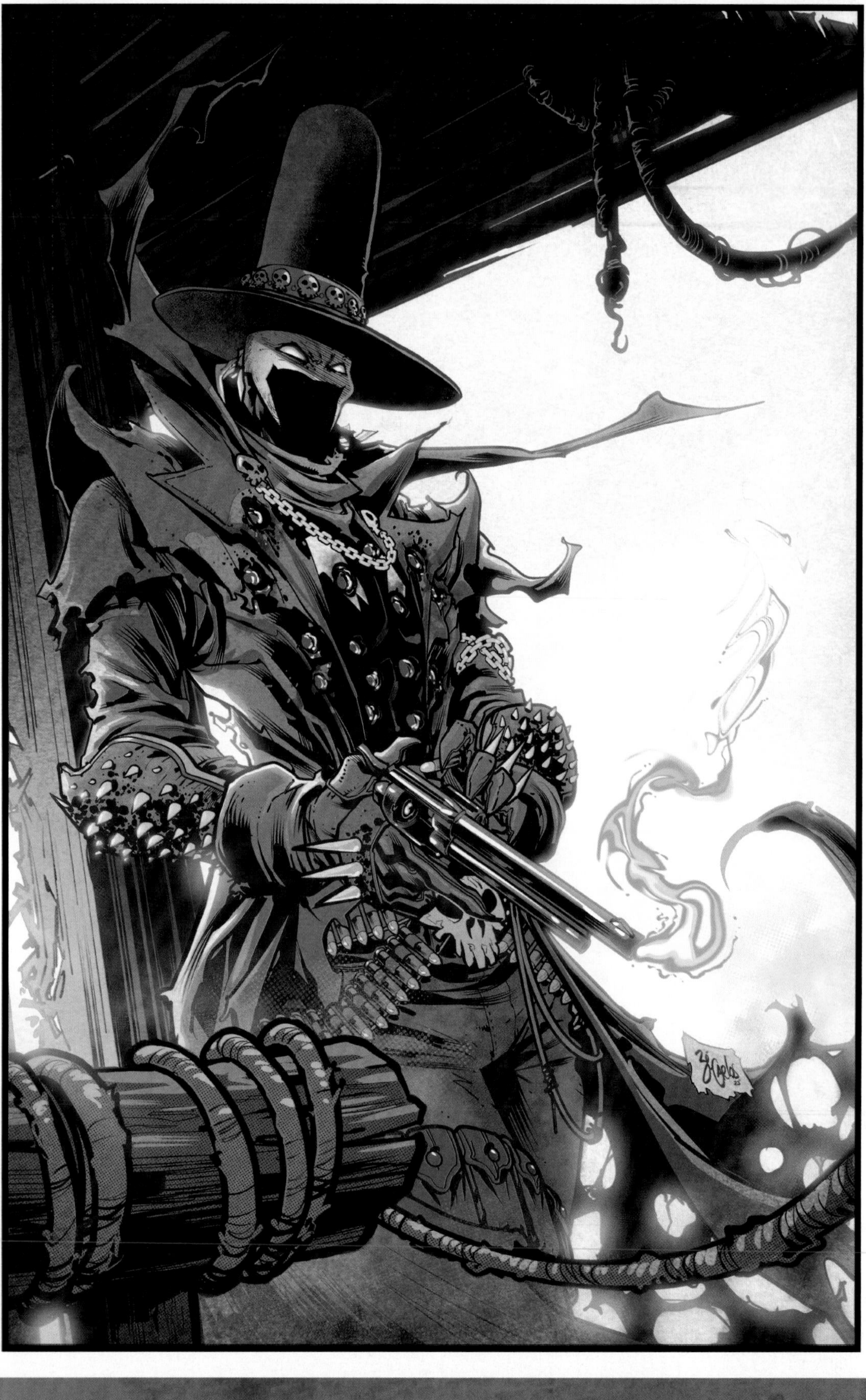

GUNSLINGER SPAWN #26 COVER 'A' BY ZÉ CARLOS

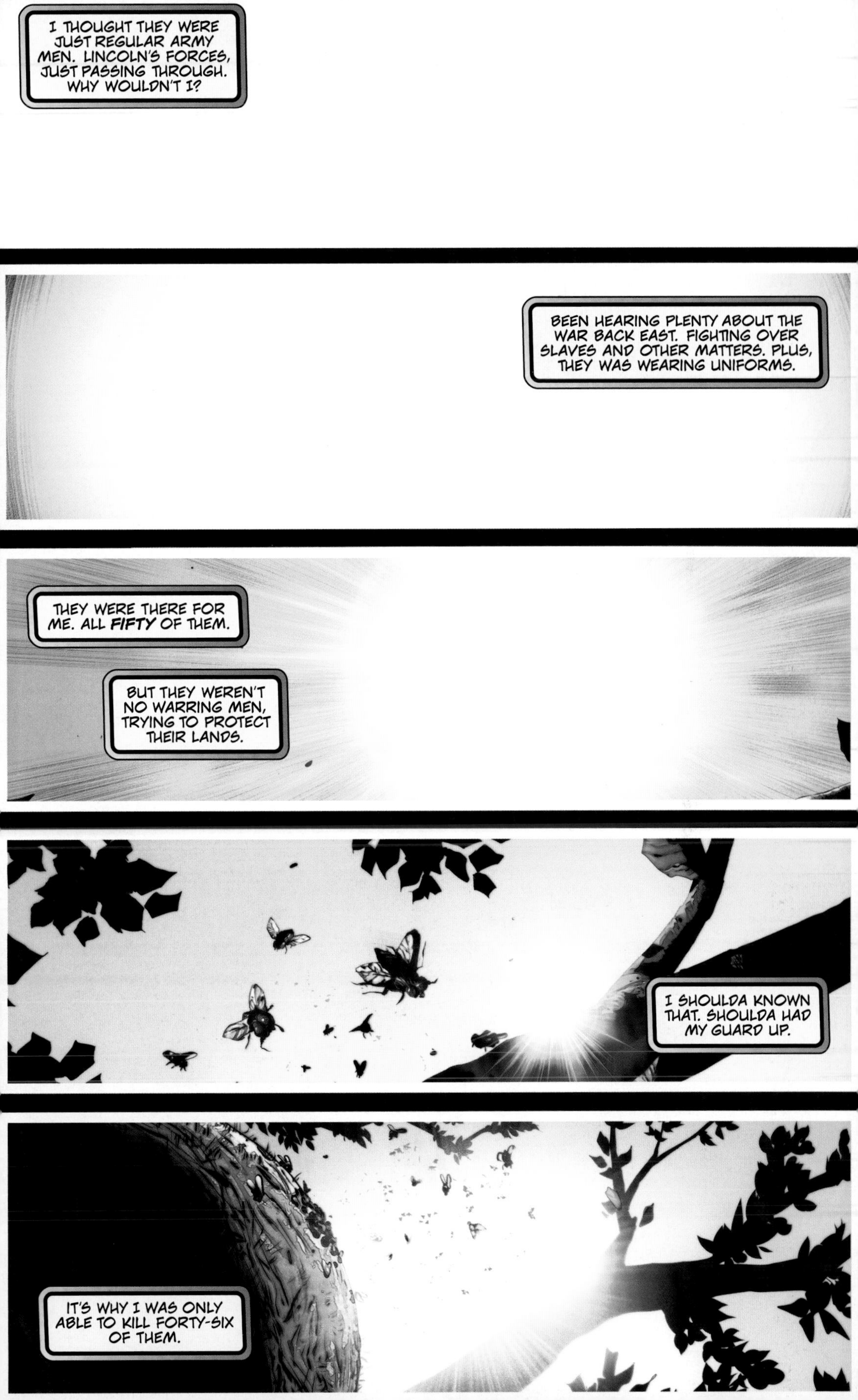
I THOUGHT THEY WERE JUST REGULAR ARMY MEN. LINCOLN'S FORCES, JUST PASSING THROUGH. WHY WOULDN'T I?
BEEN HEARING PLENTY ABOUT THE WAR BACK EAST. FIGHTING OVER SLAVES AND OTHER MATTERS. PLUS, THEY WAS WEARING UNIFORMS.
THEY WERE THERE FOR ME. ALL *FIFTY* OF THEM.
BUT THEY WEREN'T NO WARRING MEN, TRYING TO PROTECT THEIR LANDS.
I SHOULDA KNOWN THAT. SHOULDA HAD MY GUARD UP.
IT'S WHY I WAS ONLY ABLE TO KILL FORTY-SIX OF THEM.

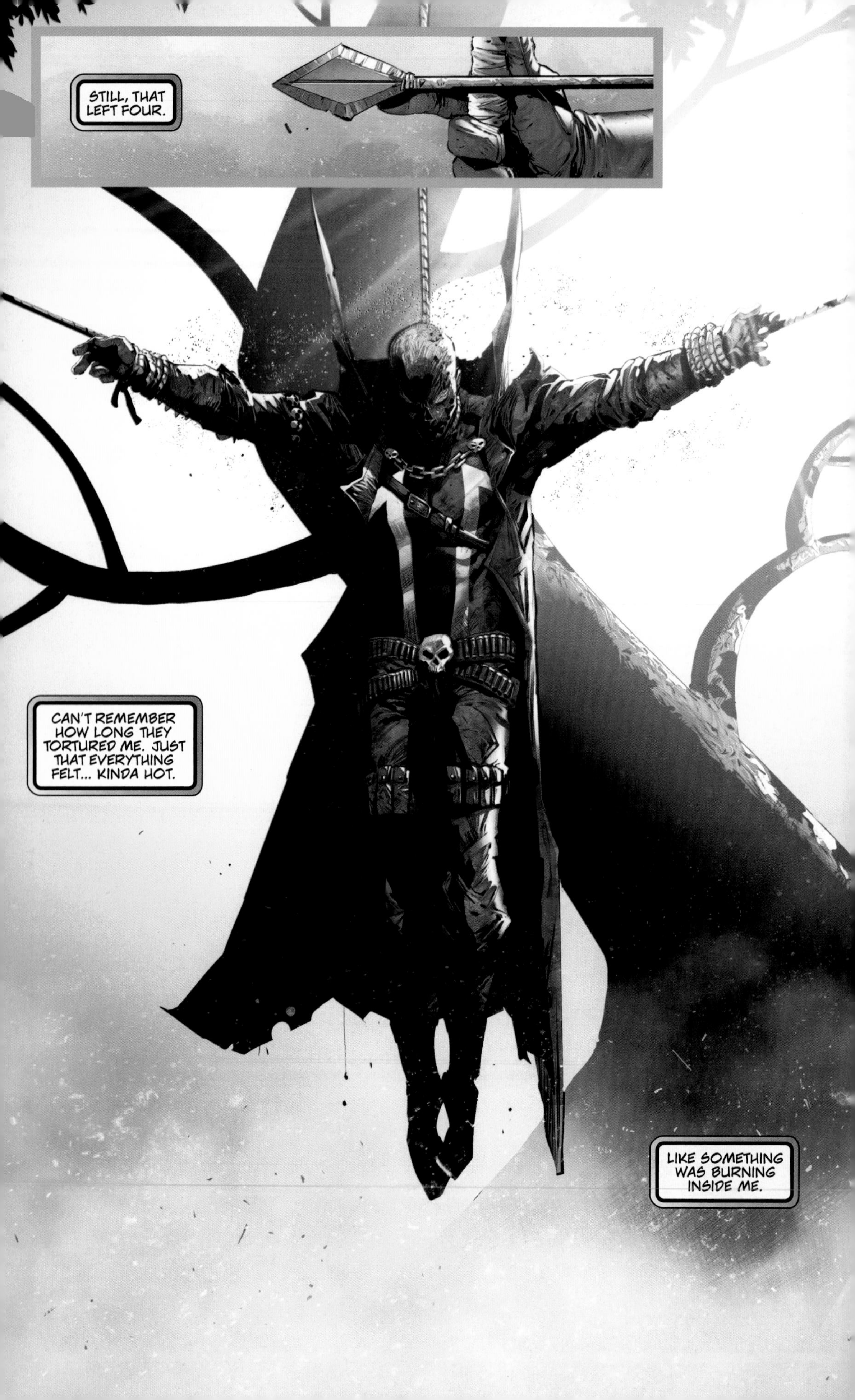
STILL, THAT LEFT FOUR.
CAN'T REMEMBER HOW LONG THEY TORTURED ME. JUST THAT EVERYTHING FELT... KINDA HOT.
LIKE SOMETHING WAS BURNING INSIDE ME.

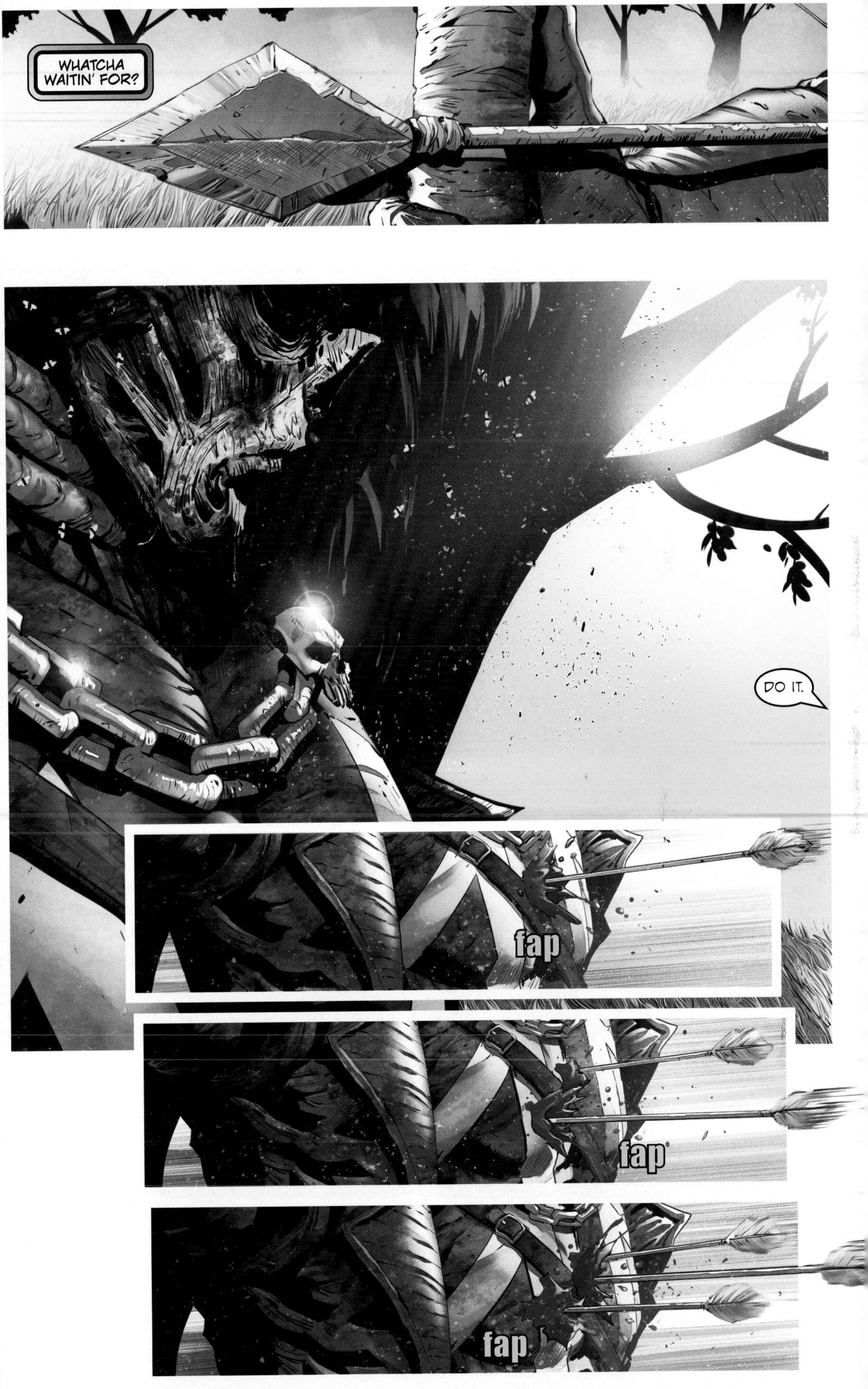
WHATCHA WAITIN' FOR?
DO IT.
fap
fap
fap

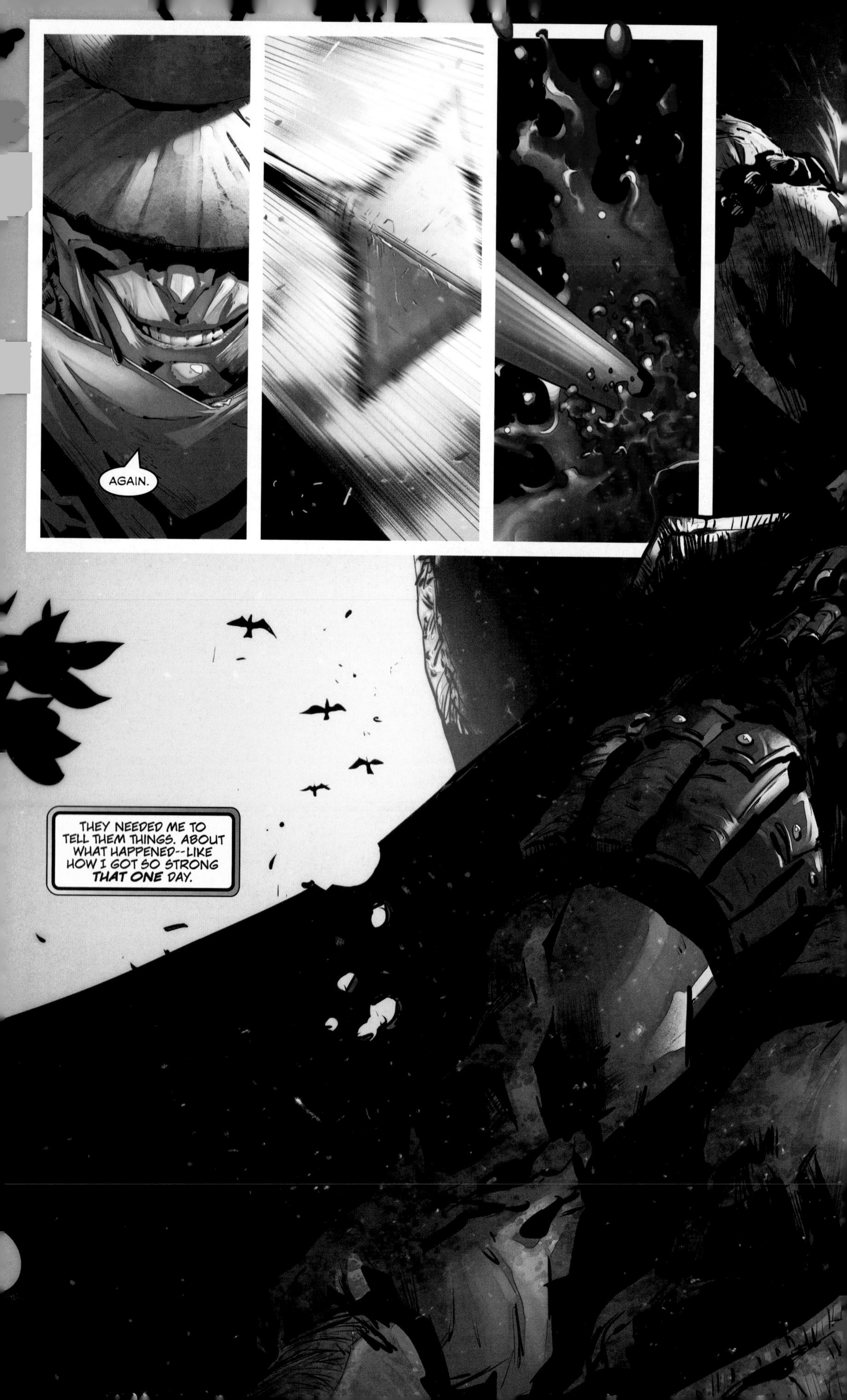
AGAIN.
THEY NEEDED ME TO TELL THEM THINGS. ABOUT WHAT HAPPENED--LIKE HOW I GOT SO STRONG THAT ONE DAY.

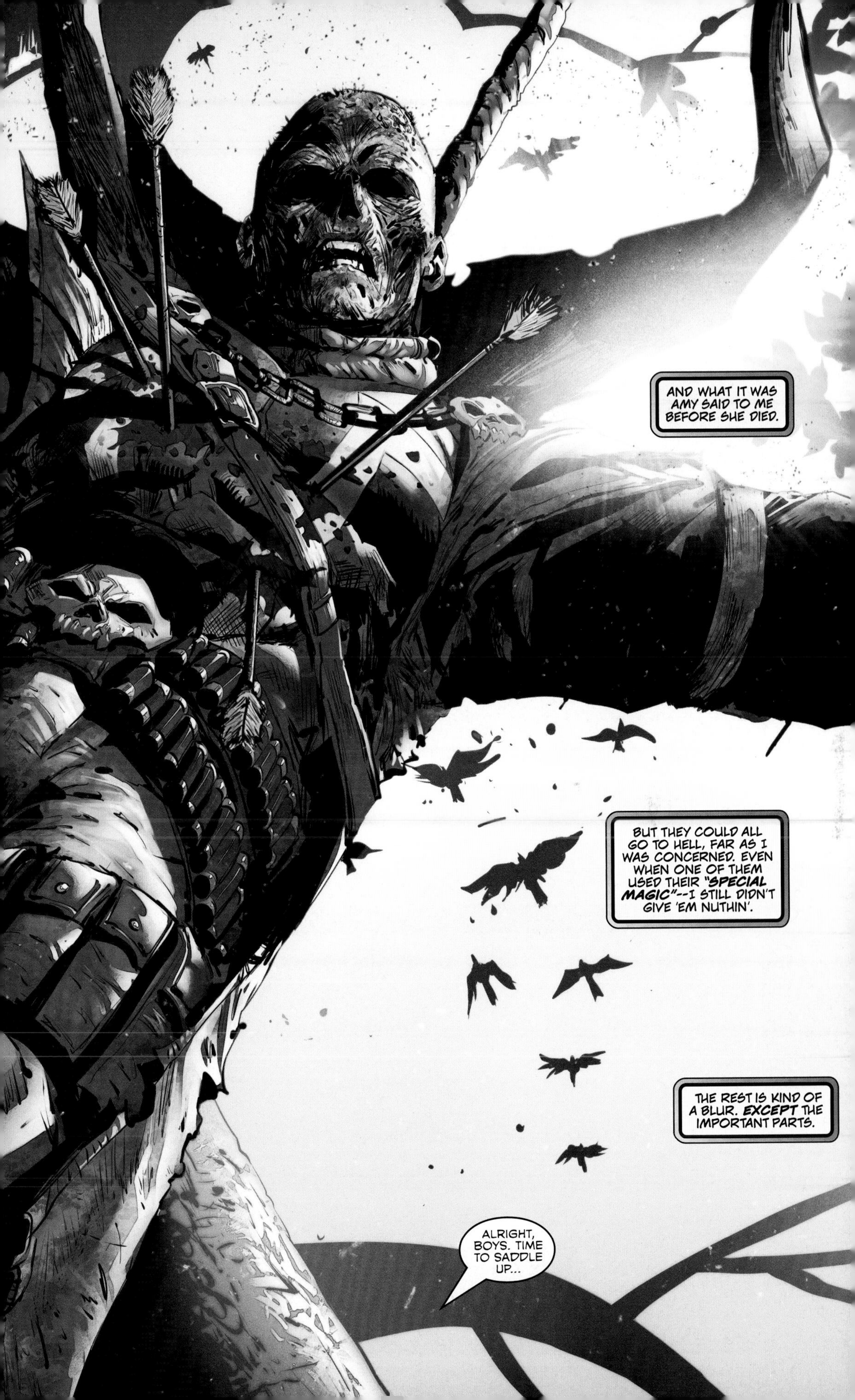
AND WHAT IT WAS AMY SAID TO ME BEFORE SHE DIED.
BUT THEY COULD ALL GO TO HELL, FAR AS I WAS CONCERNED. EVEN WHEN ONE OF THEM USED THEIR "SPECIAL MAGIC"--I STILL DIDN'T GIVE 'EM NUTHIN'.
THE REST IS KIND OF A BLUR. EXCEPT THE IMPORTANT PARTS.
ALRIGHT, BOYS. TIME TO SADDLE UP...

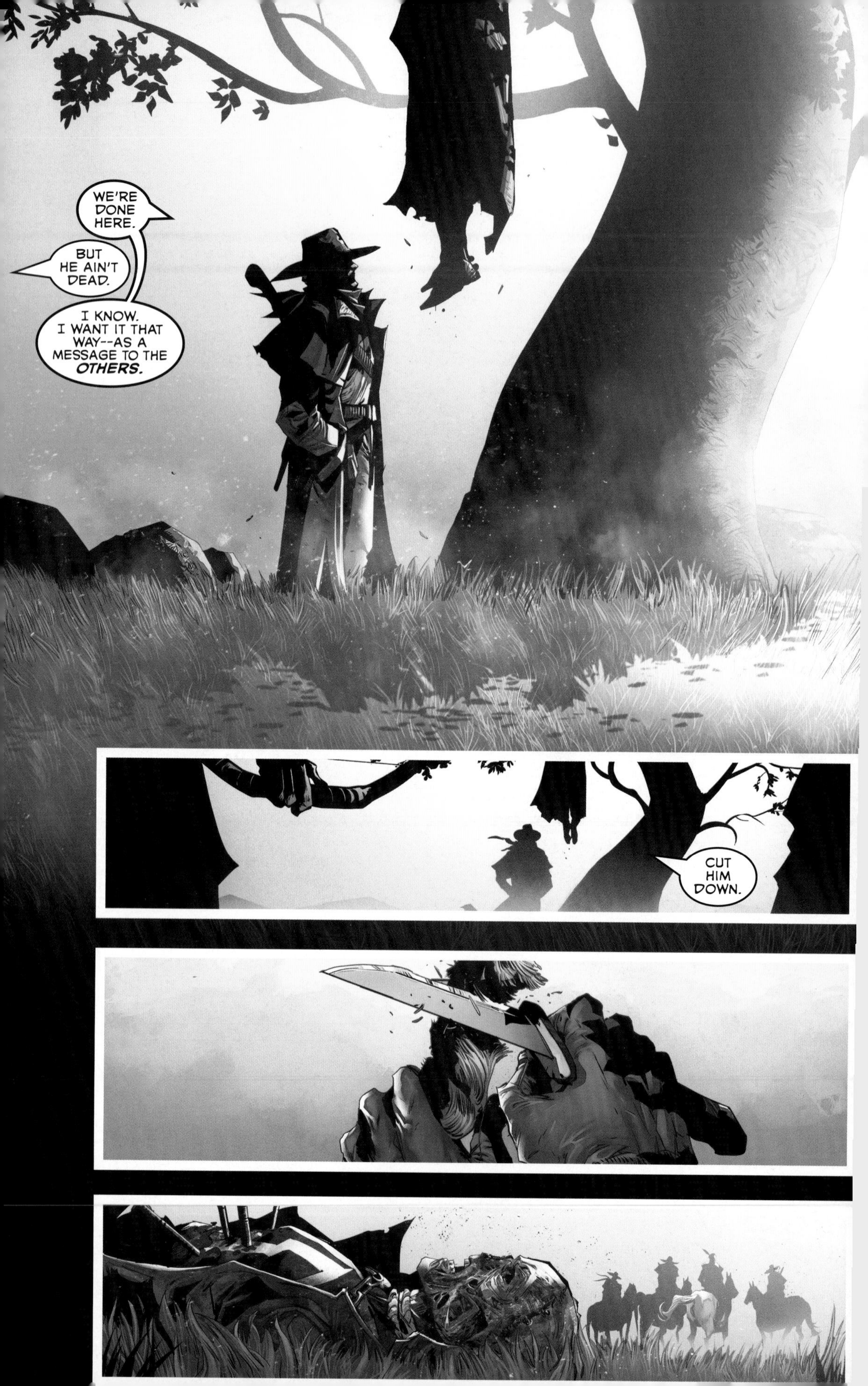
WE'RE DONE HERE.
BUT HE AIN'T DEAD.
I KNOW. I WANT IT THAT WAY--AS A MESSAGE TO THE *OTHERS.*
CUT HIM DOWN.

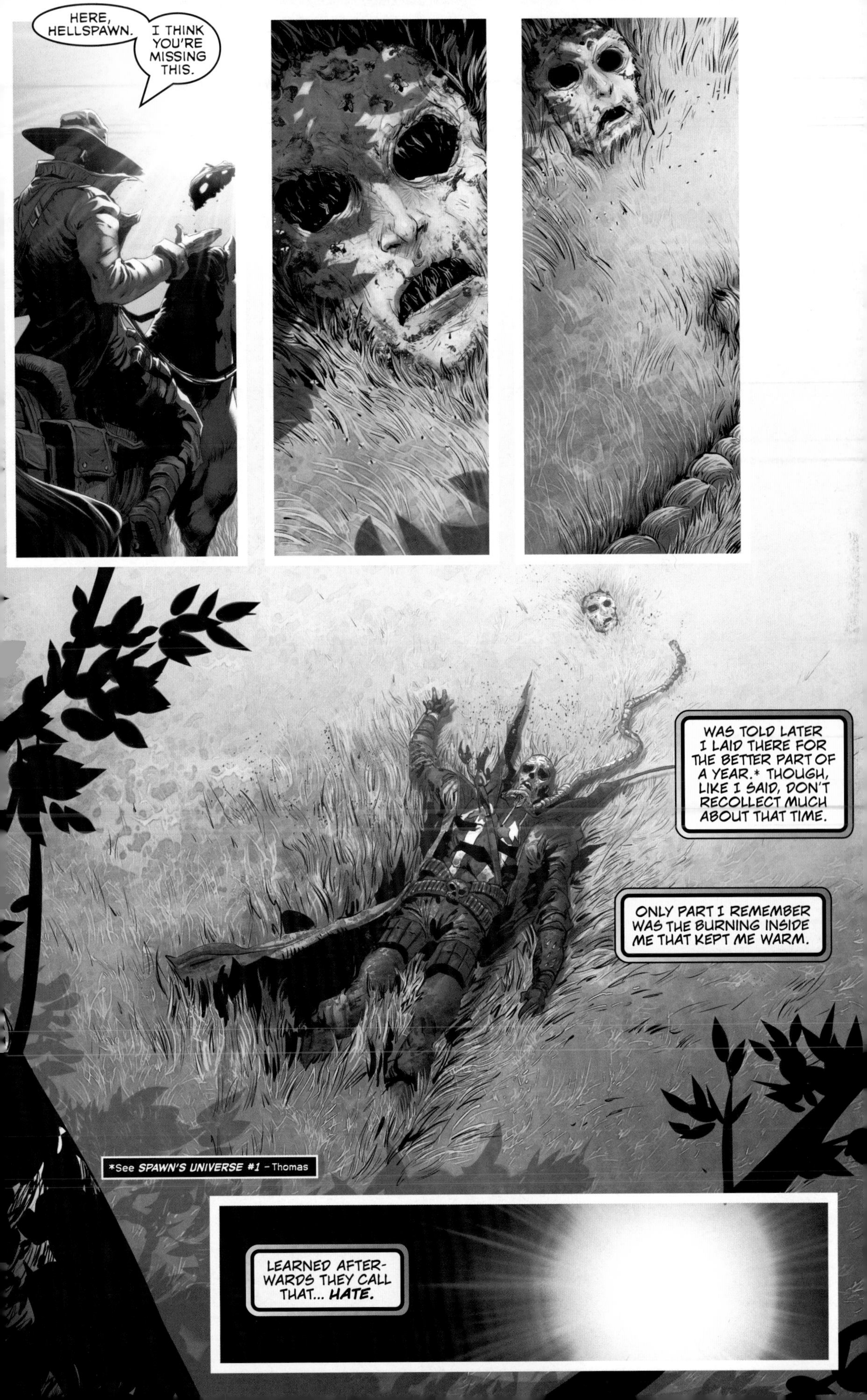

HERE, HELLSPAWN.
I THINK YOU'RE MISSING THIS.
WAS TOLD LATER I LAID THERE FOR THE BETTER PART OF A YEAR.* THOUGH, LIKE I SAID, DON'T RECOLLECT MUCH ABOUT THAT TIME.
ONLY PART I REMEMBER WAS THE BURNING INSIDE ME THAT KEPT ME WARM.
*See SPAWN'S UNIVERSE #1 – Thomas
LEARNED AFTER-WARDS THEY CALL THAT... HATE.

I'M STILL CARRYING THAT AROUND, SINCE SOMEONE TOOK *ME AWAY* FROM ITS PATH.

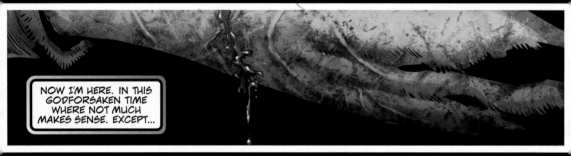

NOW I'M HERE. IN THIS GODFORSAKEN TIME WHERE NOT MUCH MAKES SENSE. EXCEPT...

...HOWEVER SPAWN BROUGHT ME HERE...

...HE ALSO DRAGGED ALONG A FEW OF *MY* ENEMIES TOO.

AND I'M FIXIN' TO GO MEET EACH AND EVERY ONE OF THEM.

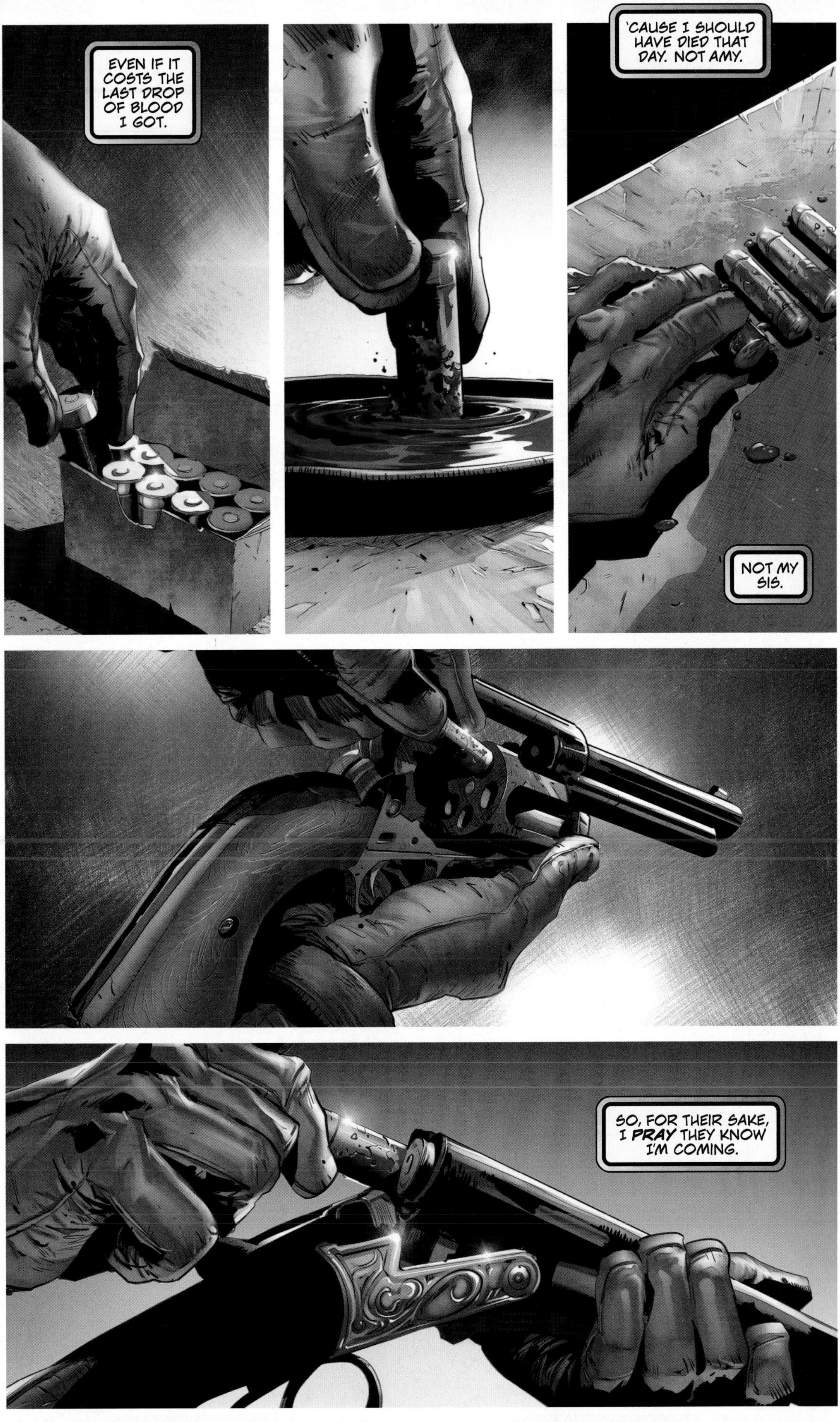
EVEN IF IT COSTS THE LAST DROP OF BLOOD I GOT.
'CAUSE I SHOULD HAVE DIED THAT DAY. NOT AMY.
NOT MY SIS.
SO, FOR THEIR SAKE, I **PRAY** THEY KNOW I'M COMING.

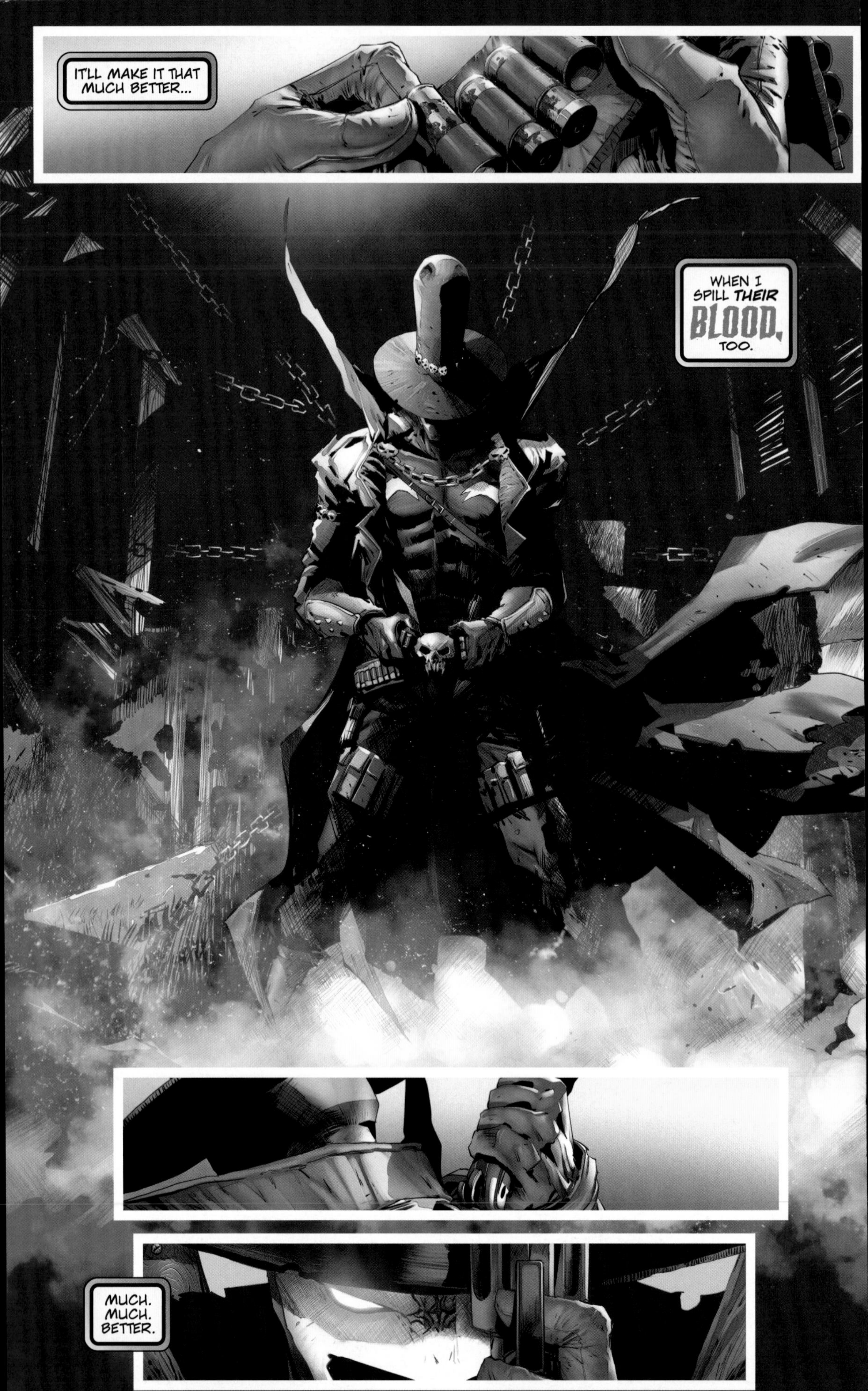
IT'LL MAKE IT THAT MUCH BETTER...
WHEN I SPILL THEIR BLOOD, TOO.
MUCH. MUCH. BETTER.

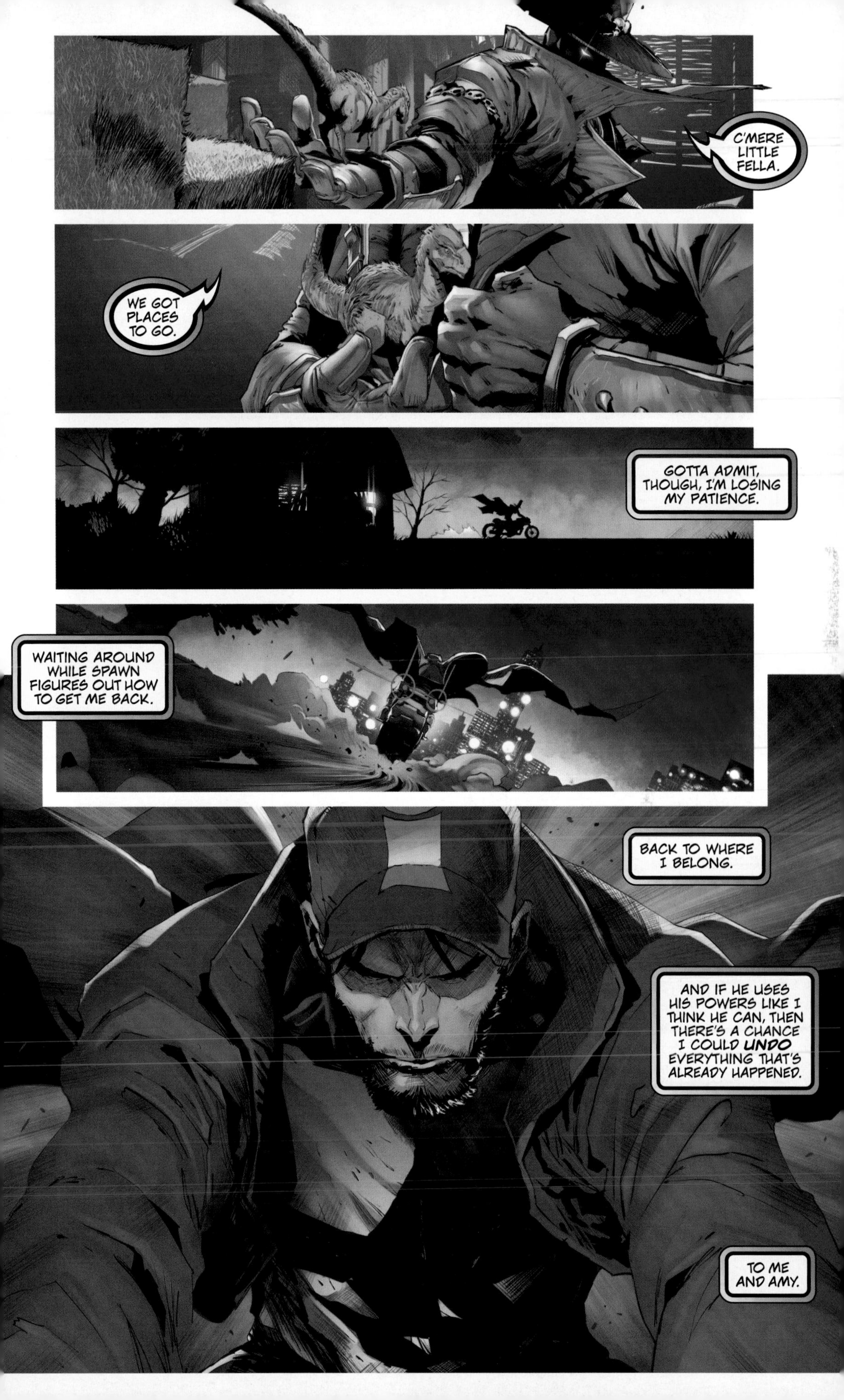

C'MERE LITTLE FELLA.
WE GOT PLACES TO GO.
GOTTA ADMIT, THOUGH, I'M LOSING MY PATIENCE.
WAITING AROUND WHILE SPAWN FIGURES OUT HOW TO GET ME BACK.
BACK TO WHERE I BELONG.
AND IF HE USES HIS POWERS LIKE I THINK HE CAN, THEN THERE'S A CHANCE I COULD UNDO EVERYTHING THAT'S ALREADY HAPPENED.
TO ME AND AMY.

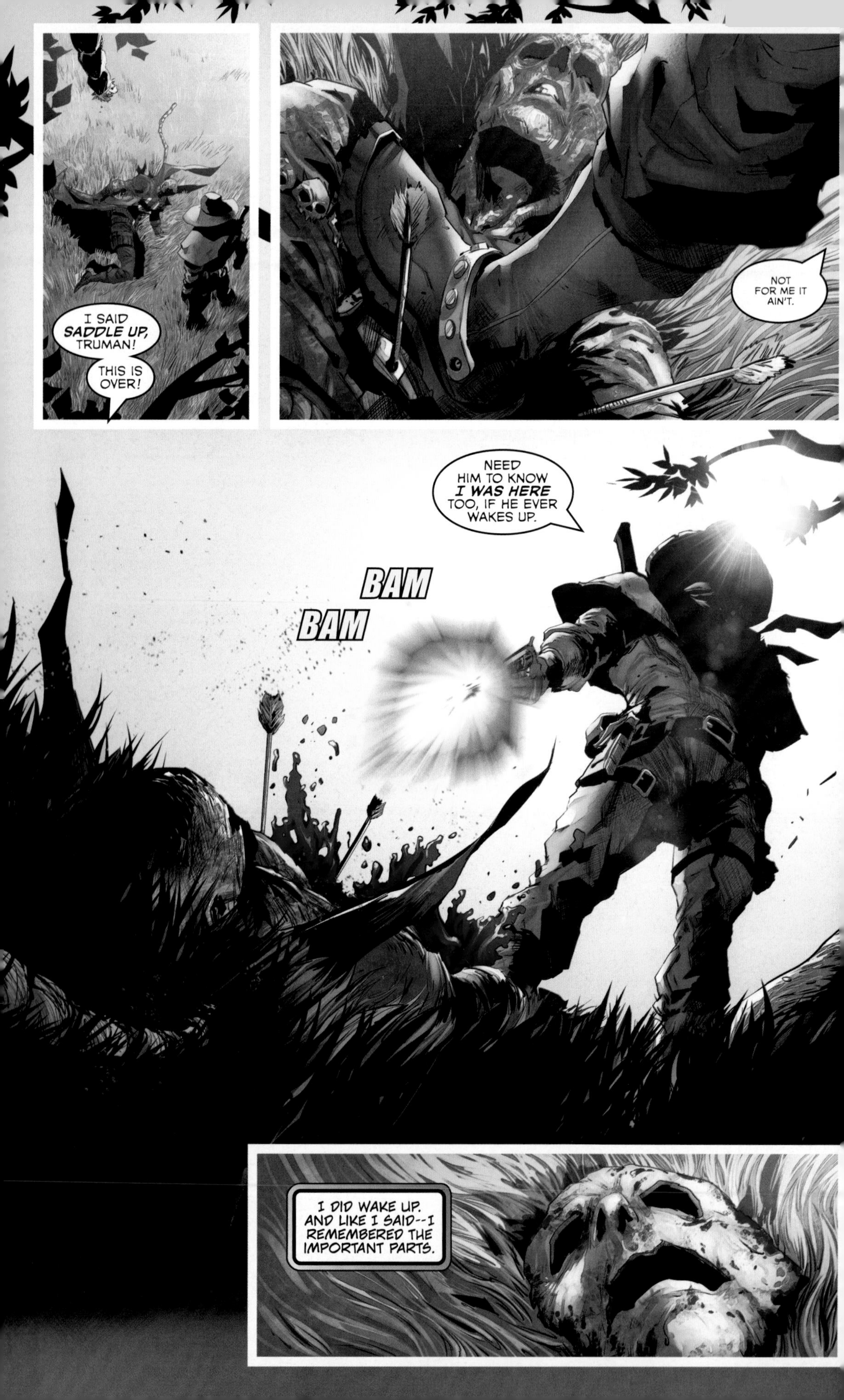
I SAID *SADDLE UP,* TRUMAN!
THIS IS OVER!
NOT FOR ME IT AIN'T.
NEED HIM TO KNOW *I WAS HERE* TOO, IF HE EVER WAKES UP.
BAM
BAM
I DID WAKE UP. AND LIKE I SAID--I REMEMBERED THE IMPORTANT PARTS.

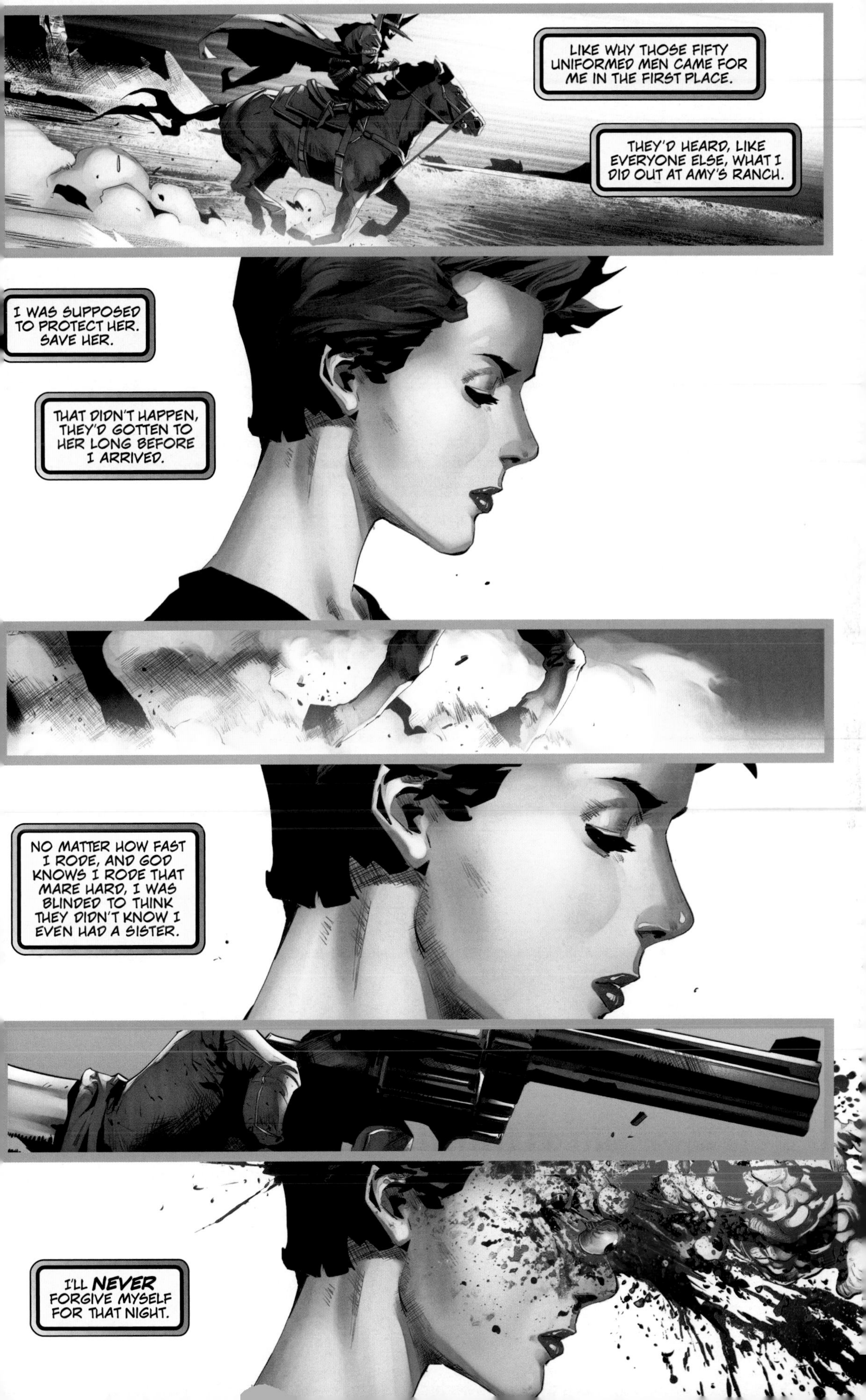
LIKE WHY THOSE FIFTY UNIFORMED MEN CAME FOR ME IN THE FIRST PLACE.
THEY'D HEARD, LIKE EVERYONE ELSE, WHAT I DID OUT AT AMY'S RANCH.
I WAS SUPPOSED TO PROTECT HER. SAVE HER.
THAT DIDN'T HAPPEN, THEY'D GOTTEN TO HER LONG BEFORE I ARRIVED.
NO MATTER HOW FAST I RODE, AND GOD KNOWS I RODE THAT MARE HARD, I WAS BLINDED TO THINK THEY DIDN'T KNOW I EVEN HAD A SISTER.
I'LL **NEVER** FORGIVE MYSELF FOR THAT NIGHT.

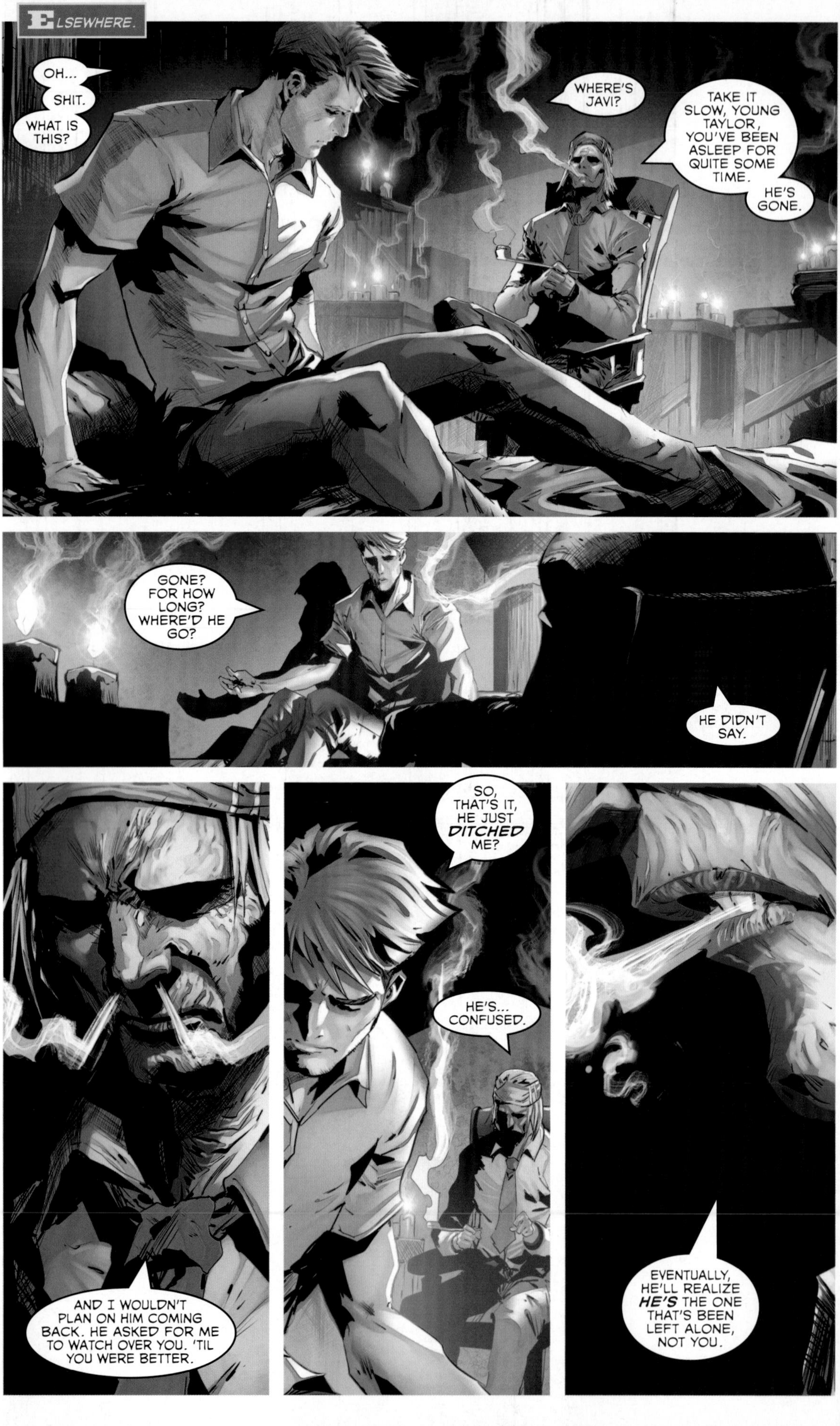
ELSEWHERE.
OH...
SHIT.
WHAT IS THIS?
WHERE'S JAVI?
TAKE IT SLOW, YOUNG TAYLOR, YOU'VE BEEN ASLEEP FOR QUITE SOME TIME.
HE'S GONE.
GONE? FOR HOW LONG? WHERE'D HE GO?
HE DIDN'T SAY.
AND I WOULDN'T PLAN ON HIM COMING BACK. HE ASKED FOR ME TO WATCH OVER YOU. 'TIL YOU WERE BETTER.
SO, THAT'S IT, HE JUST *DITCHED* ME?
HE'S... CONFUSED.
EVENTUALLY, HE'LL REALIZE ***HE'S*** THE ONE THAT'S BEEN LEFT ALONE, NOT YOU.

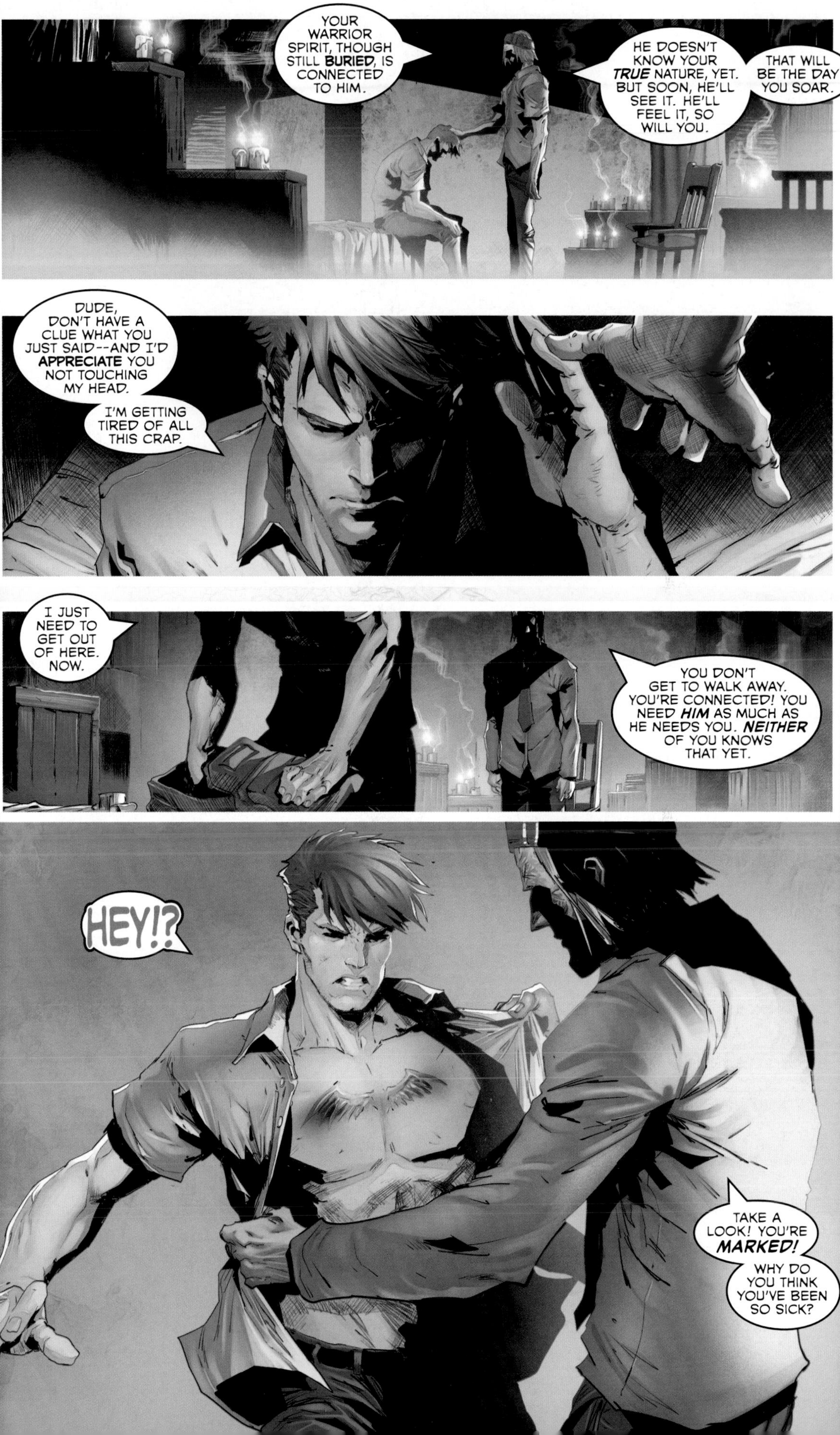
YOUR WARRIOR SPIRIT, THOUGH STILL BURIED, IS CONNECTED TO HIM.
HE DOESN'T KNOW YOUR TRUE NATURE, YET. BUT SOON, HE'LL SEE IT. HE'LL FEEL IT, SO WILL YOU.
THAT WILL BE THE DAY YOU SOAR.
DUDE, DON'T HAVE A CLUE WHAT YOU JUST SAID--AND I'D APPRECIATE YOU NOT TOUCHING MY HEAD.
I'M GETTING TIRED OF ALL THIS CRAP.
I JUST NEED TO GET OUT OF HERE. NOW.
YOU DON'T GET TO WALK AWAY. YOU'RE CONNECTED! YOU NEED HIM AS MUCH AS HE NEEDS YOU. NEITHER OF YOU KNOWS THAT YET.
HEY!?
TAKE A LOOK! YOU'RE MARKED!
WHY DO YOU THINK YOU'VE BEEN SO SICK?

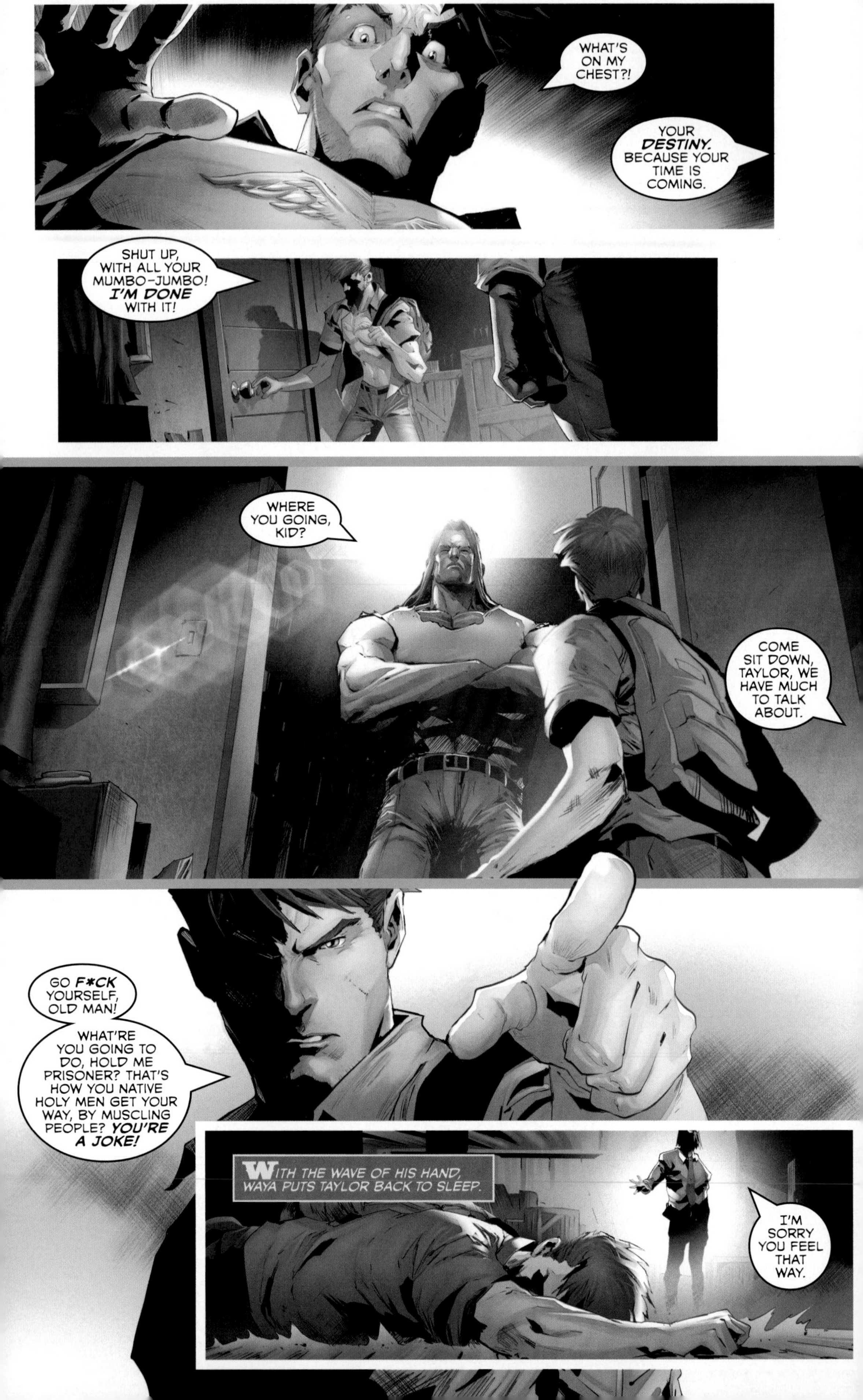
WHAT'S ON MY CHEST?!
YOUR **DESTINY.** BECAUSE YOUR TIME IS COMING.
SHUT UP, WITH ALL YOUR MUMBO-JUMBO! ***I'M DONE*** WITH IT!
WHERE YOU GOING, KID?
COME SIT DOWN, TAYLOR, WE HAVE MUCH TO TALK ABOUT.
GO ***F*CK*** YOURSELF, OLD MAN!
WHAT'RE YOU GOING TO DO, HOLD ME PRISONER? THAT'S HOW YOU NATIVE HOLY MEN GET YOUR WAY, BY MUSCLING PEOPLE? ***YOU'RE A JOKE!***
WITH THE WAVE OF HIS HAND, WAYA PUTS TAYLOR BACK TO SLEEP.
I'M SORRY YOU FEEL THAT WAY.

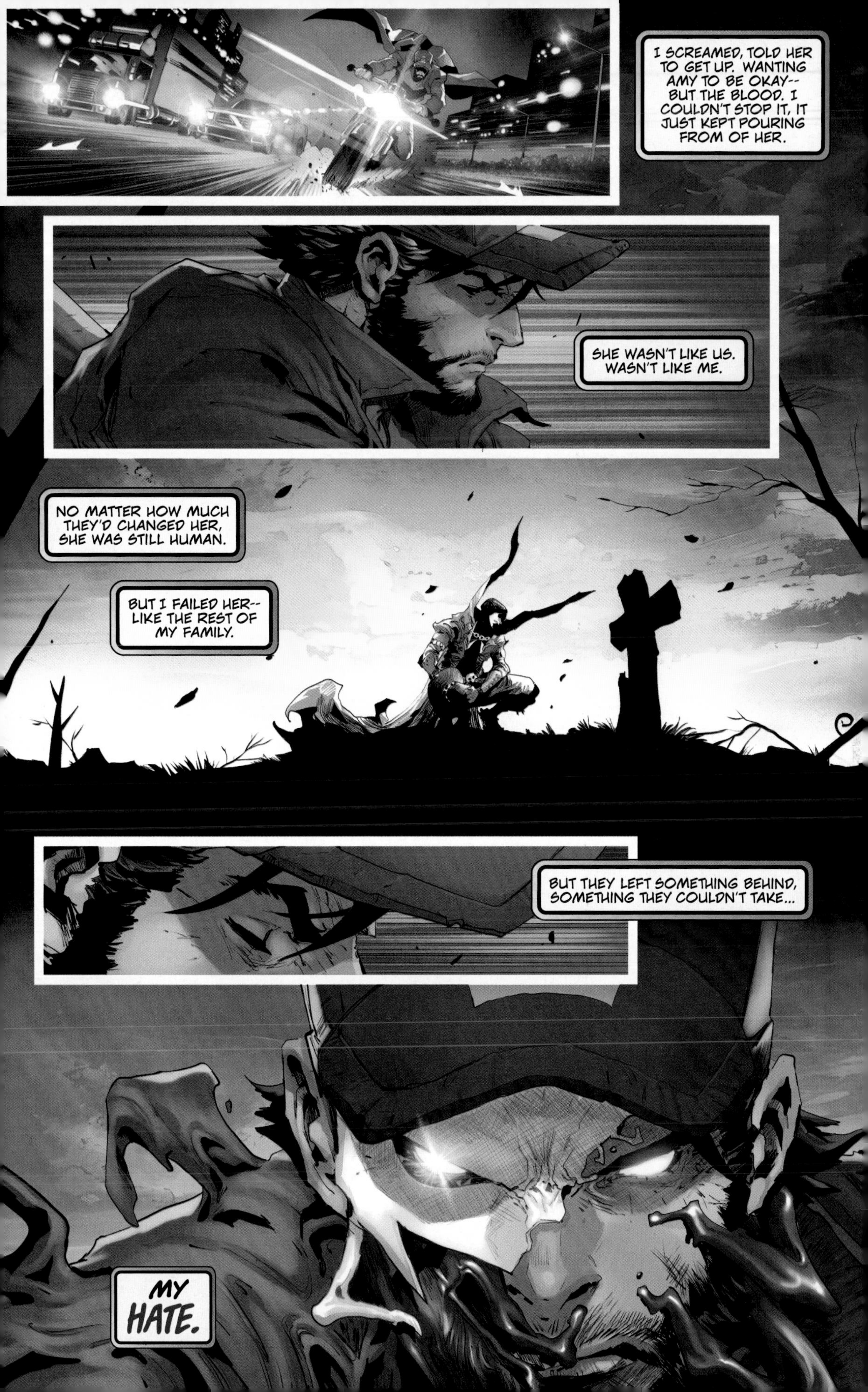
I SCREAMED, TOLD HER TO GET UP. WANTING AMY TO BE OKAY-- BUT THE BLOOD. I COULDN'T STOP IT, IT JUST KEPT POURING FROM OF HER.
SHE WASN'T LIKE US. WASN'T LIKE ME.
NO MATTER HOW MUCH THEY'D CHANGED HER, SHE WAS STILL HUMAN.
BUT I FAILED HER-- LIKE THE REST OF MY FAMILY.
BUT THEY LEFT SOMETHING BEHIND, SOMETHING THEY COULDN'T TAKE...
MY HATE.

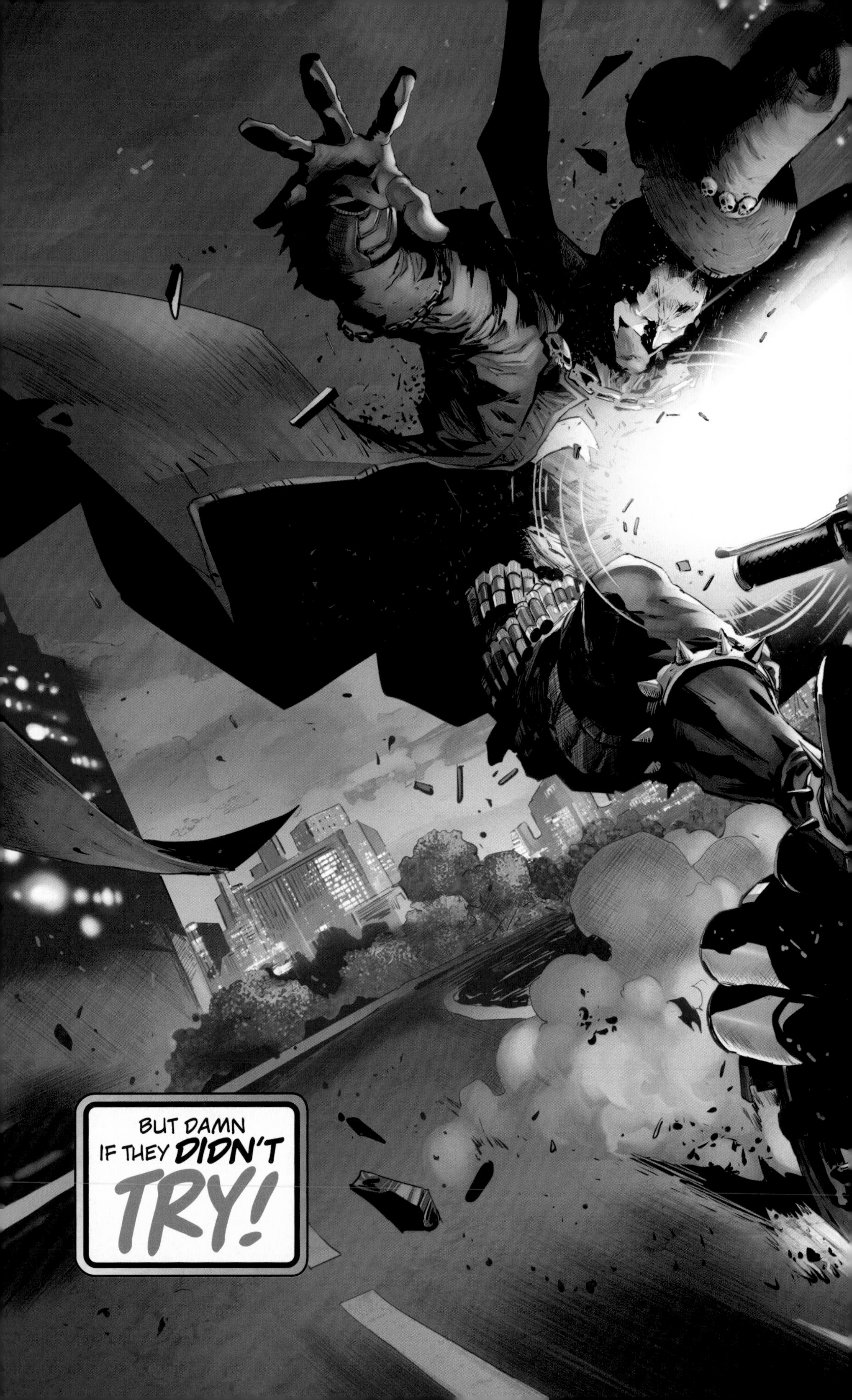
BUT DAMN
IF THEY DIDN'T
TRY!

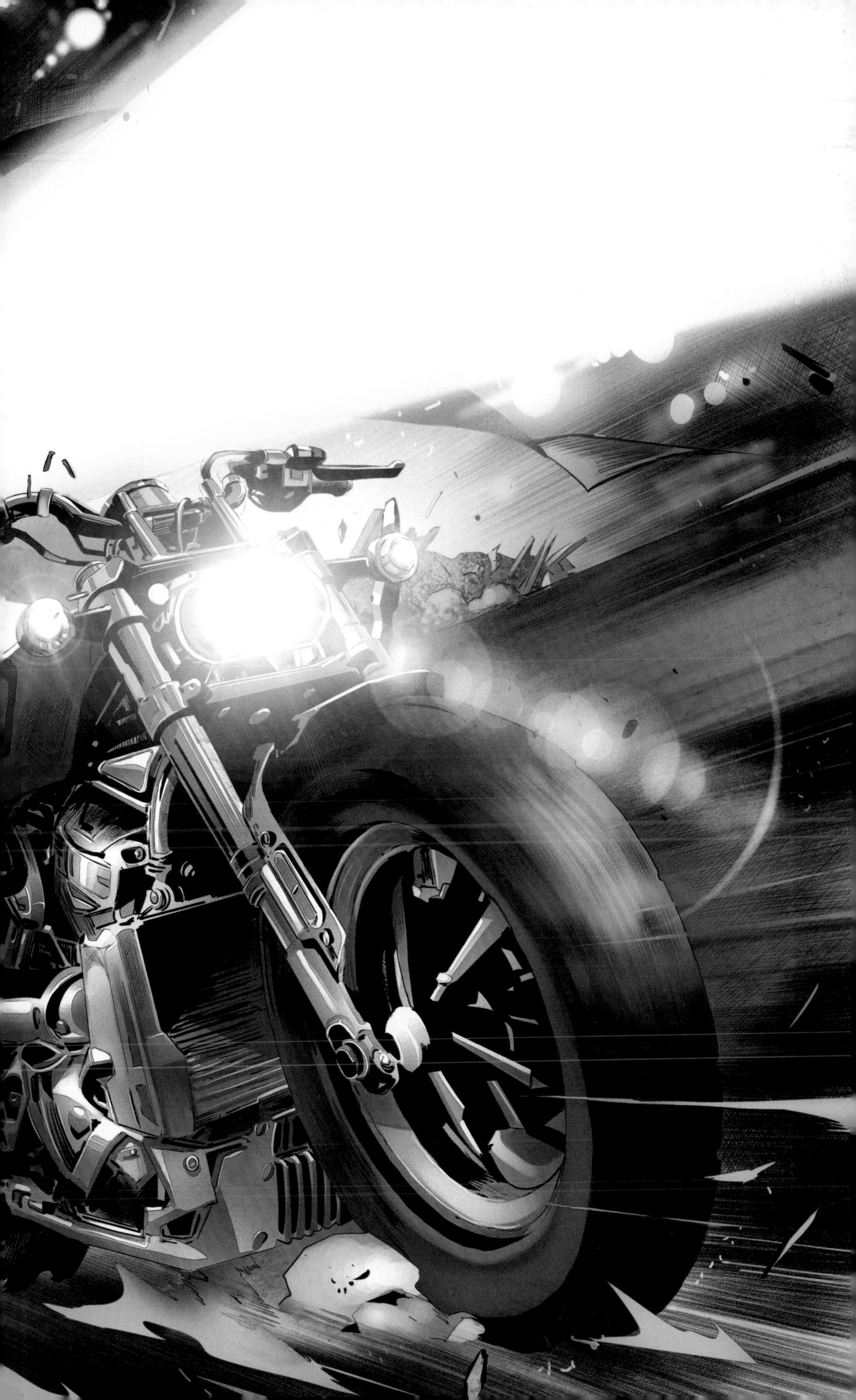

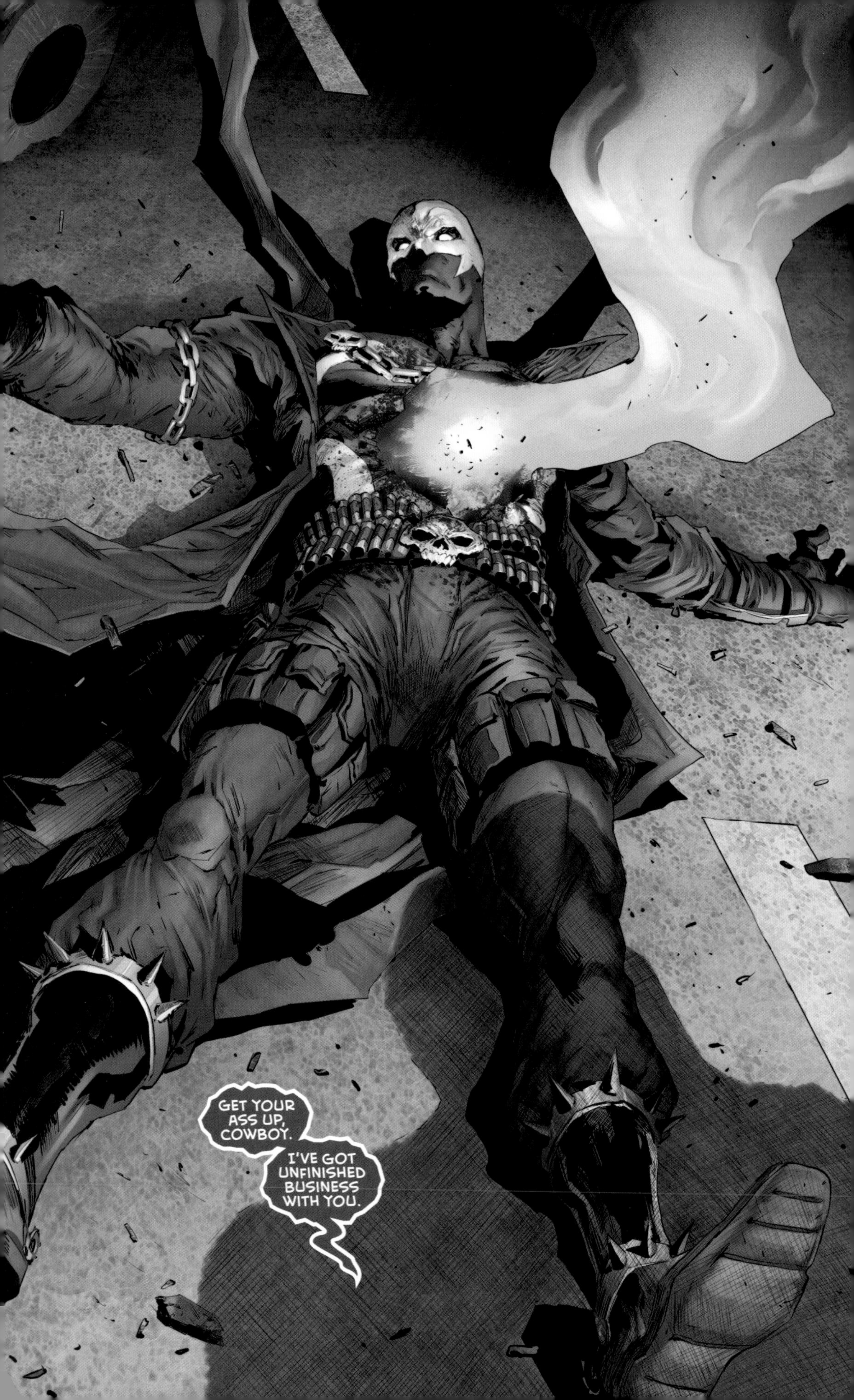
GET YOUR ASS UP, COWBOY.
I'VE GOT UNFINISHED BUSINESS WITH YOU.

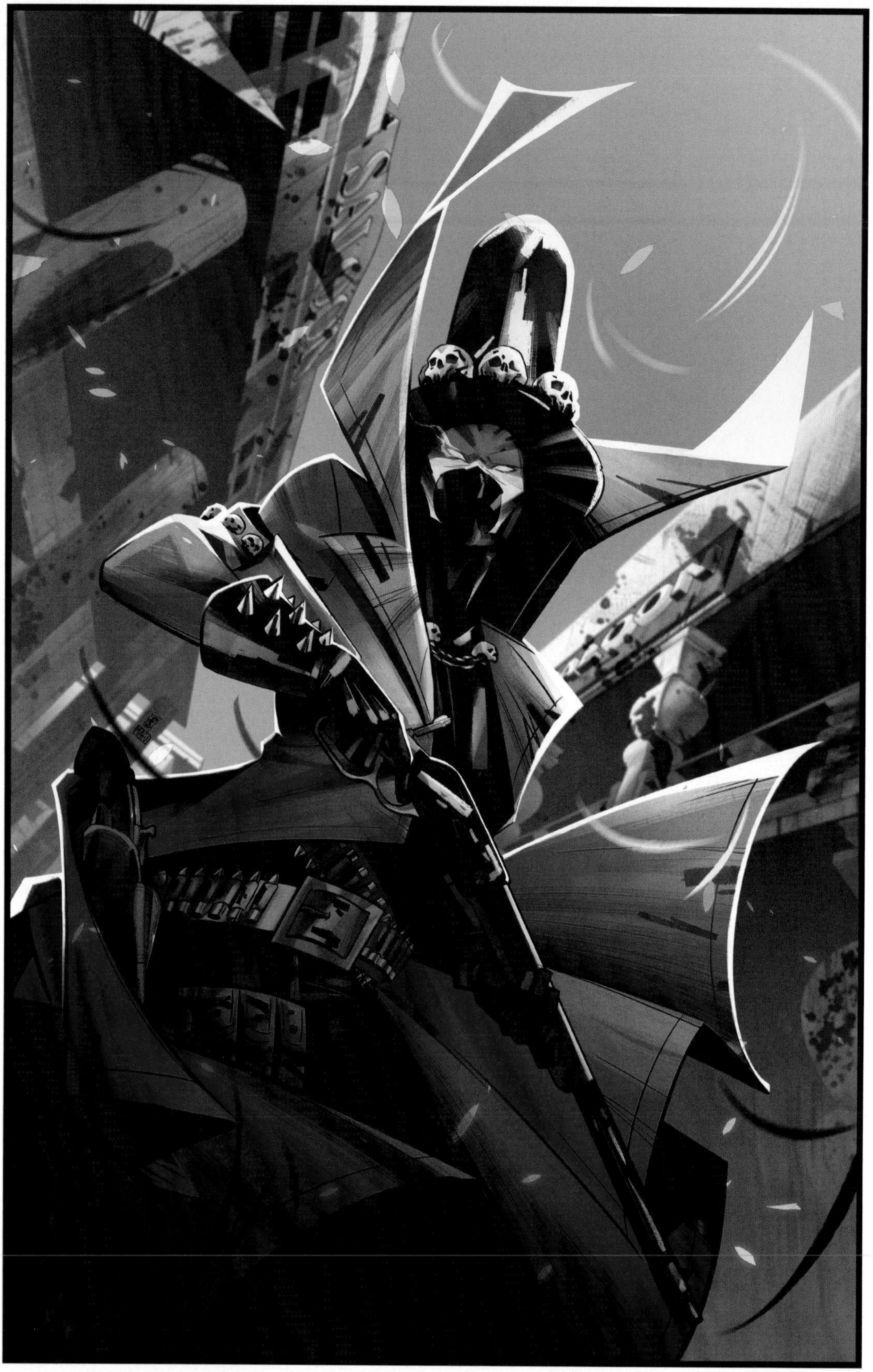

GUNSLINGER SPAWN #27 COVER 'A' BY FEDERICO SABBATINI

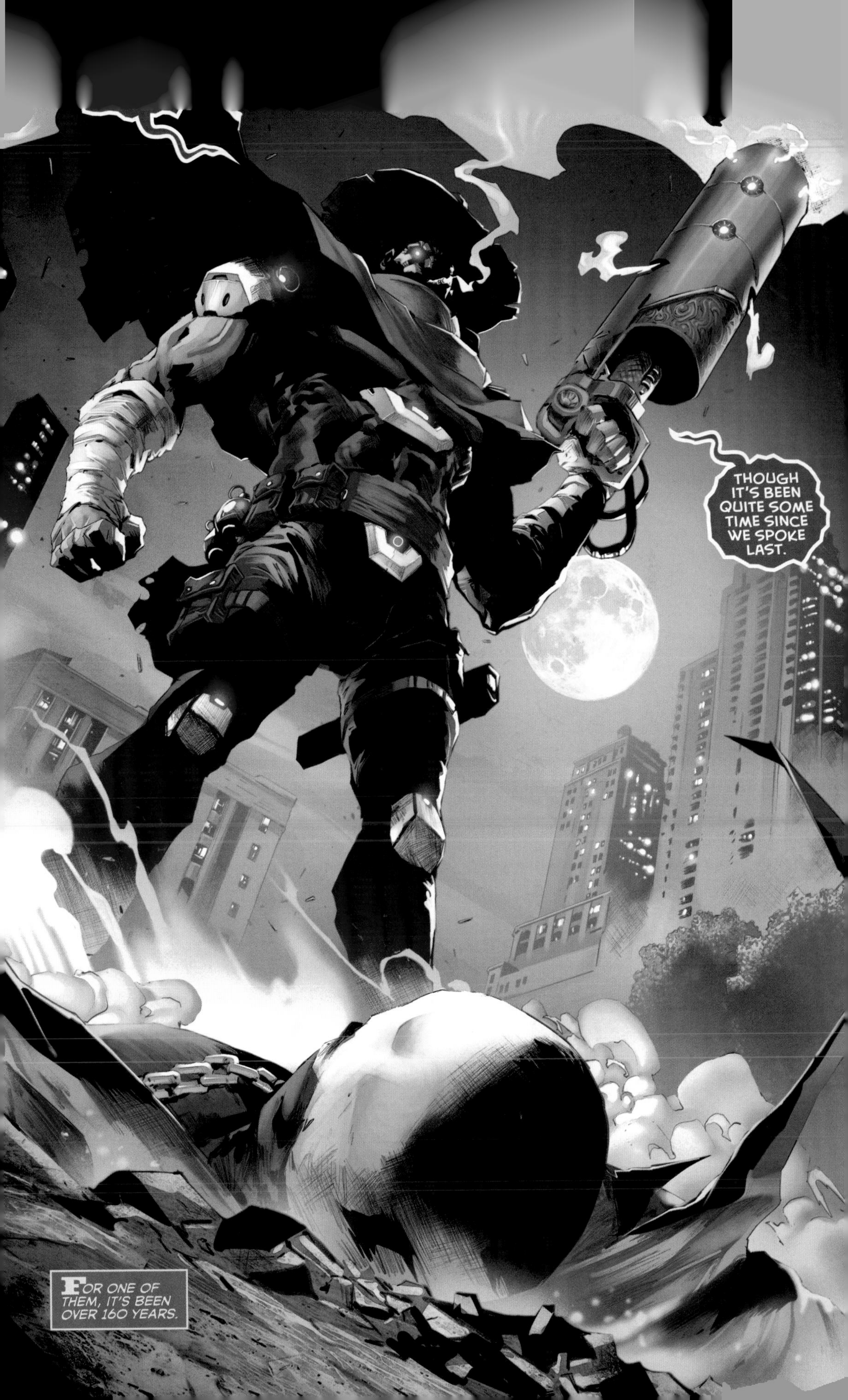
THOUGH IT'S BEEN QUITE SOME TIME SINCE WE SPOKE LAST.
FOR ONE OF THEM, IT'S BEEN OVER 160 YEARS.

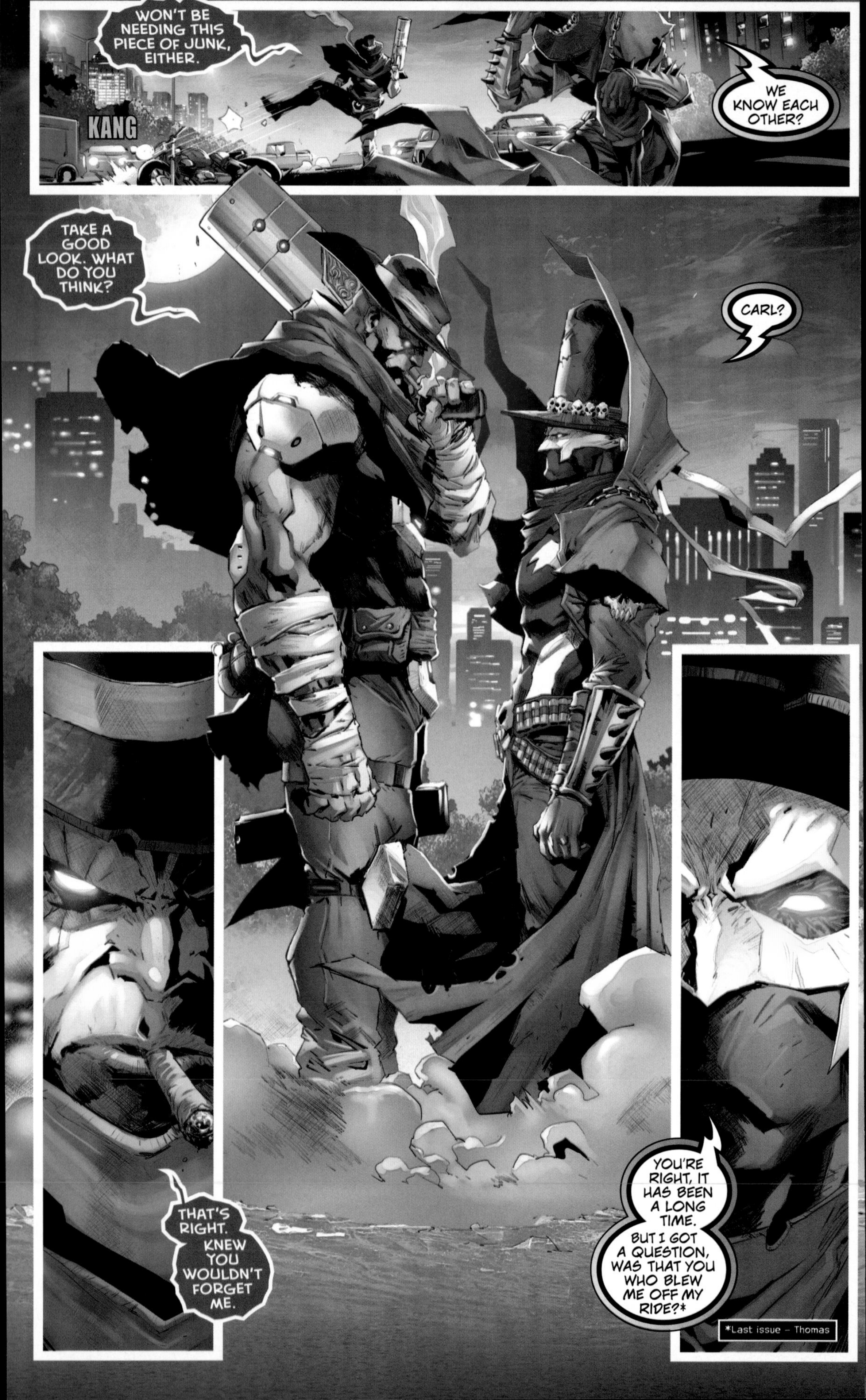
WON'T BE NEEDING THIS PIECE OF JUNK, EITHER.
KANG
WE KNOW EACH OTHER?
TAKE A GOOD LOOK. WHAT DO YOU THINK?
CARL?
THAT'S RIGHT.
KNEW YOU WOULDN'T FORGET ME.
YOU'RE RIGHT, IT HAS BEEN A LONG TIME.
BUT I GOT A QUESTION, WAS THAT YOU WHO BLEW ME OFF MY RIDE?*
*Last issue – Thomas

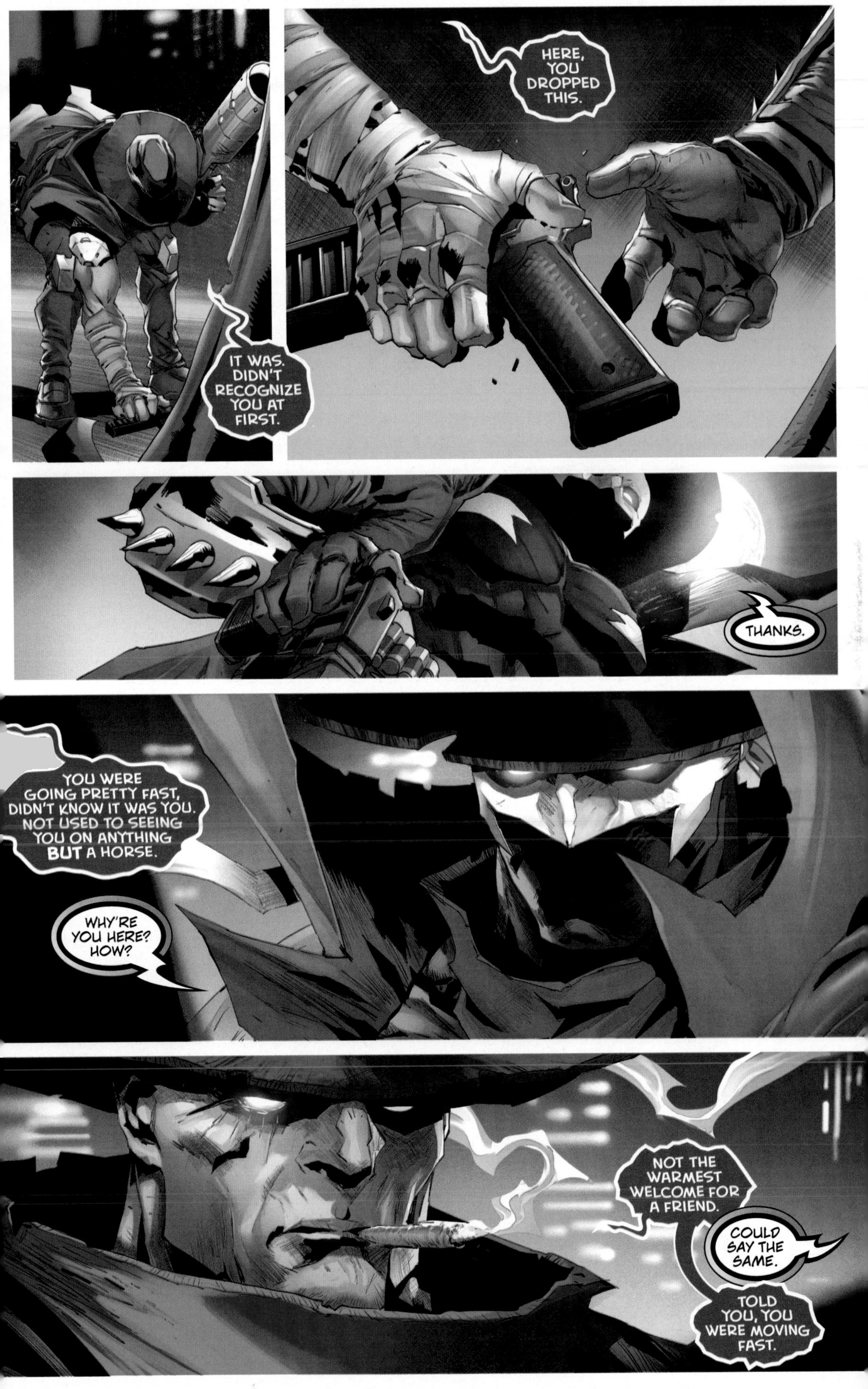

IT WAS. DIDN'T RECOGNIZE YOU AT FIRST.
HERE, YOU DROPPED THIS.
THANKS.
YOU WERE GOING PRETTY FAST, DIDN'T KNOW IT WAS YOU. NOT USED TO SEEING YOU ON ANYTHING **BUT** A HORSE.
WHY'RE YOU HERE? HOW?
NOT THE WARMEST WELCOME FOR A FRIEND.
COULD SAY THE SAME.
TOLD YOU, YOU WERE MOVING FAST.

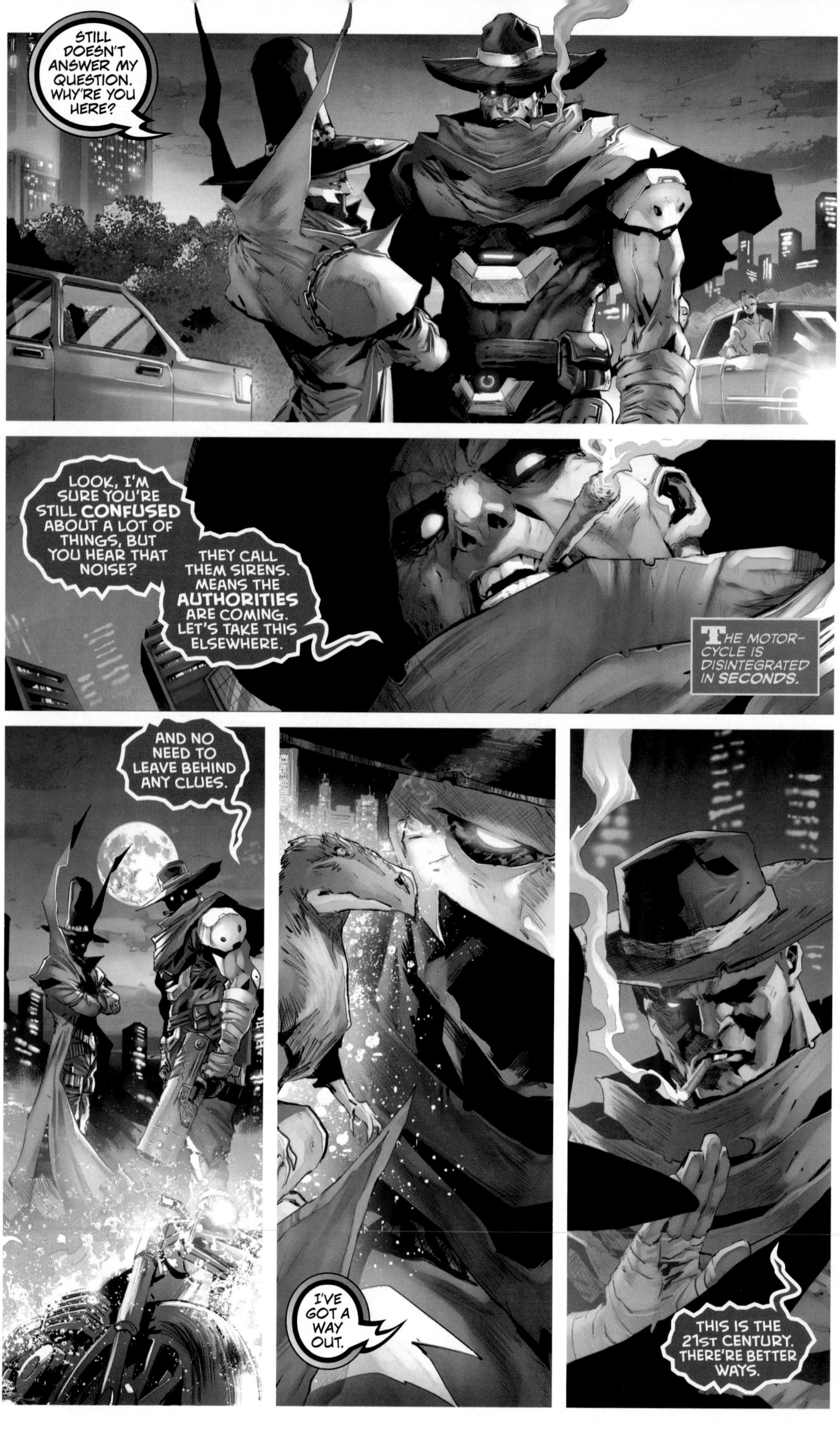
STILL DOESN'T ANSWER MY QUESTION. WHY'RE YOU HERE?
LOOK, I'M SURE YOU'RE STILL CONFUSED ABOUT A LOT OF THINGS, BUT YOU HEAR THAT NOISE?
THEY CALL THEM SIRENS. MEANS THE AUTHORITIES ARE COMING. LET'S TAKE THIS ELSEWHERE.
THE MOTORCYCLE IS DISINTEGRATED IN SECONDS.
AND NO NEED TO LEAVE BEHIND ANY CLUES.
I'VE GOT A WAY OUT.
THIS IS THE 21ST CENTURY. THERE'RE BETTER WAYS.

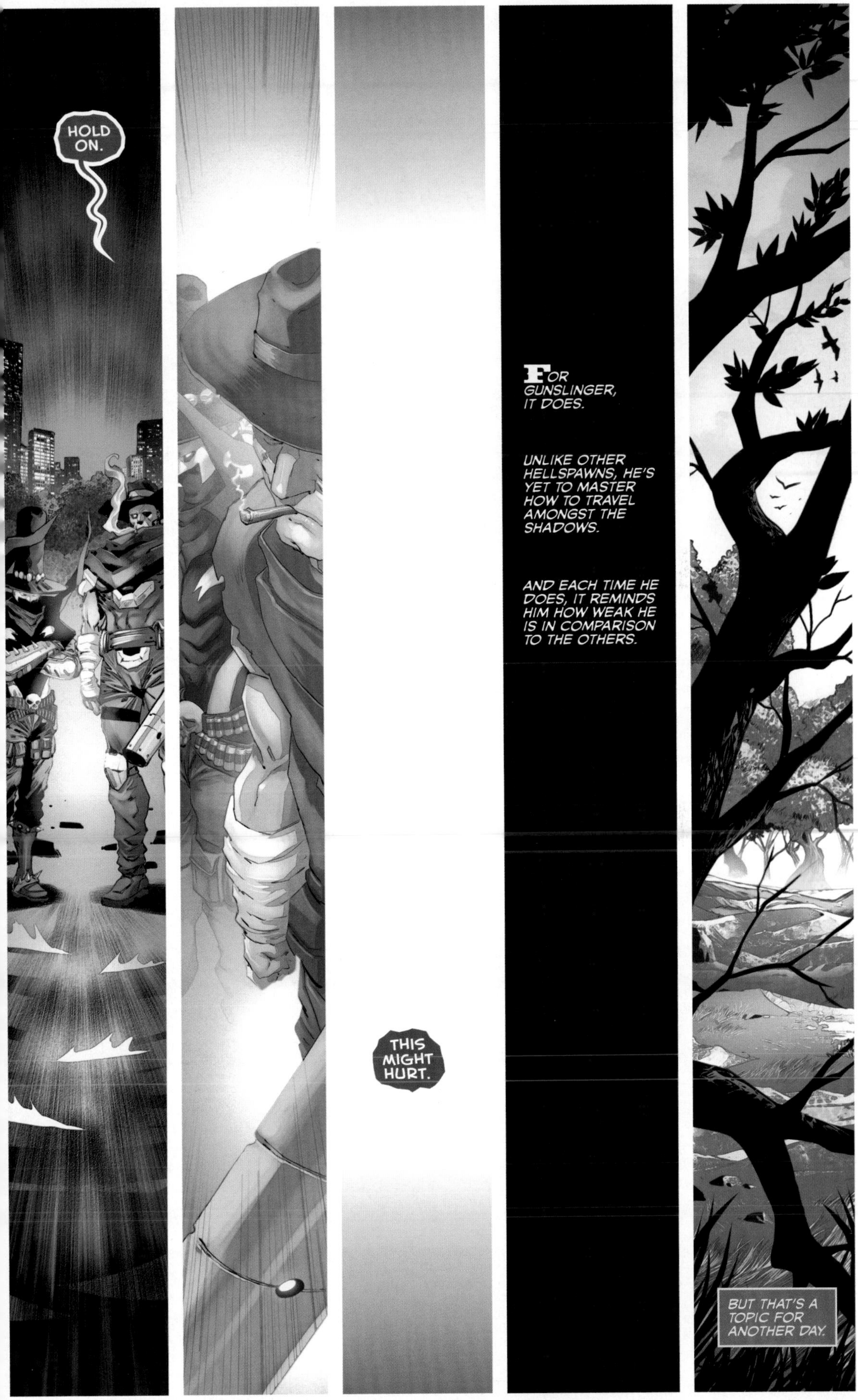
HOLD ON.
THIS MIGHT HURT.
FOR GUNSLINGER, IT DOES.
UNLIKE OTHER HELLSPAWNS, HE'S YET TO MASTER HOW TO TRAVEL AMONGST THE SHADOWS.
AND EACH TIME HE DOES, IT REMINDS HIM HOW WEAK HE IS IN COMPARISON TO THE OTHERS.
BUT THAT'S A TOPIC FOR ANOTHER DAY.

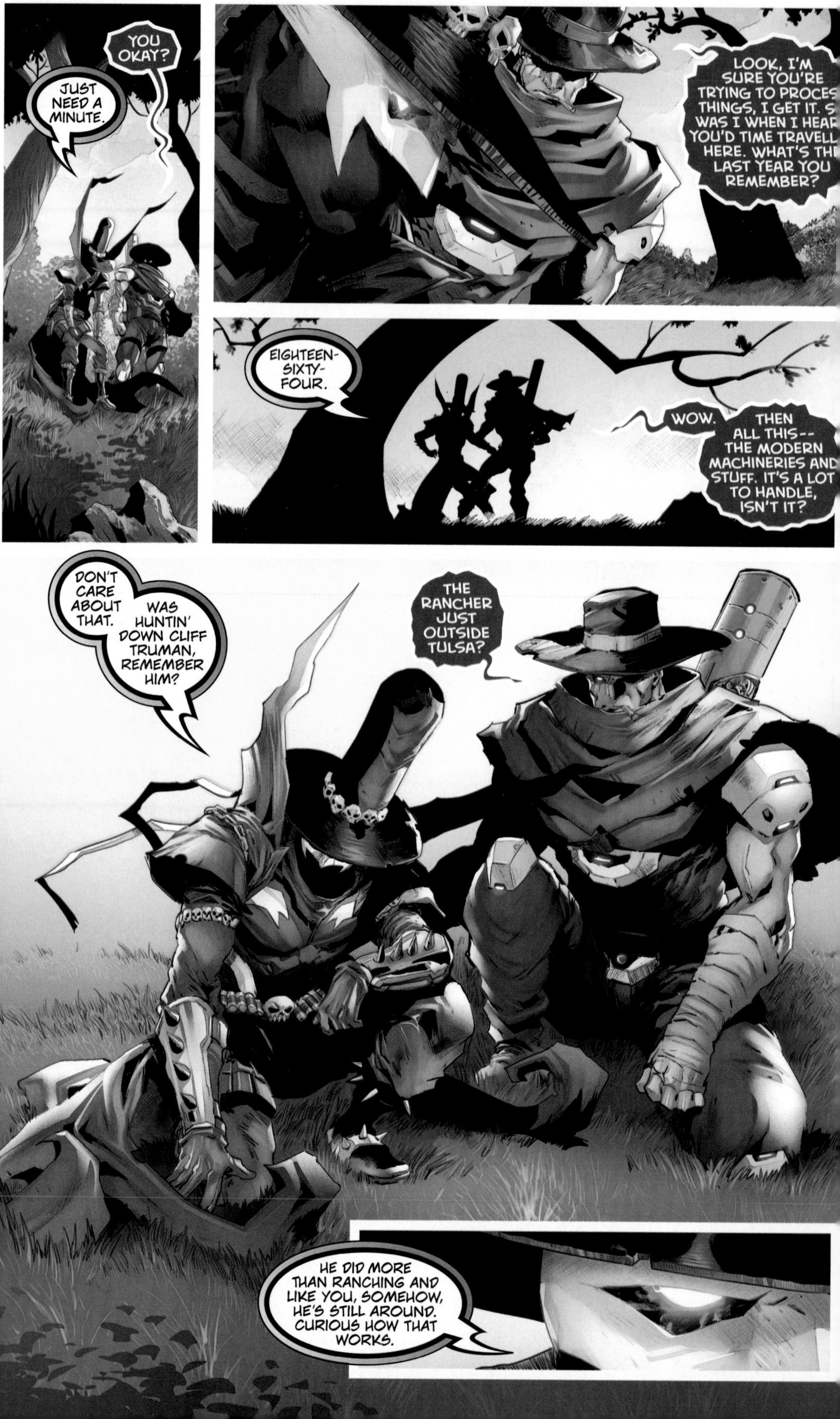
YOU OKAY?
JUST NEED A MINUTE.
LOOK, I'M SURE YOU'RE TRYING TO PROCES THINGS, I GET IT. S WAS I WHEN I HEAR YOU'D TIME TRAVELL HERE. WHAT'S TH LAST YEAR YOU REMEMBER?
EIGHTEEN-SIXTY-FOUR.
WOW.
THEN ALL THIS-- THE MODERN MACHINERIES AND STUFF. IT'S A LOT TO HANDLE, ISN'T IT?
DON'T CARE ABOUT THAT.
WAS HUNTIN' DOWN CLIFF TRUMAN, REMEMBER HIM?
THE RANCHER JUST OUTSIDE TULSA?
HE DID MORE THAN RANCHING AND LIKE YOU, SOMEHOW, HE'S STILL AROUND. CURIOUS HOW THAT WORKS.

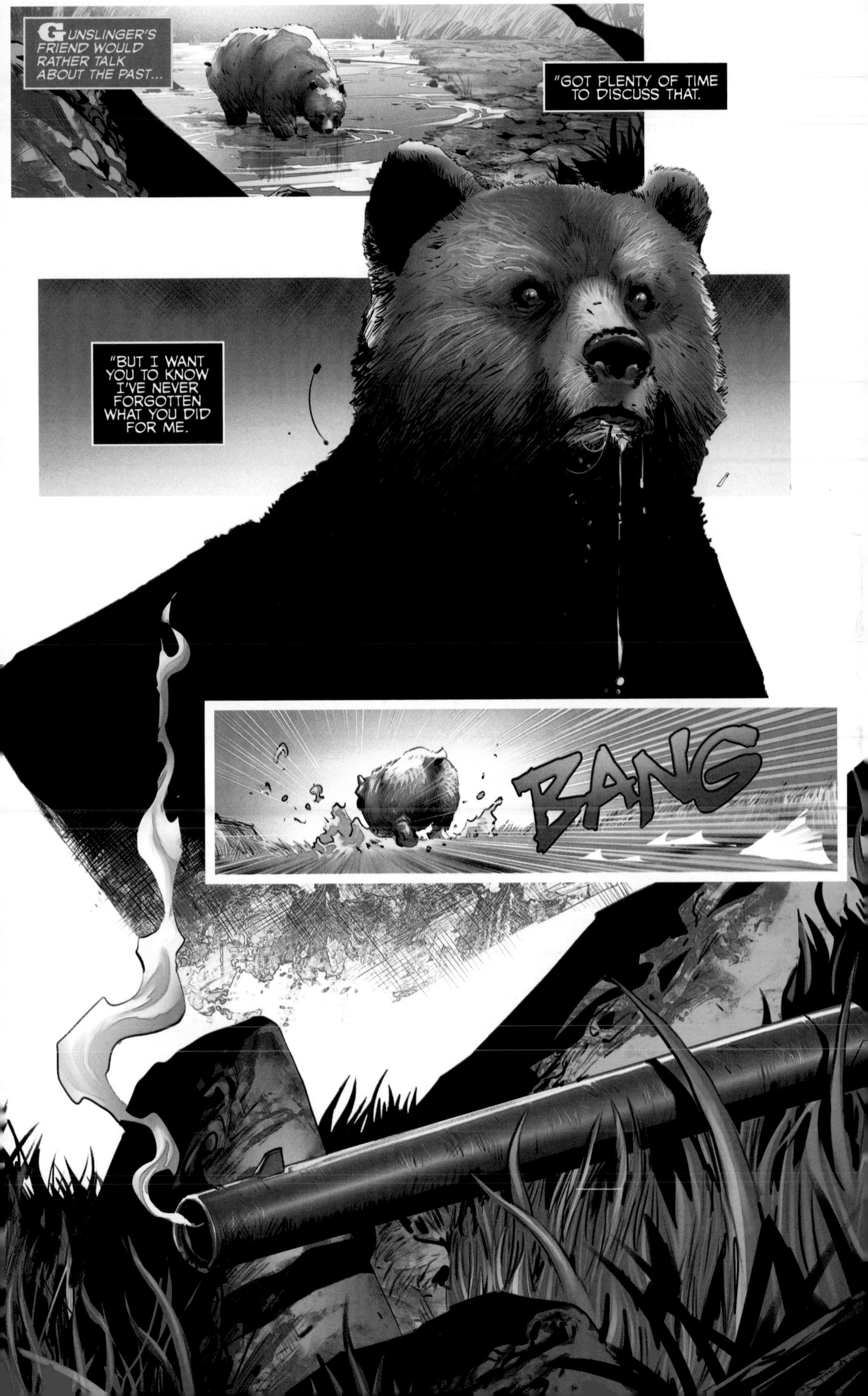
GUNSLINGER'S FRIEND WOULD RATHER TALK ABOUT THE PAST...
"GOT PLENTY OF TIME TO DISCUSS THAT.
"BUT I WANT YOU TO KNOW I'VE NEVER FORGOTTEN WHAT YOU DID FOR ME.
BANG

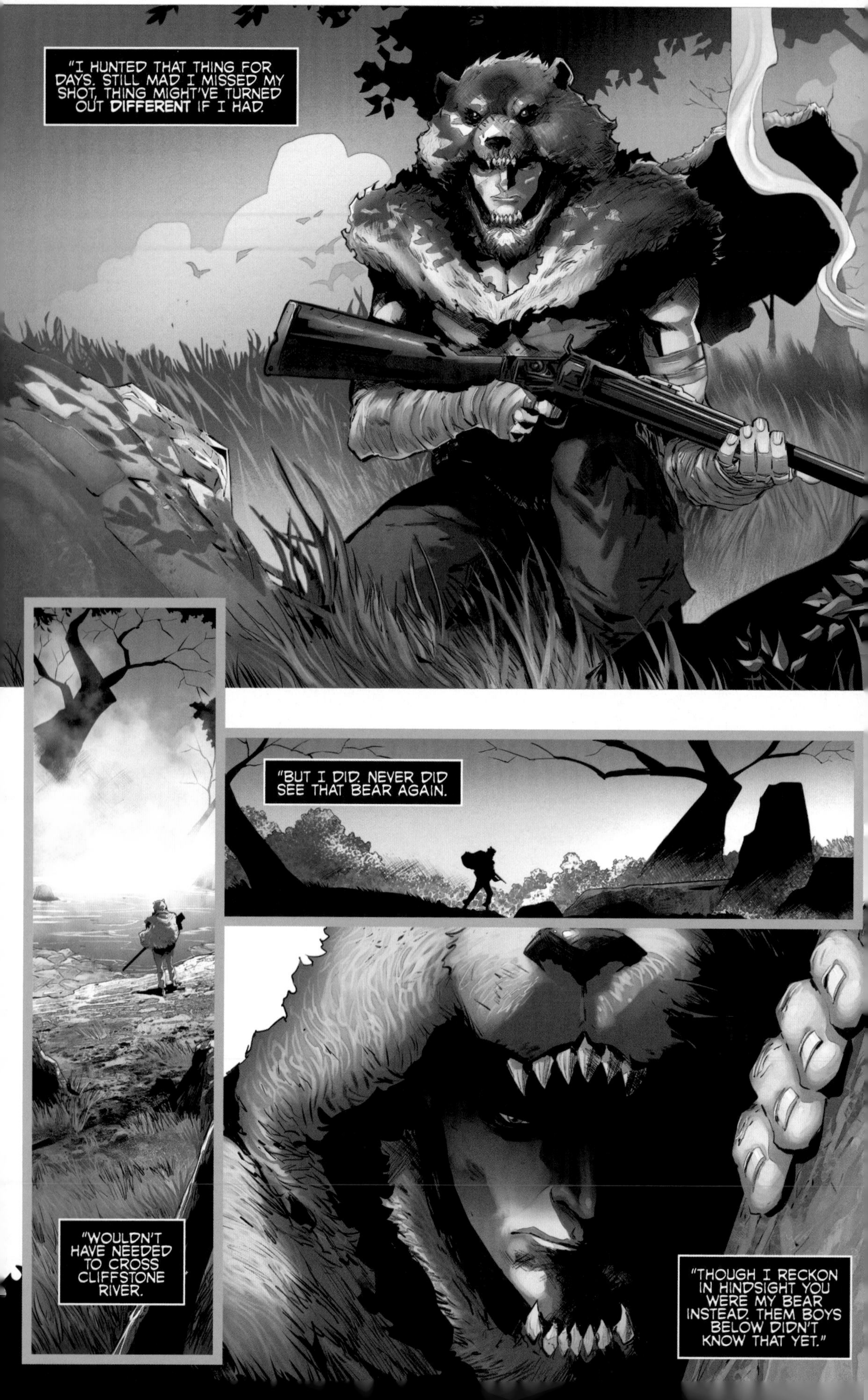
"I HUNTED THAT THING FOR DAYS. STILL MAD I MISSED MY SHOT, THING MIGHT'VE TURNED OUT **DIFFERENT** IF I HAD.
"WOULDN'T HAVE NEEDED TO CROSS CLIFFSTONE RIVER.
"BUT I DID. NEVER DID SEE THAT BEAR AGAIN.
"THOUGH I RECKON IN HINDSIGHT YOU WERE MY BEAR INSTEAD. THEM BOYS BELOW DIDN'T KNOW THAT YET."

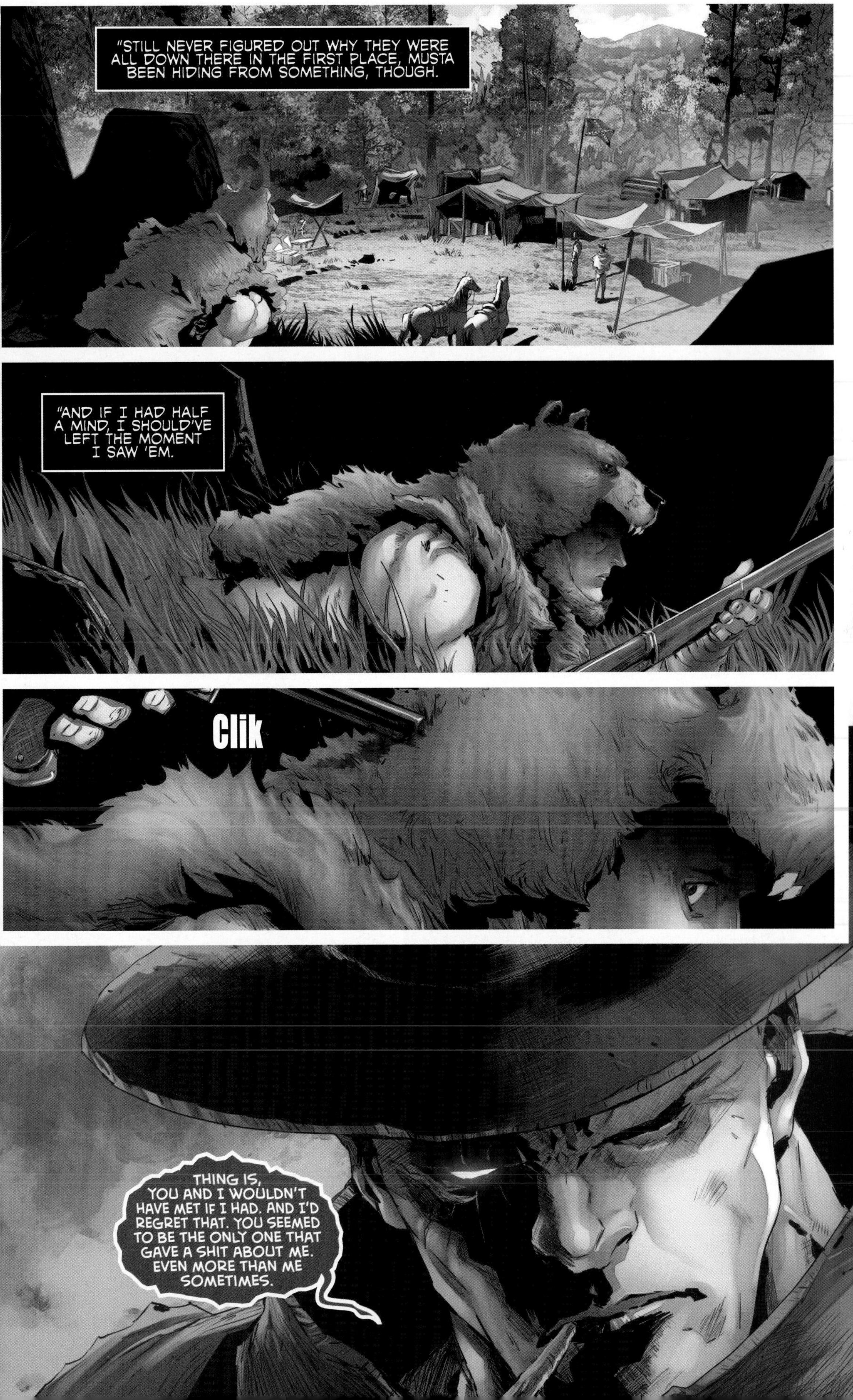
"STILL NEVER FIGURED OUT WHY THEY WERE ALL DOWN THERE IN THE FIRST PLACE, MUSTA BEEN HIDING FROM SOMETHING, THOUGH.
"AND IF I HAD HALF A MIND, I SHOULD'VE LEFT THE MOMENT I SAW 'EM.
Clik
THING IS, YOU AND I WOULDN'T HAVE MET IF I HAD. AND I'D REGRET THAT. YOU SEEMED TO BE THE ONLY ONE THAT GAVE A SHIT ABOUT ME. EVEN MORE THAN ME SOMETIMES.

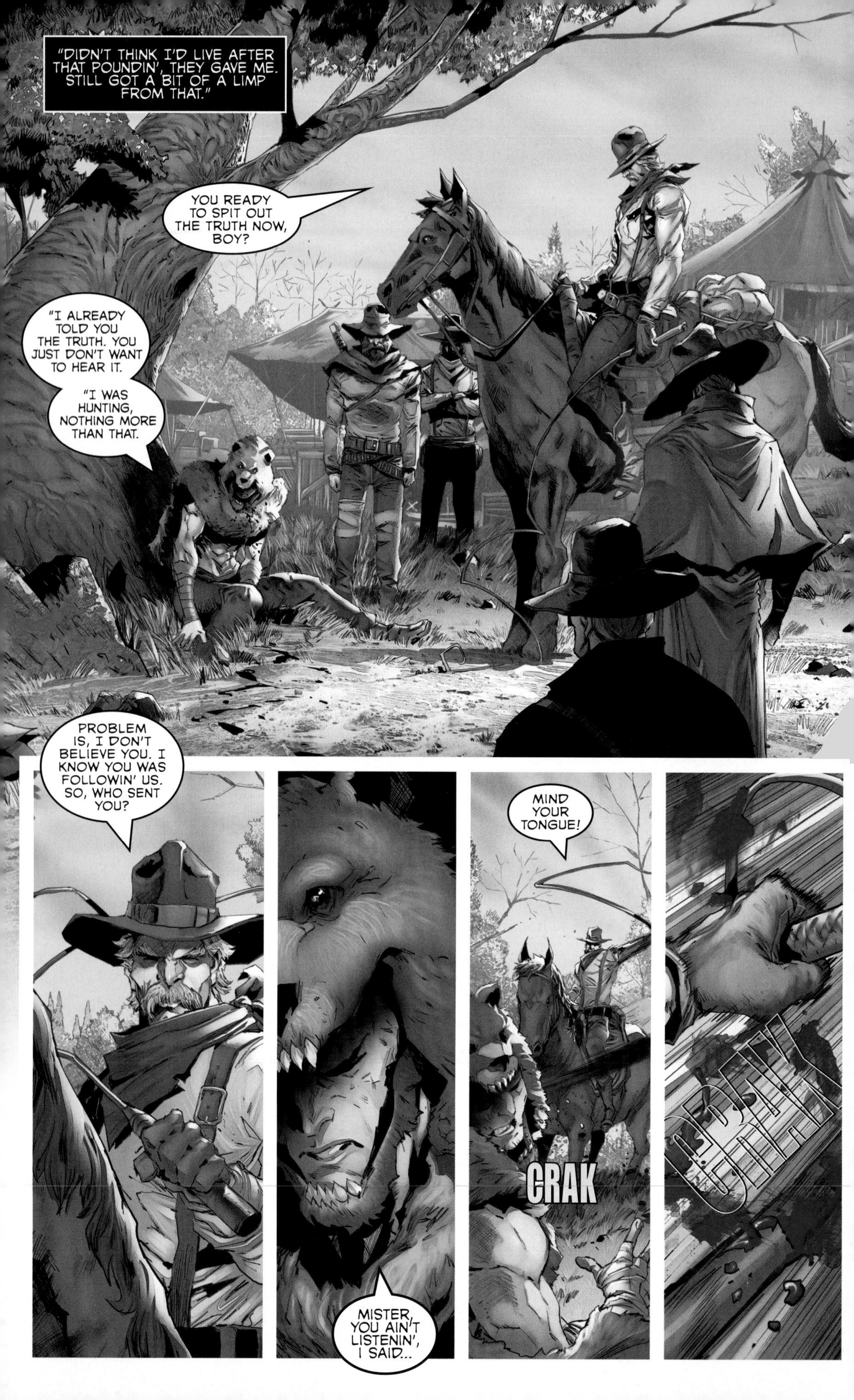
"DIDN'T THINK I'D LIVE AFTER THAT POUNDIN', THEY GAVE ME. STILL GOT A BIT OF A LIMP FROM THAT."
YOU READY TO SPIT OUT THE TRUTH NOW, BOY?
"I ALREADY TOLD YOU THE TRUTH. YOU JUST DON'T WANT TO HEAR IT.
"I WAS HUNTING, NOTHING MORE THAN THAT.
PROBLEM IS, I DON'T BELIEVE YOU. I KNOW YOU WAS FOLLOWIN' US. SO, WHO SENT YOU?
MISTER, YOU AIN'T LISTENIN', I SAID...
MIND YOUR TONGUE!
CRAK

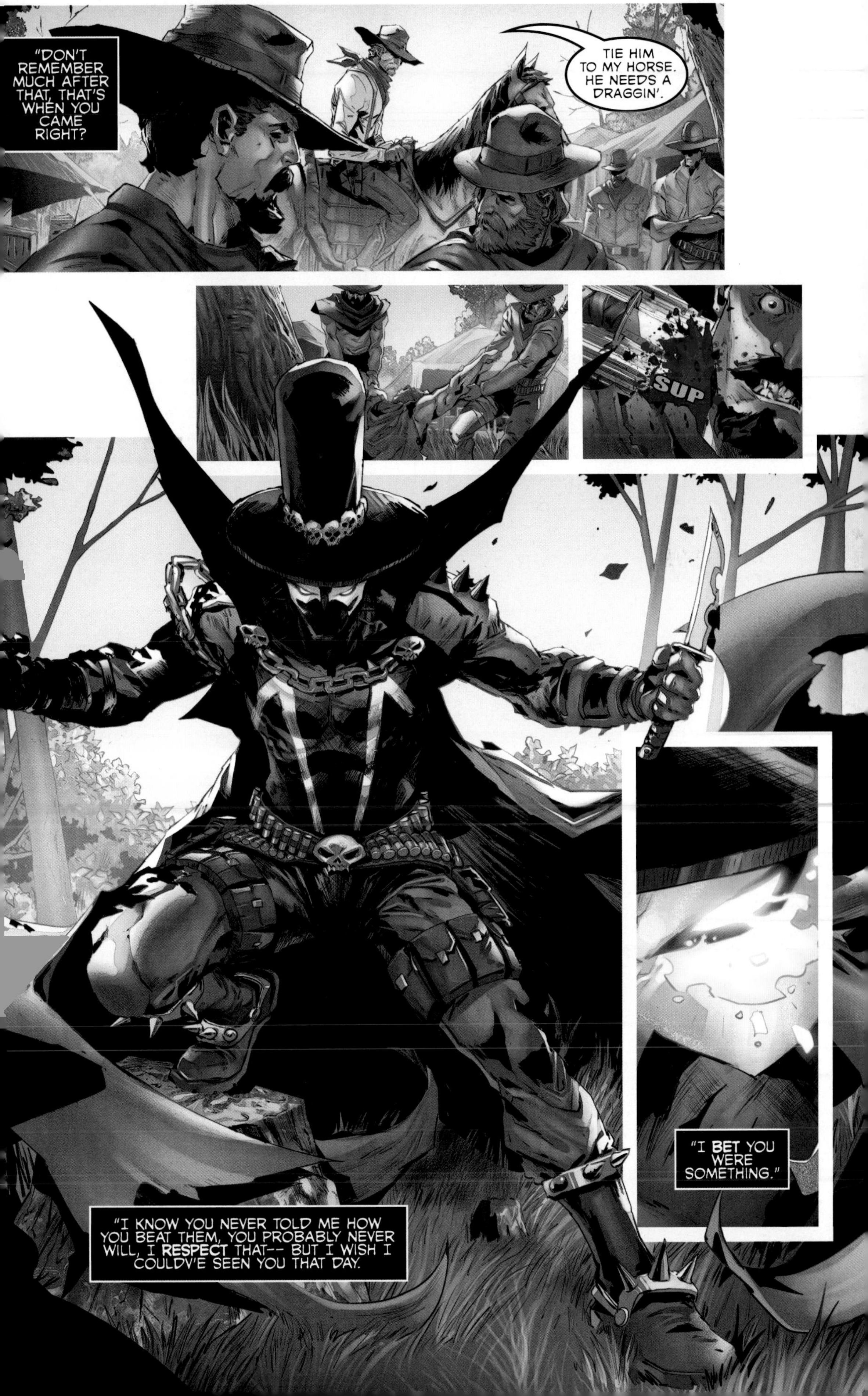
"DON'T REMEMBER MUCH AFTER THAT, THAT'S WHEN YOU CAME RIGHT?
TIE HIM TO MY HORSE. HE NEEDS A DRAGGIN'.
SUP
"I KNOW YOU NEVER TOLD ME HOW YOU BEAT THEM, YOU PROBABLY NEVER WILL, I RESPECT THAT-- BUT I WISH I COULDV'E SEEN YOU THAT DAY.
"I BET YOU WERE SOMETHING."

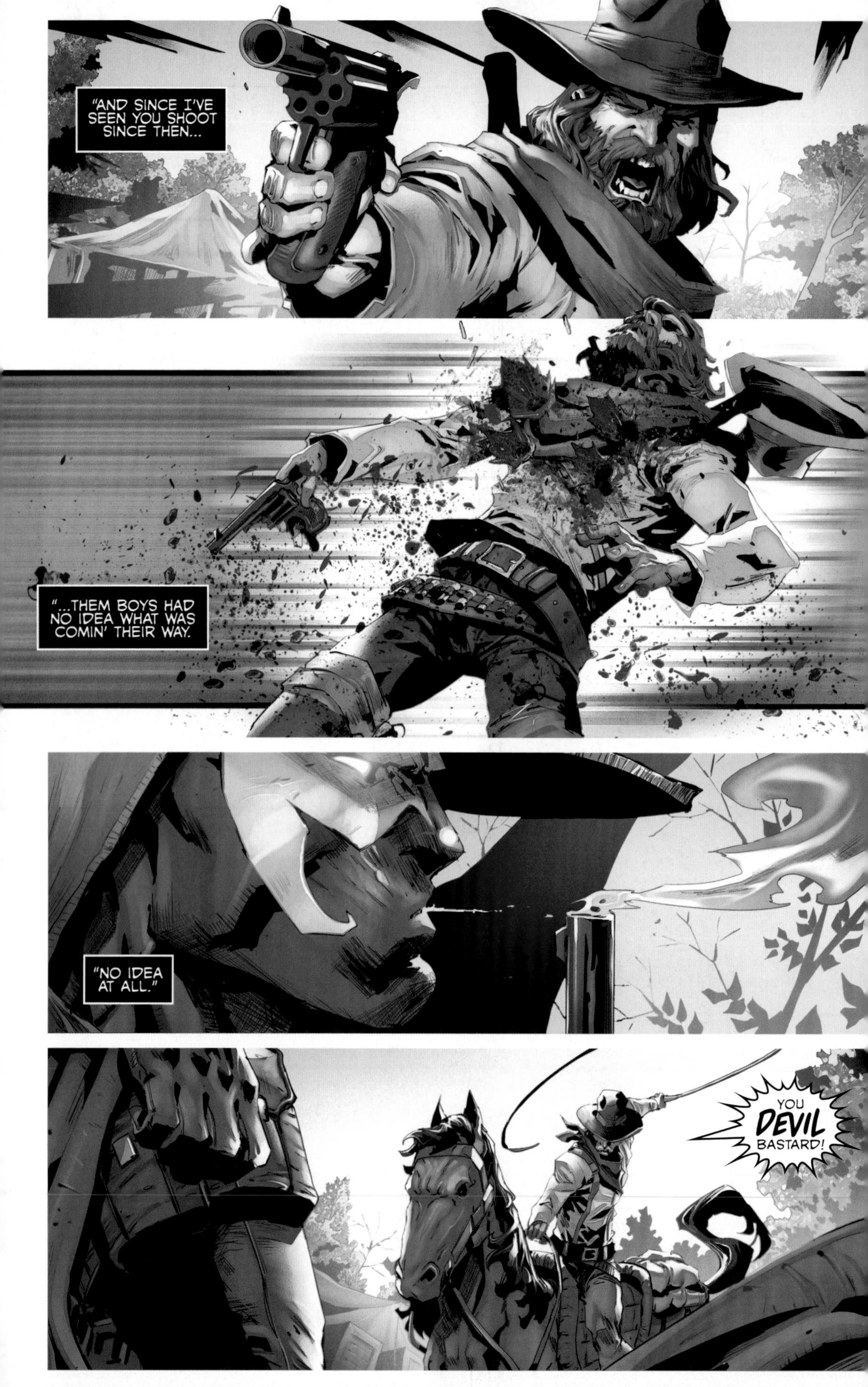
"AND SINCE I'VE SEEN YOU SHOOT SINCE THEN...
"...THEM BOYS HAD NO IDEA WHAT WAS COMIN' THEIR WAY.
"NO IDEA AT ALL."
YOU DEVIL BASTARD!

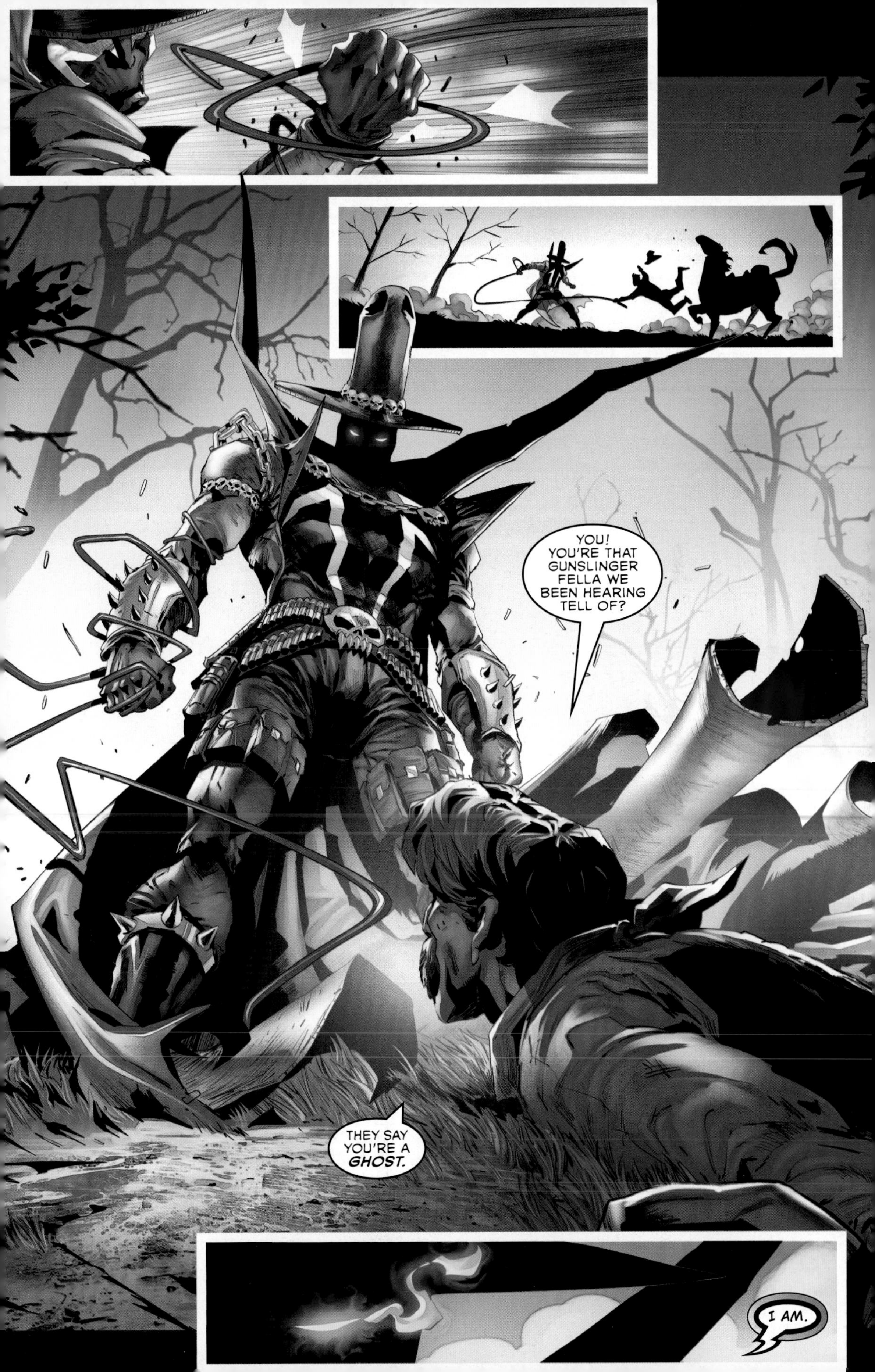
YOU! YOU'RE THAT GUNSLINGER FELLA WE BEEN HEARING TELL OF?
THEY SAY YOU'RE A *GHOST.*
I AM.

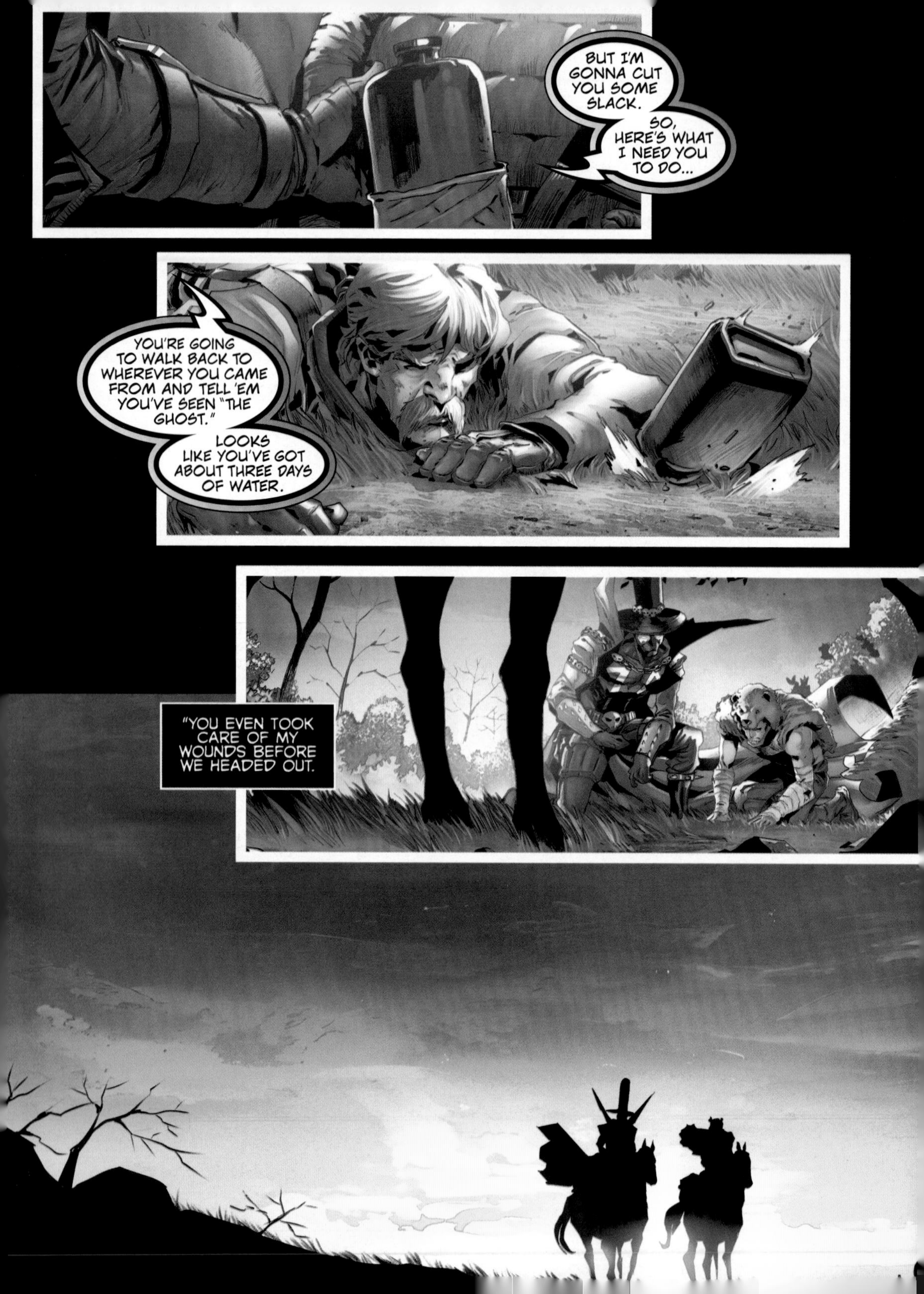
BUT I'M GONNA CUT YOU SOME SLACK.
SO, HERE'S WHAT I NEED YOU TO DO...
YOU'RE GOING TO WALK BACK TO WHEREVER YOU CAME FROM AND TELL 'EM YOU'VE SEEN "THE GHOST."
LOOKS LIKE YOU'VE GOT ABOUT THREE DAYS OF WATER.
"YOU EVEN TOOK CARE OF MY WOUNDS BEFORE WE HEADED OUT.

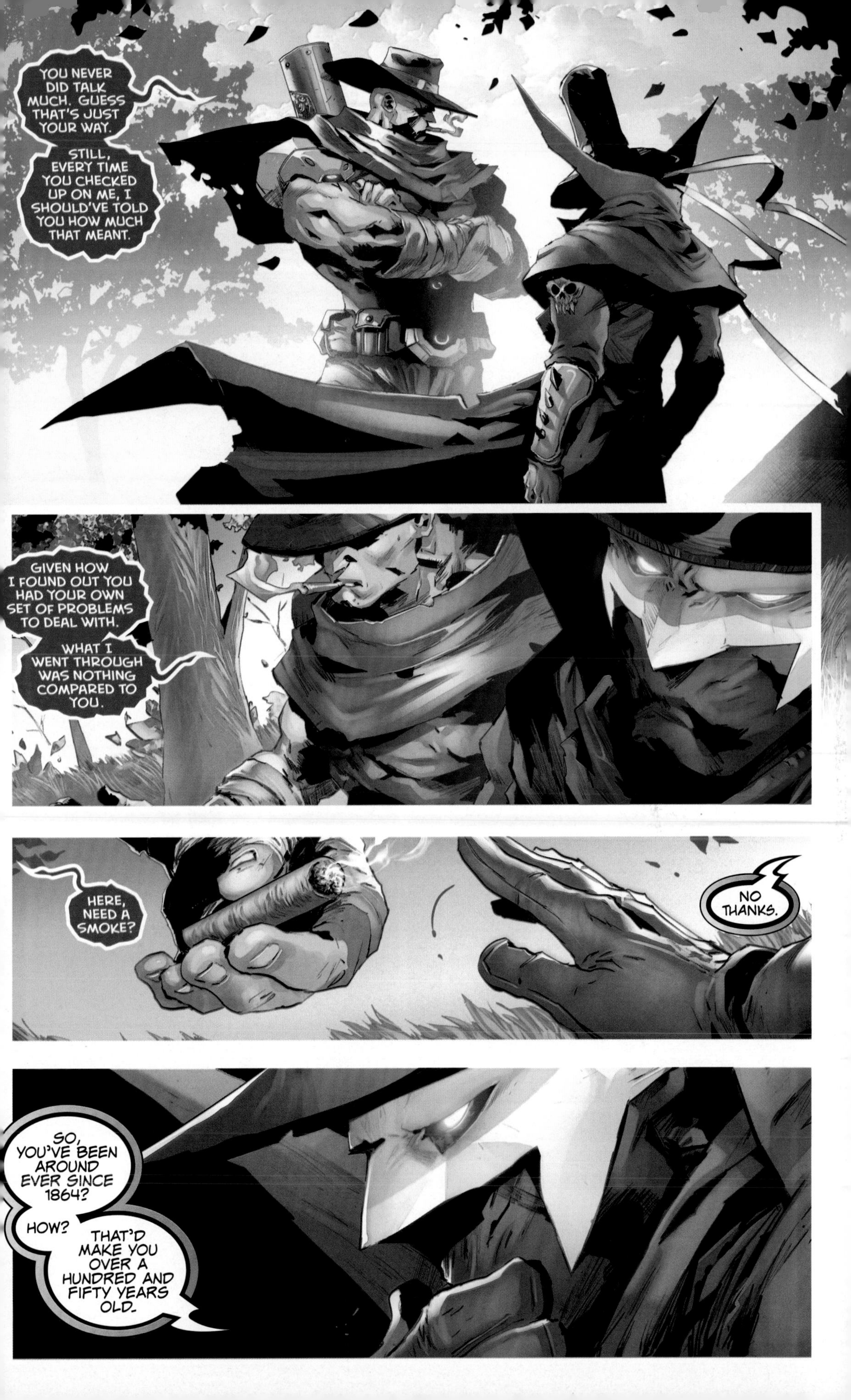
YOU NEVER DID TALK MUCH. GUESS THAT'S JUST YOUR WAY.
STILL, EVERY TIME YOU CHECKED UP ON ME, I SHOULD'VE TOLD YOU HOW MUCH THAT MEANT.
GIVEN HOW I FOUND OUT YOU HAD YOUR OWN SET OF PROBLEMS TO DEAL WITH.
WHAT I WENT THROUGH WAS NOTHING COMPARED TO YOU.
HERE, NEED A SMOKE?
NO THANKS.
SO, YOU'VE BEEN AROUND EVER SINCE 1864?
HOW?
THAT'D MAKE YOU OVER A HUNDRED AND FIFTY YEARS OLD.

LET'S JUST SAY THINGS GOT 'STRANGE' OVER TIME. BUT BEFORE I FORGET, WHAT DID HAPPEN TO AMY?

SHE'S DEAD.

I KNOW. YOU TOLD ME. BUT WHO KILLED HER?

THE ONES I'M HUNTING. YOU KNOW THINGS ABOUT THAT?

THE MAN WALKS AWAY, TO THE SHADOWS OF A NEARBY TALL TREE.

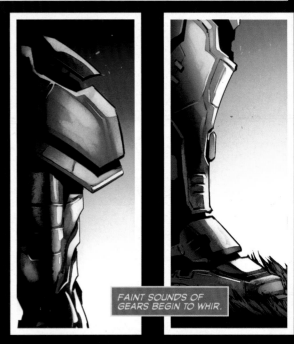

FAINT SOUNDS OF GEARS BEGIN TO WHIR.

AS I SAID... STRANGE THINGS HAPPENED TO ME ALONG THE WAY.

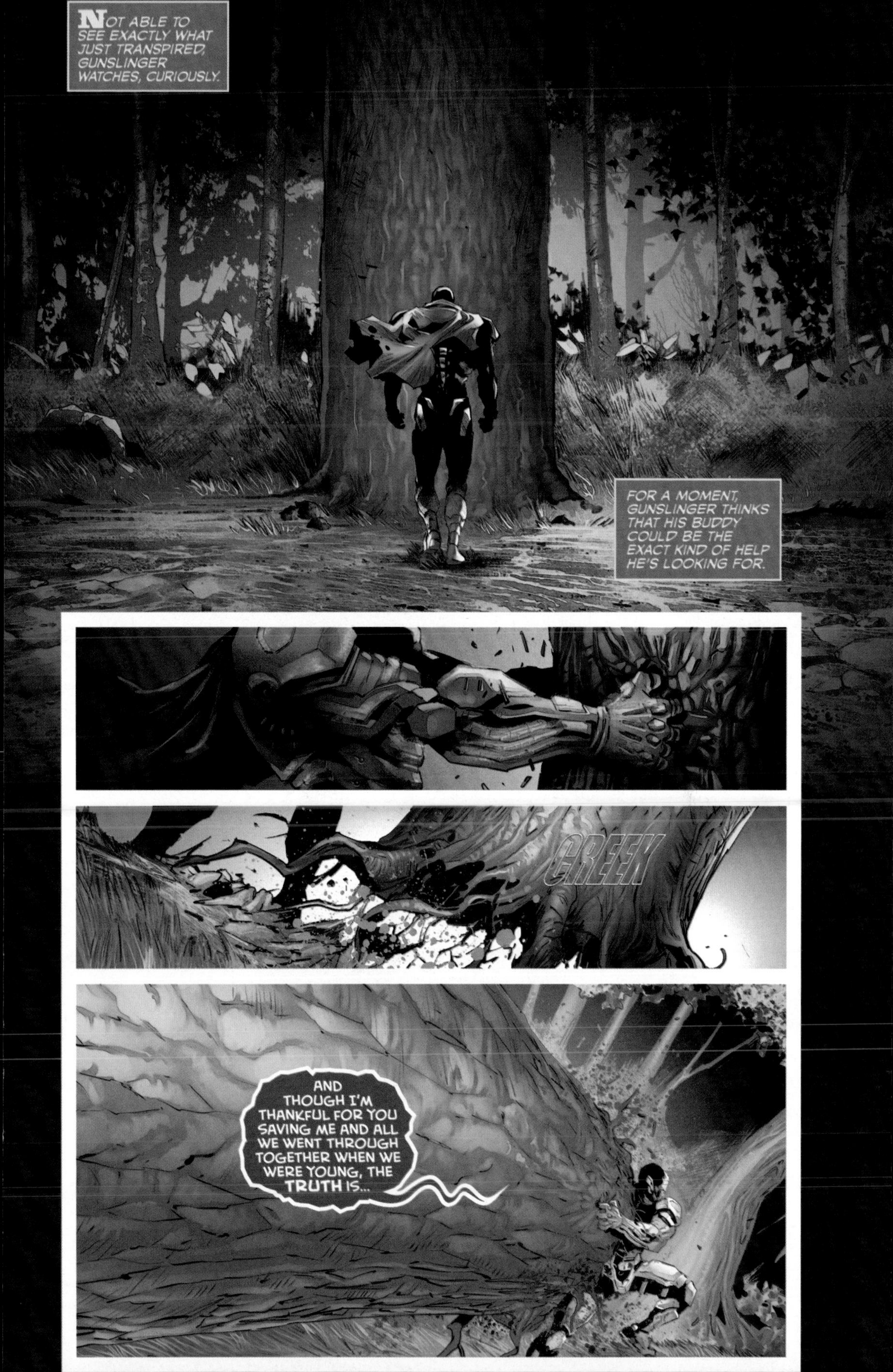
NOT ABLE TO SEE EXACTLY WHAT JUST TRANSPIRED, GUNSLINGER WATCHES, CURIOUSLY.
FOR A MOMENT, GUNSLINGER THINKS THAT HIS BUDDY COULD BE THE EXACT KIND OF HELP HE'S LOOKING FOR.
CREEK
AND THOUGH I'M THANKFUL FOR YOU SAVING ME AND ALL WE WENT THROUGH TOGETHER WHEN WE WERE YOUNG, THE TRUTH IS...

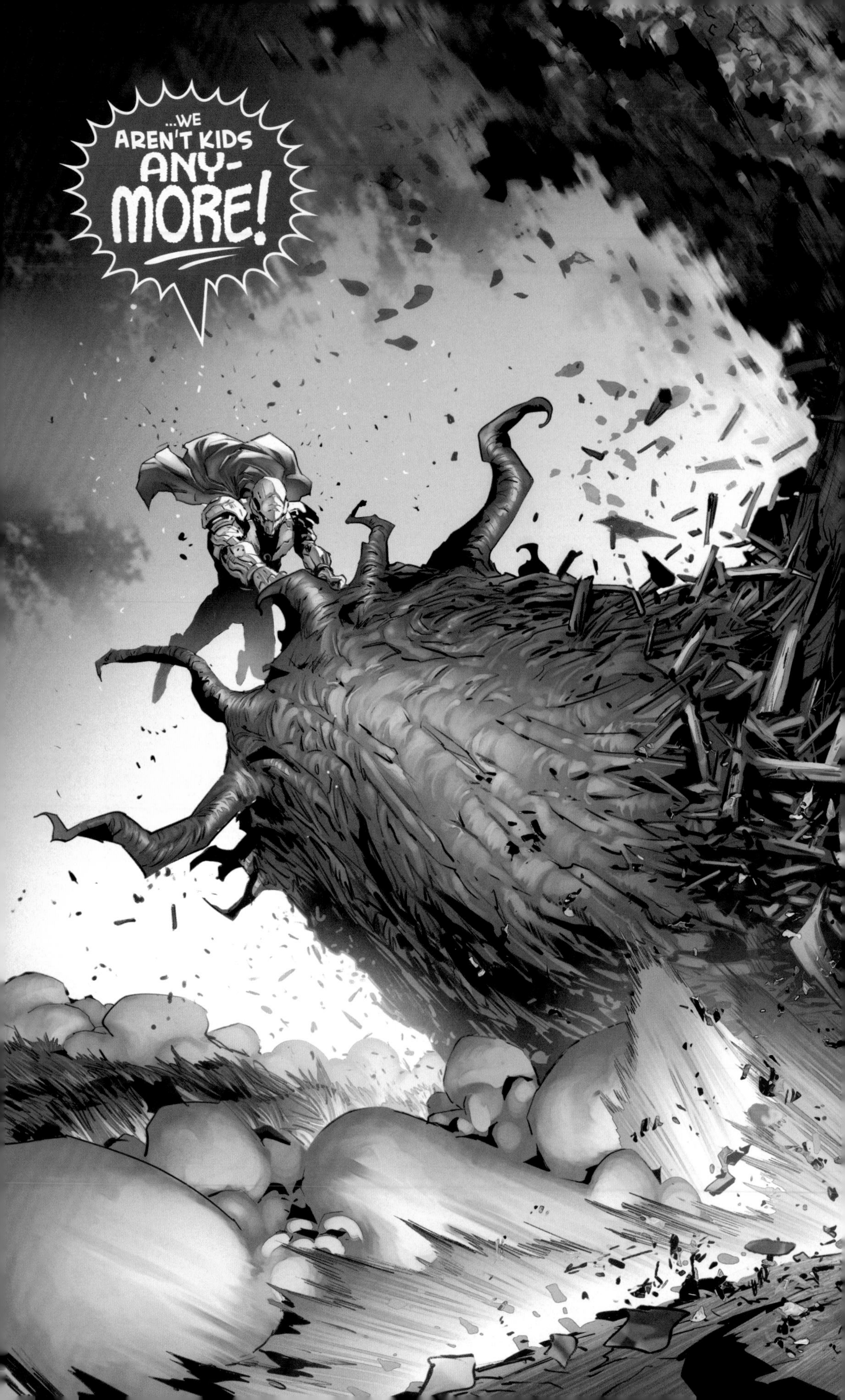
...WE AREN'T KIDS ANY-MORE!

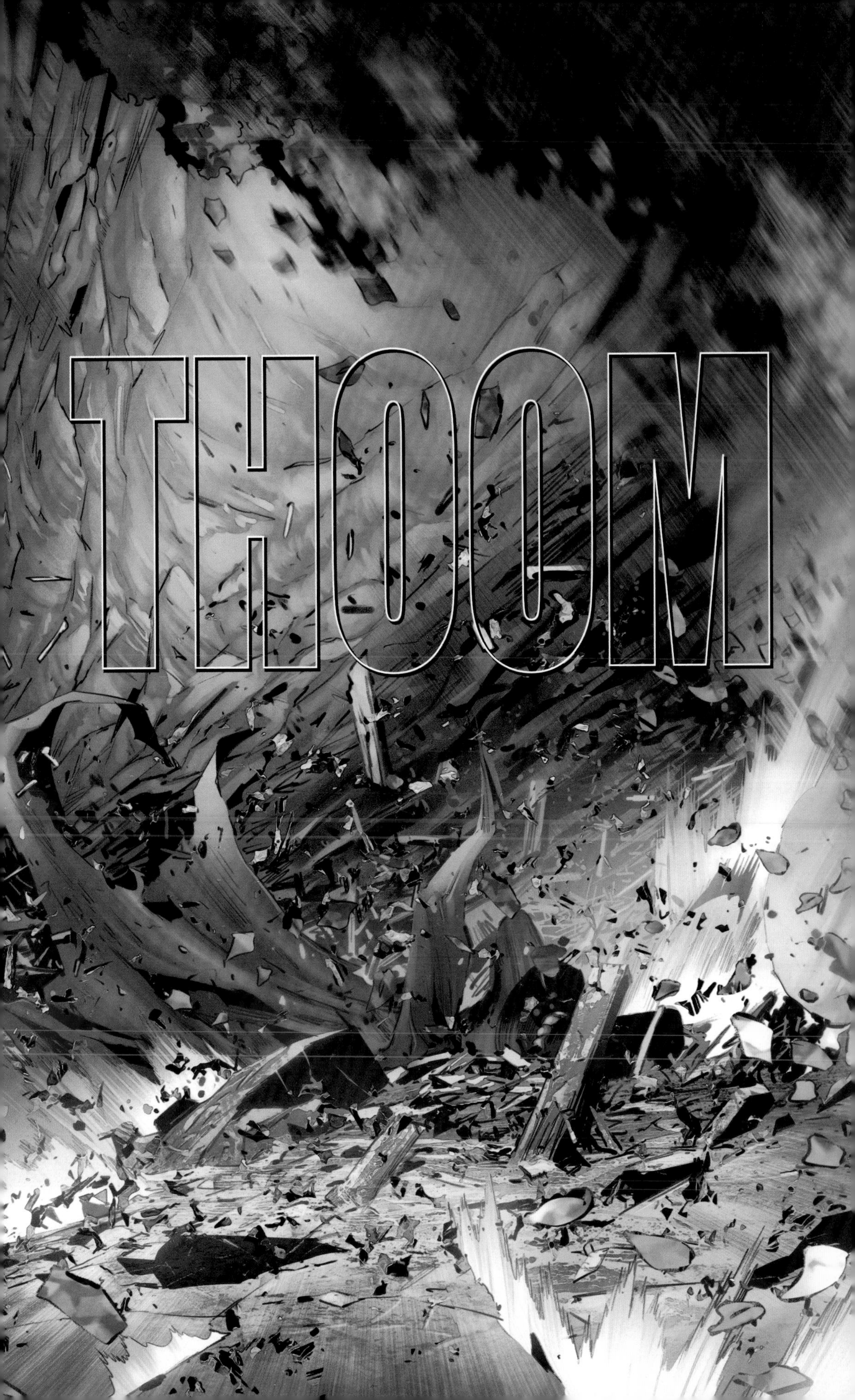
THOOM

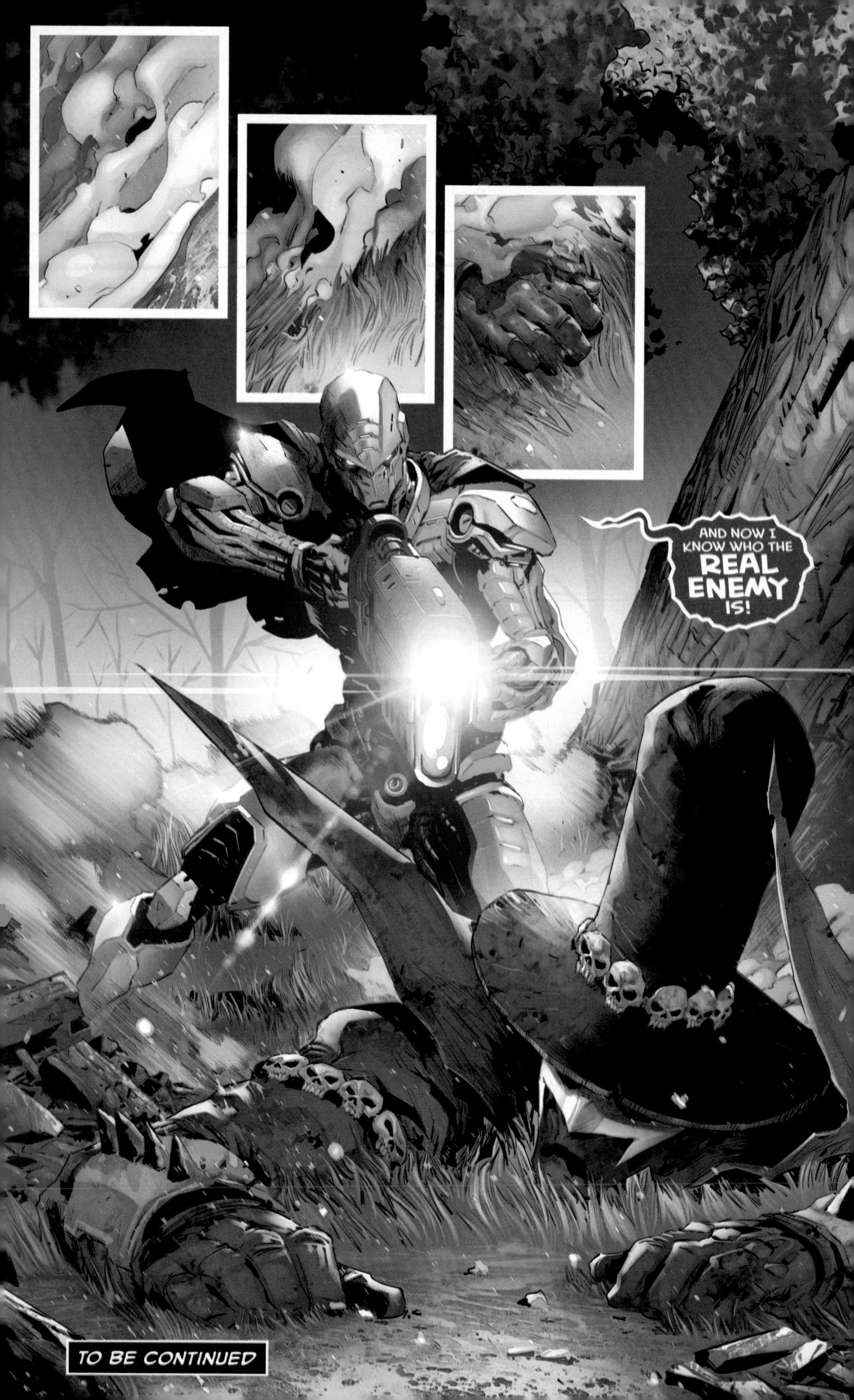
AND NOW I KNOW WHO THE REAL ENEMY IS!
TO BE CONTINUED

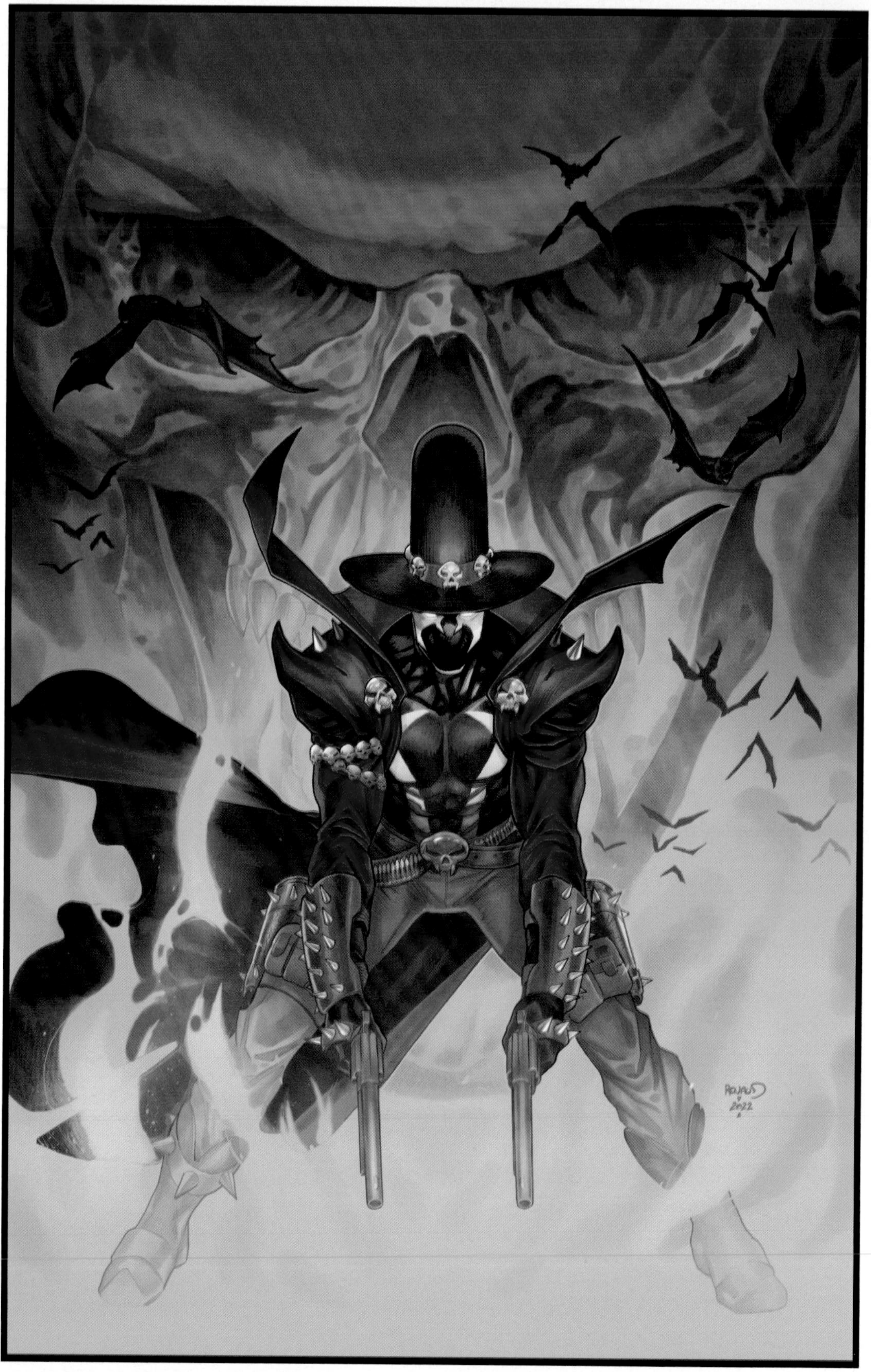
RENAUD
2022

GUNSLINGER SPAWN #28 COVER 'A' BY PAUL RENAUD

SINCE BEING 'PULLED' INTO OUR MODERN TIMES, GUNSLINGER HAS PRETTY MUCH BEEN A LONER.

HIS PERSONALITY WAS NEVER ONE THAT NEEDED A BUNCH OF PEOPLE IN HIS LIFE.

IN FACT, THE FEWER WHO KNEW HE WAS ALIVE, THE BETTER. SO, HE ONLY LET A FEW INTO HIS CIRCLE.

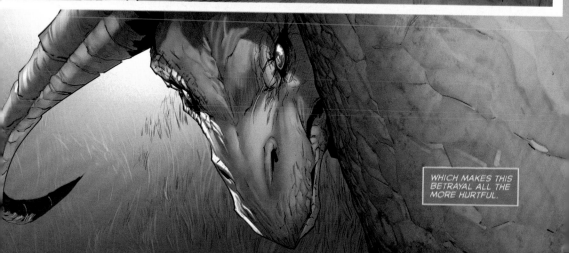

WHICH MAKES THIS BETRAYAL ALL THE MORE HURTFUL.

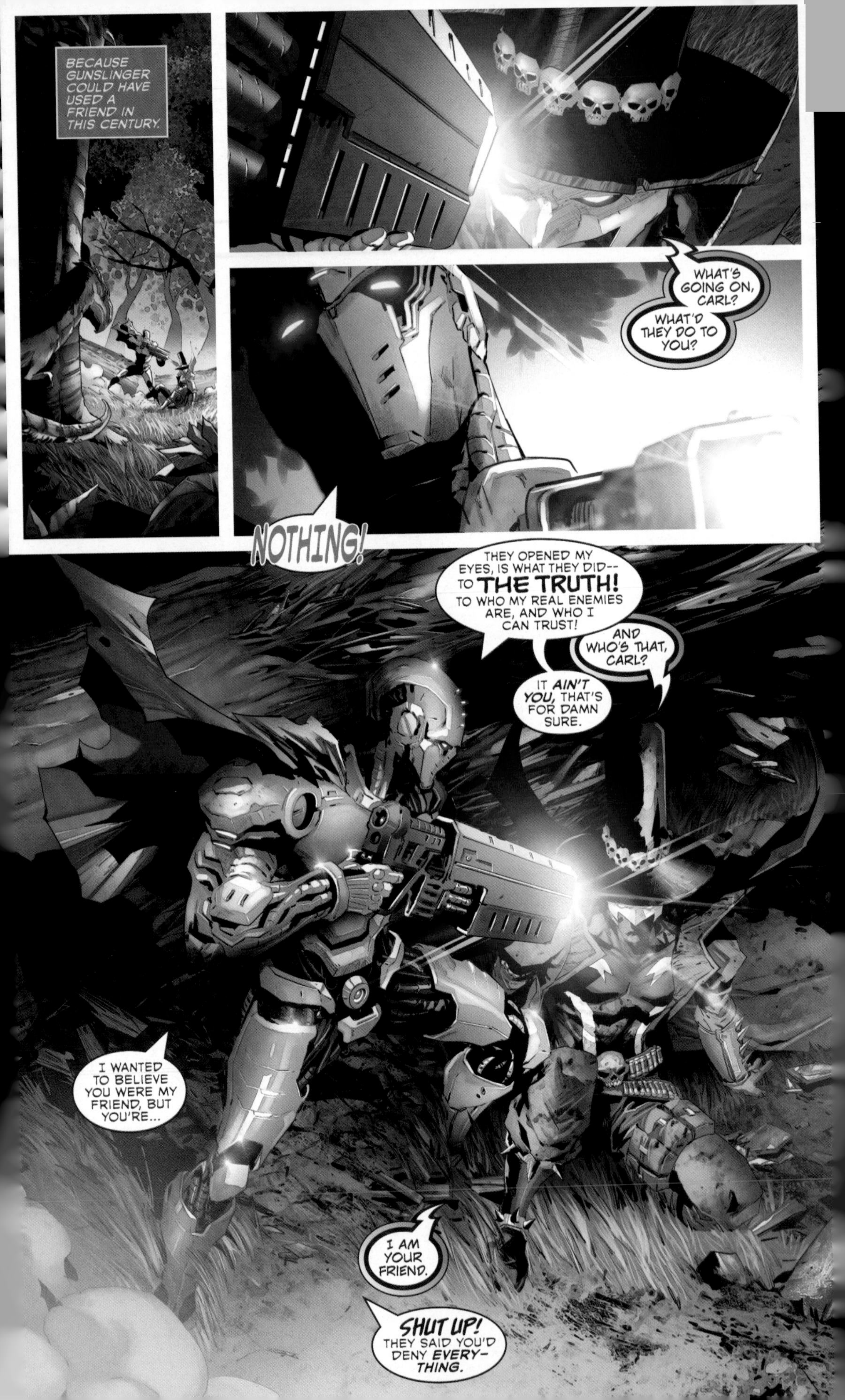
BECAUSE GUNSLINGER COULD HAVE USED A FRIEND IN THIS CENTURY.
WHAT'S GOING ON, CARL?
WHAT'D THEY DO TO YOU?
NOTHING!
THEY OPENED MY EYES, IS WHAT THEY DID-- TO THE TRUTH! TO WHO MY REAL ENEMIES ARE, AND WHO I CAN TRUST!
AND WHO'S THAT, CARL?
IT AIN'T YOU, THAT'S FOR DAMN SURE.
I WANTED TO BELIEVE YOU WERE MY FRIEND, BUT YOU'RE...
I AM YOUR FRIEND.
SHUT UP! THEY SAID YOU'D DENY EVERY-THING.

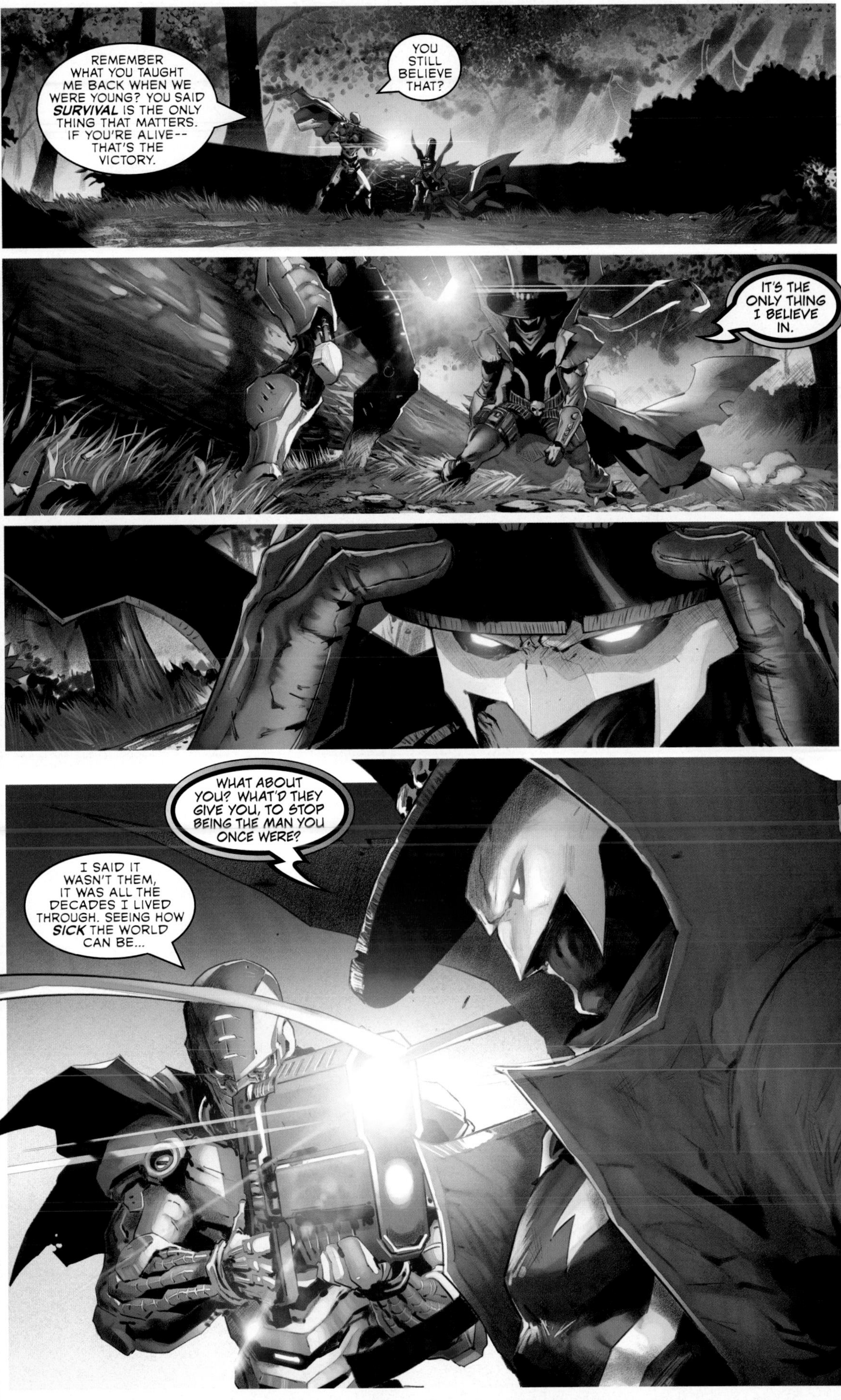
REMEMBER WHAT YOU TAUGHT ME BACK WHEN WE WERE YOUNG? YOU SAID SURVIVAL IS THE ONLY THING THAT MATTERS. IF YOU'RE ALIVE-- THAT'S THE VICTORY.
YOU STILL BELIEVE THAT?
IT'S THE ONLY THING I BELIEVE IN.
WHAT ABOUT YOU? WHAT'D THEY GIVE YOU, TO STOP BEING THE MAN YOU ONCE WERE?
I SAID IT WASN'T THEM, IT WAS ALL THE DECADES I LIVED THROUGH. SEEING HOW SICK THE WORLD CAN BE...

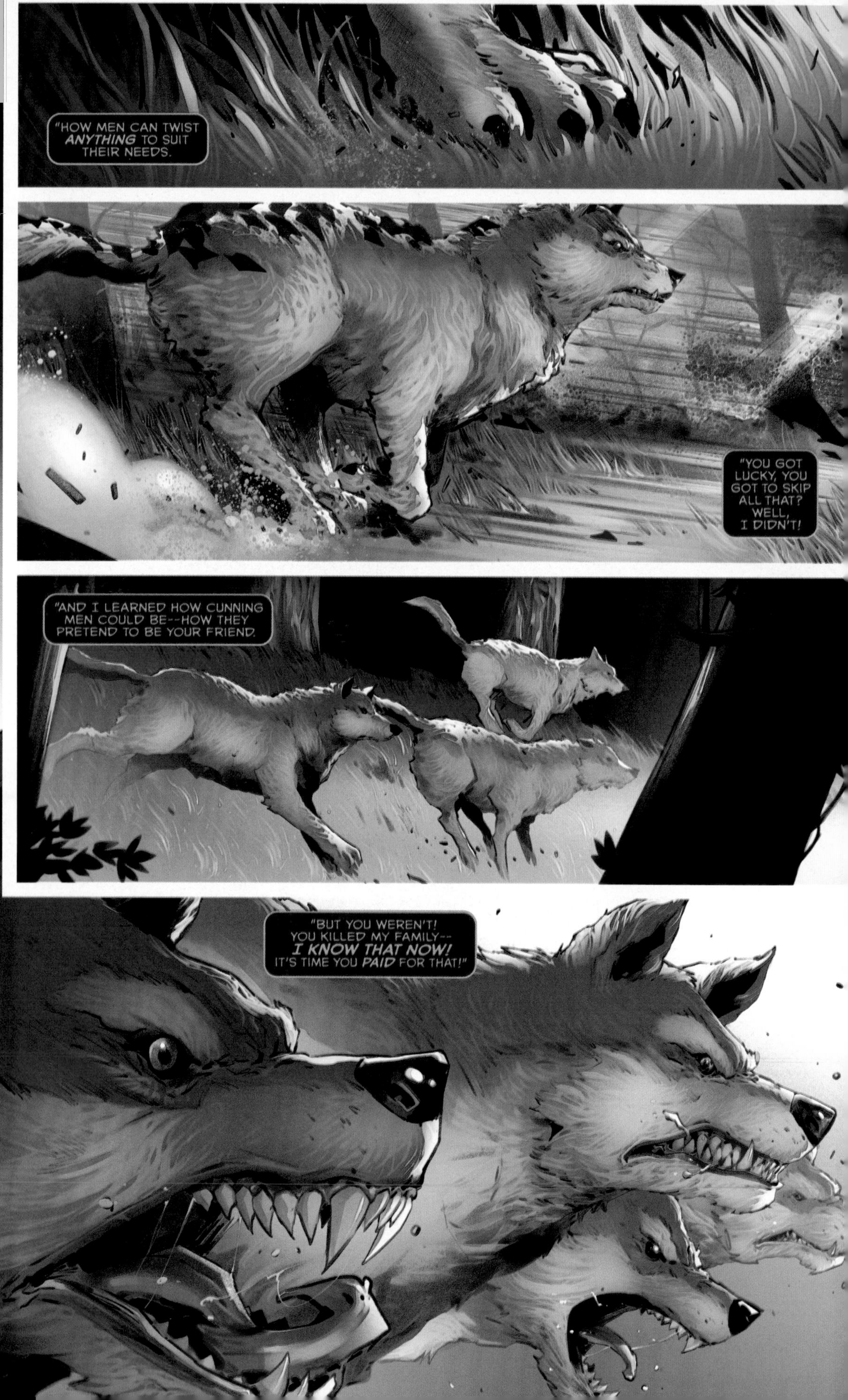
"HOW MEN CAN TWIST *ANYTHING* TO SUIT THEIR NEEDS.
"YOU GOT LUCKY, YOU GOT TO SKIP ALL THAT? WELL, I DIDN'T!
"AND I LEARNED HOW CUNNING MEN COULD BE--HOW THEY PRETEND TO BE YOUR FRIEND.
"BUT YOU WEREN'T! YOU KILLED MY FAMILY-- *I KNOW THAT NOW!* IT'S TIME YOU *PAID* FOR THAT!"

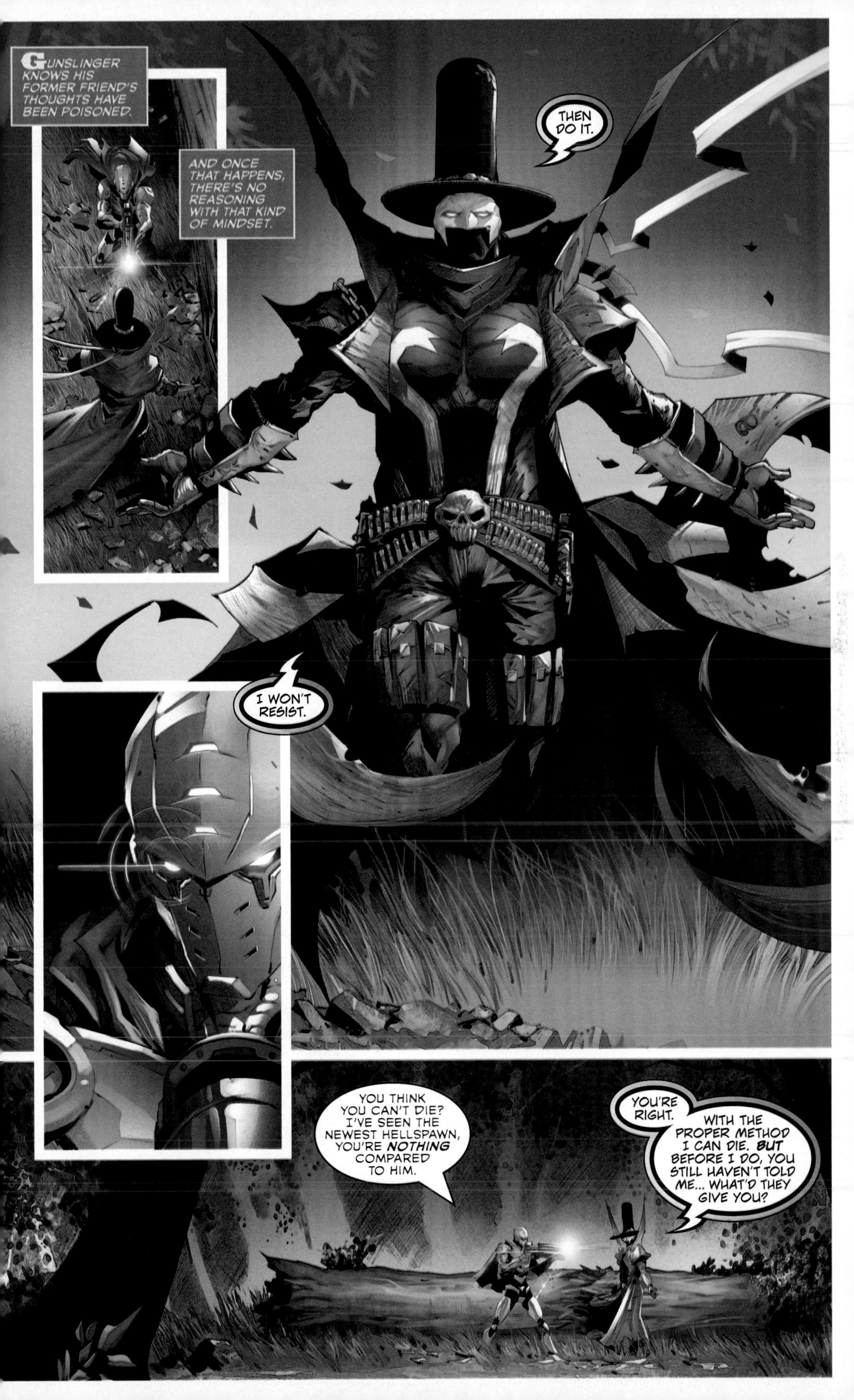
GUNSLINGER KNOWS HIS FORMER FRIEND'S THOUGHTS HAVE BEEN POISONED.
AND ONCE THAT HAPPENS, THERE'S NO REASONING WITH THAT KIND OF MINDSET.
THEN DO IT.
I WON'T RESIST.
YOU THINK YOU CAN'T DIE? I'VE SEEN THE NEWEST HELLSPAWN, YOU'RE **NOTHING** COMPARED TO HIM.
YOU'RE RIGHT.
WITH THE PROPER METHOD I CAN DIE. **BUT** BEFORE I DO, YOU STILL HAVEN'T TOLD ME... WHAT'D THEY GIVE YOU?

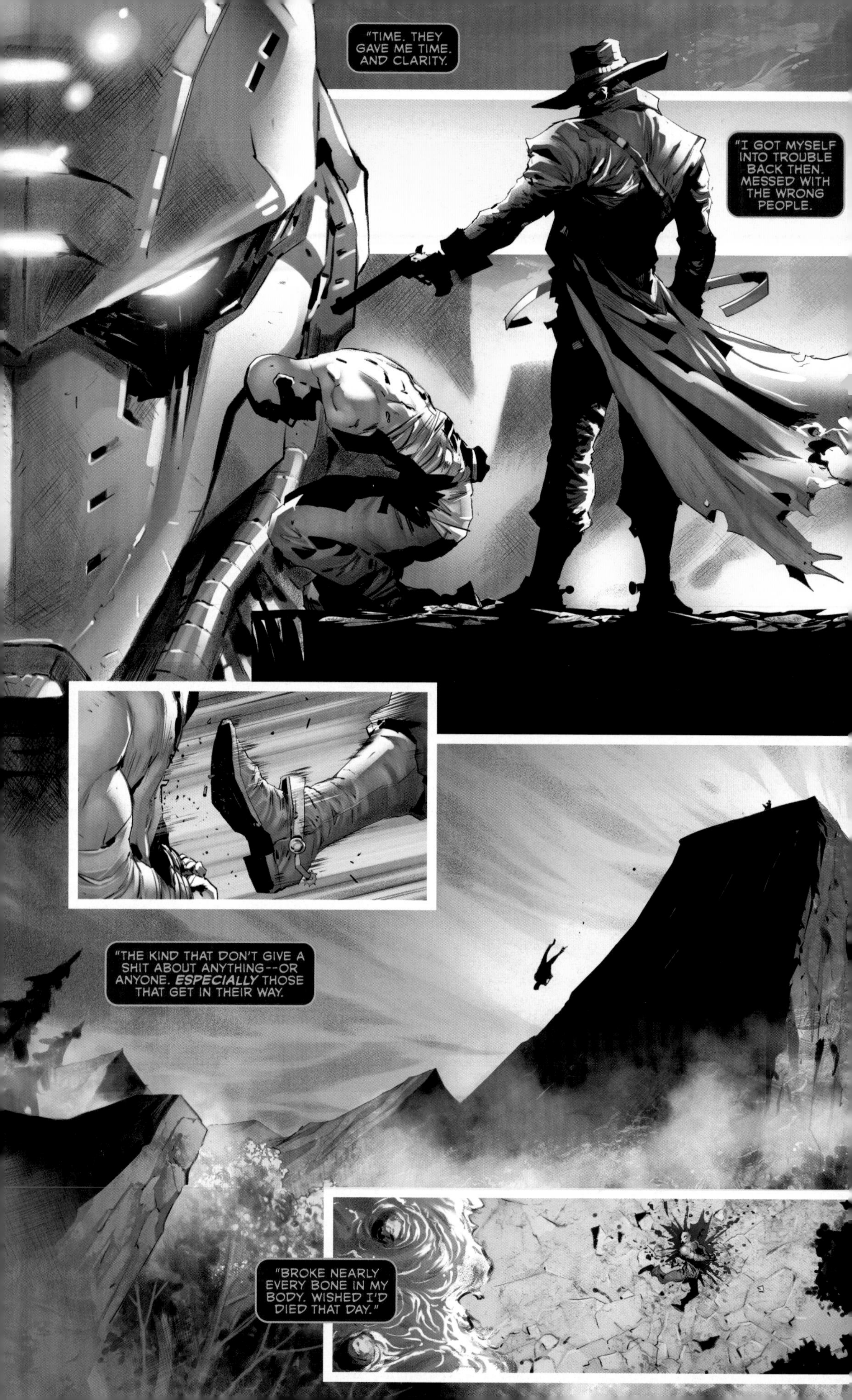
"TIME. THEY GAVE ME TIME. AND CLARITY.
"I GOT MYSELF INTO TROUBLE BACK THEN. MESSED WITH THE WRONG PEOPLE.
"THE KIND THAT DON'T GIVE A SHIT ABOUT ANYTHING--OR ANYONE. *ESPECIALLY* THOSE THAT GET IN THEIR WAY.
"BROKE NEARLY EVERY BONE IN MY BODY. WISHED I'D DIED THAT DAY."

"INSTEAD SOMEONE FOUND ME, TOOK ME IN, KEPT ME ALIVE SOMEHOW.

"TOOK YEARS BEFORE I COULD EVEN DO THE SIMPLE THINGS AGAIN, LIKE FEED MYSELF.

"BUT THIS MAN, THE ONE YOU'RE HUNTING, HE MADE SURE I WAS IN AS LITTLE PAIN AS POSSIBLE.

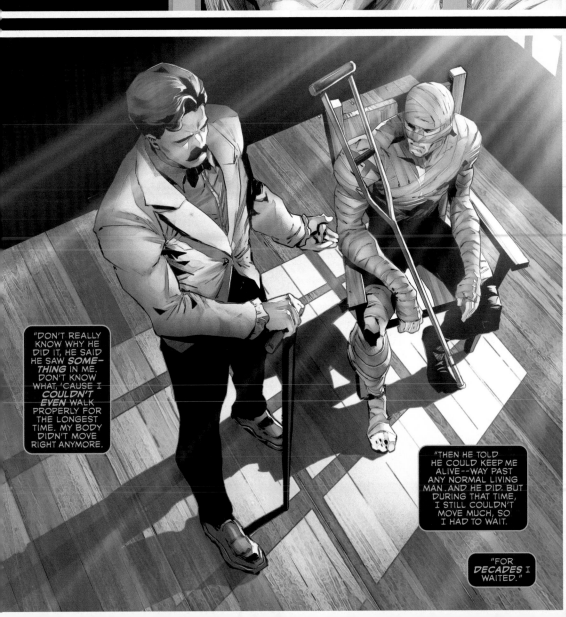

"DON'T REALLY KNOW WHY HE DID IT, HE SAID HE SAW SOME-THING IN ME. DON'T KNOW WHAT, 'CAUSE I COULDN'T EVEN WALK PROPERLY FOR THE LONGEST TIME. MY BODY DIDN'T MOVE RIGHT ANYMORE.

"THEN HE TOLD HE COULD KEEP ME ALIVE--WAY PAST ANY NORMAL LIVING MAN. AND HE DID. BUT DURING THAT TIME, I STILL COULDN'T MOVE MUCH, SO I HAD TO WAIT.

"FOR DECADES I WAITED."

"SEE, THE DOCTORS COULDN'T FIX ME. THEY DIDN'T HAVE THE KNOW-HOW.

"SO, I BEGAN TO LEARN ABOUT THINGS, HEARD ABOUT WHAT WAS HAPPENING OUTSIDE MY WINDOW.

"THEY TAUGHT ME HOW TO READ. TO WRITE.

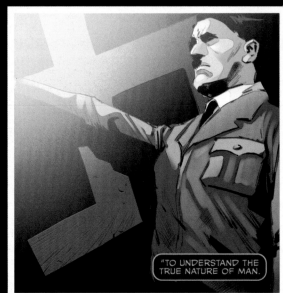

"TO UNDERSTAND THE TRUE NATURE OF MAN.

"SOME WERE BETTER THAN OTHERS, BUT THE LUST FOR POWER WAS THE THING THEY **ALL HAD** IN COMMON.

"EVENTUALLY, THE WAITING WAS OVER. TECHNOLOGY AND SCIENCE WAS FINALLY ABLE TO HELP ME."

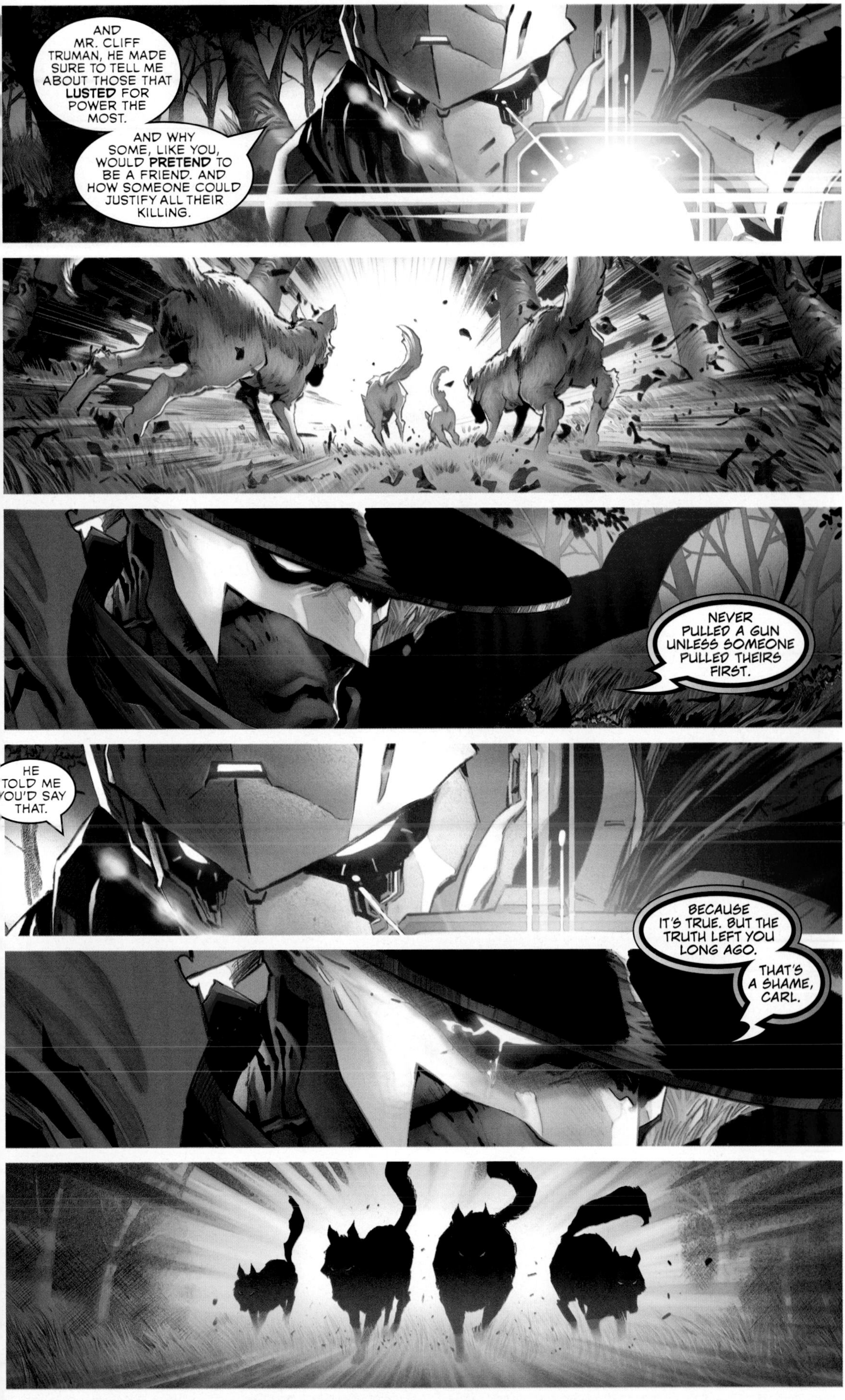
AND MR. CLIFF TRUMAN, HE MADE SURE TO TELL ME ABOUT THOSE THAT **LUSTED** FOR POWER THE MOST.
AND WHY SOME, LIKE YOU, WOULD **PRETEND** TO BE A FRIEND. AND HOW SOMEONE COULD JUSTIFY ALL THEIR KILLING.
NEVER PULLED A GUN UNLESS SOMEONE PULLED THEIRS FIRST.
HE TOLD ME YOU'D SAY THAT.
BECAUSE IT'S TRUE. BUT THE TRUTH LEFT YOU LONG AGO.
THAT'S A SHAME, CARL.

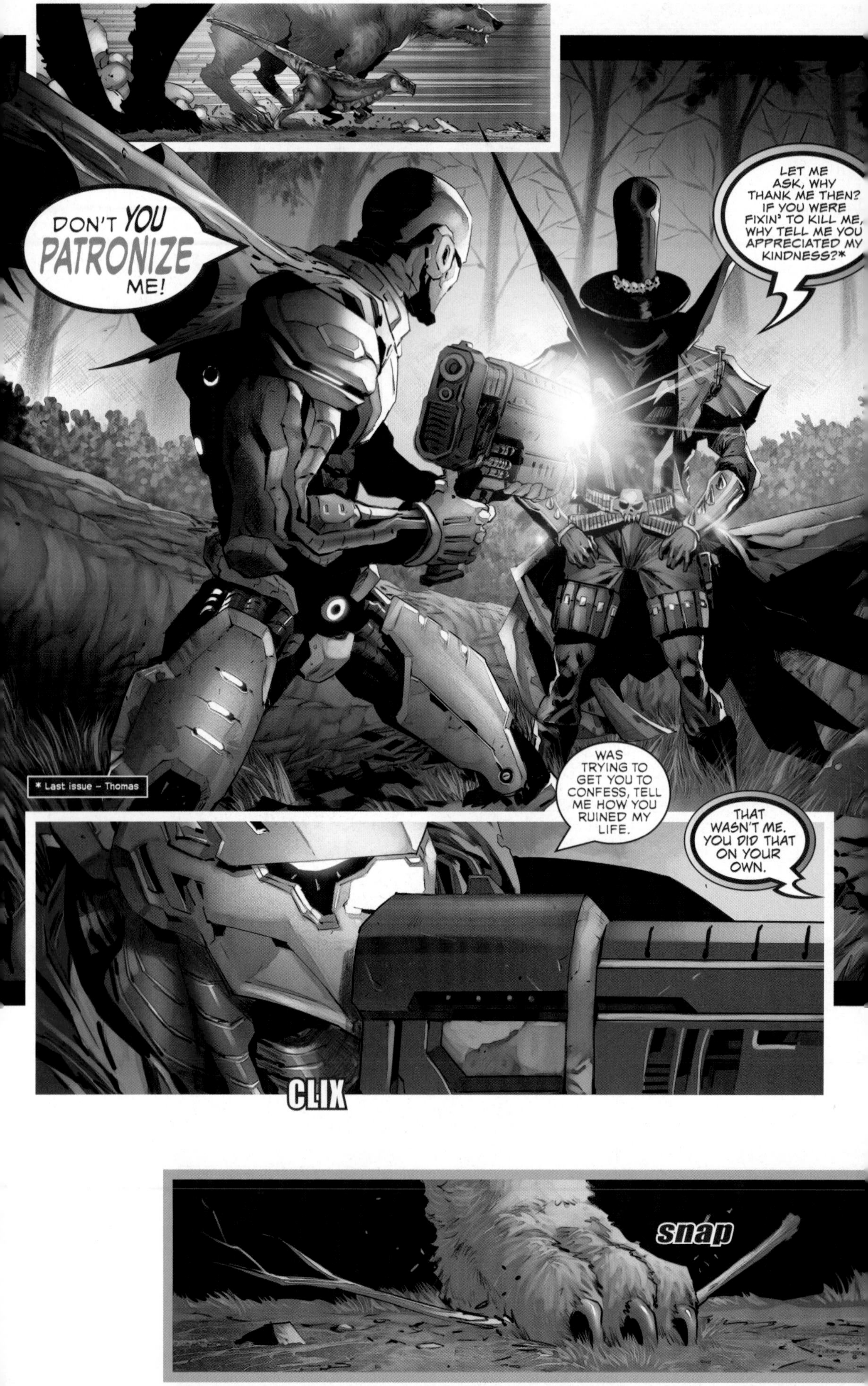

DON'T YOU PATRONIZE ME!
LET ME ASK, WHY THANK ME THEN? IF YOU WERE FIXIN' TO KILL ME, WHY TELL ME YOU APPRECIATED MY KINDNESS?*
* Last issue - Thomas
WAS TRYING TO GET YOU TO CONFESS, TELL ME HOW YOU RUINED MY LIFE.
THAT WASN'T ME. YOU DID THAT ON YOUR OWN.
CLIX
snap

HE SPINS AT THE SOUND BEHIND HIM.

BECAUSE CARL WAS RIGHT, GUNSLINGER WOULD HAVE DIED TONIGHT. HIS HELLSPAWN BODY WOULDN'T HAVE BEEN ABLE TO WITHSTAND THE IONIC BLAST OF CARL'S BIOWEAPON.

AS THE WEAKEST OF THE HELLSPAWN, GUNSLINGER KNEW THAT. SO, HE DEVISED ANOTHER PLAN TO ENSURE HIS SURVIVAL.

TO STALL. TO BUY TIME UNTIL HIS REINFORCEMENTS APPEARED. WHICH HE KNEW THEY WOULD.

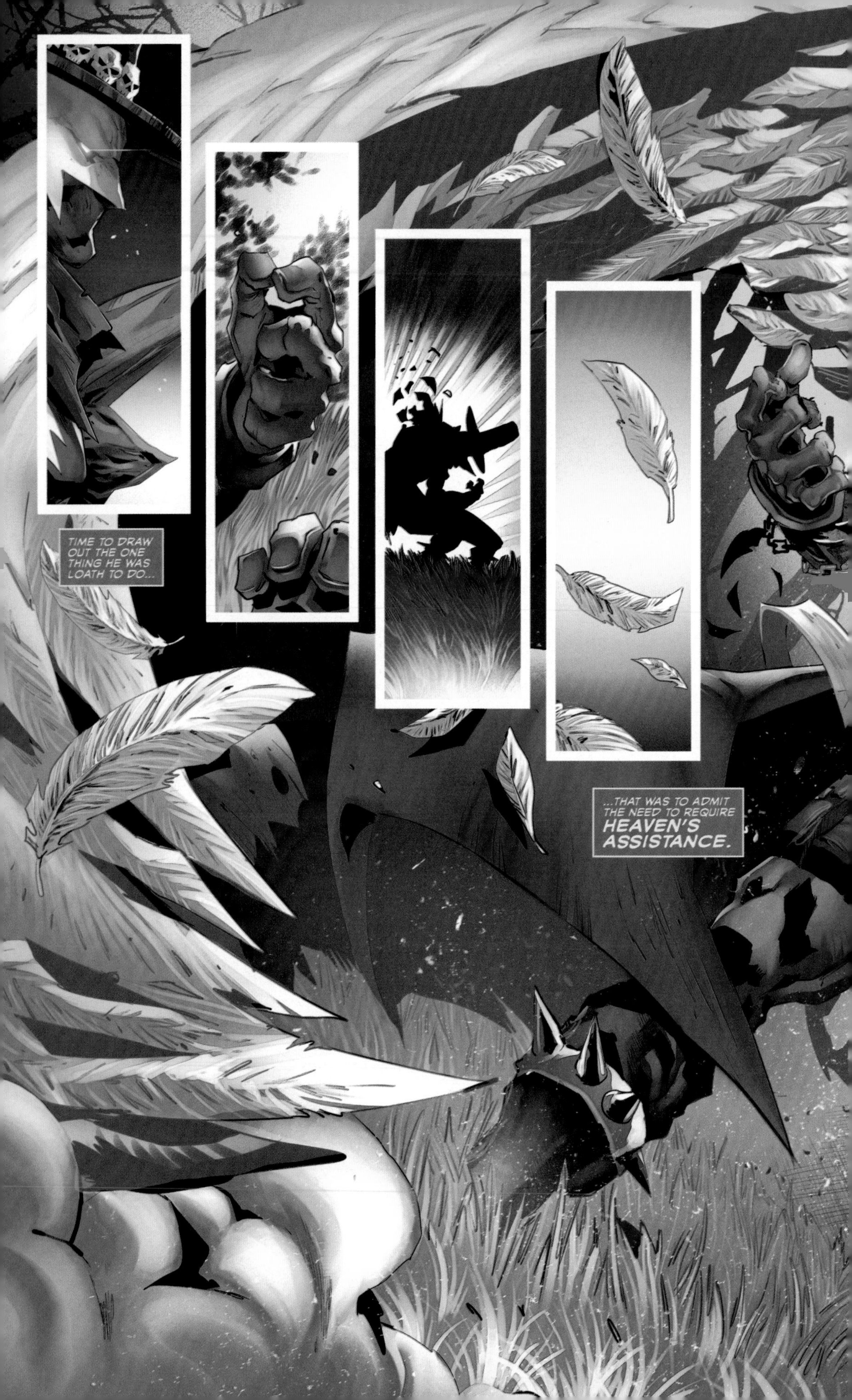
TIME TO DRAW OUT THE ONE THING HE WAS LOATH TO DO...
...THAT WAS TO ADMIT THE NEED TO REQUIRE HEAVEN'S ASSISTANCE.

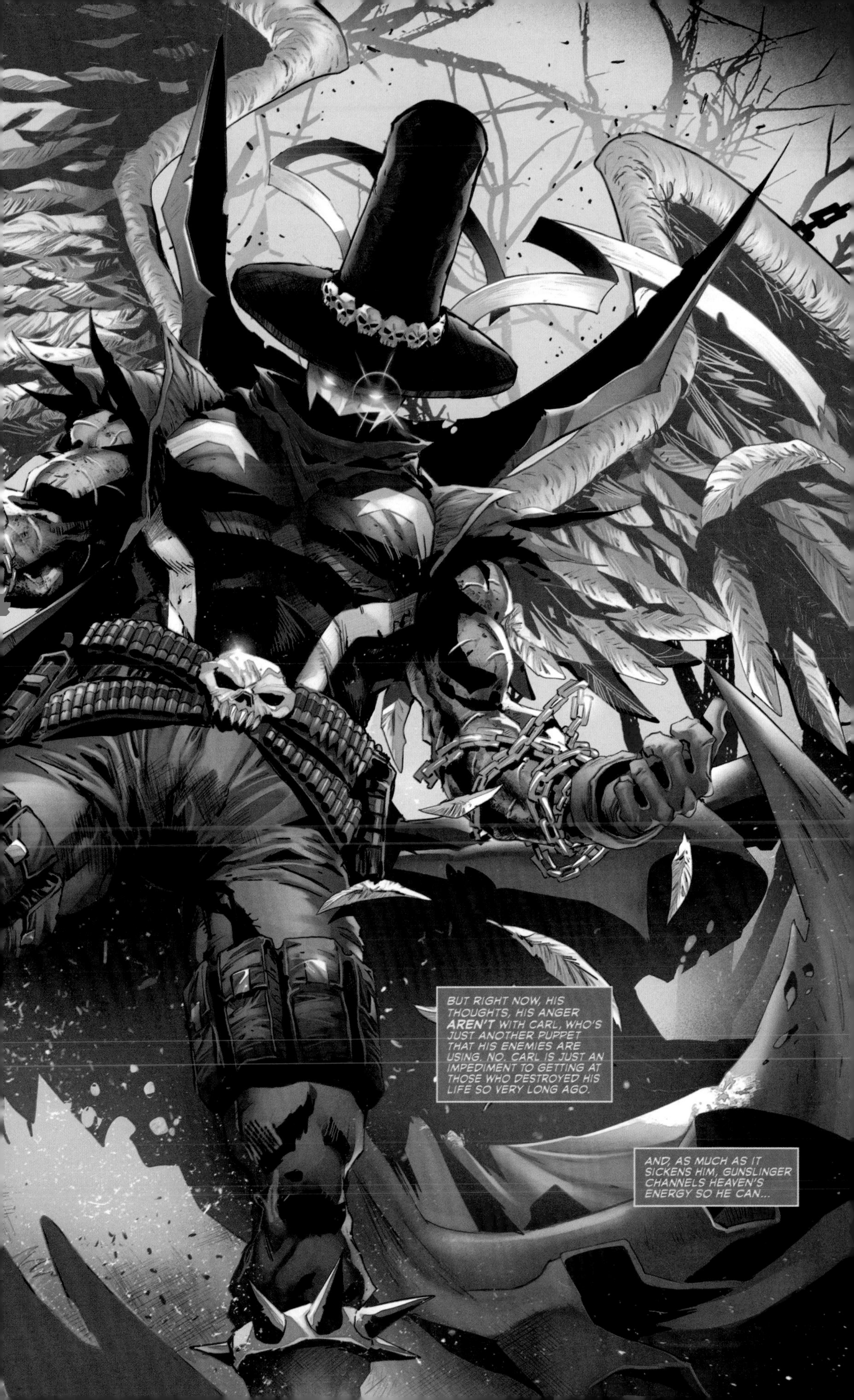
BUT RIGHT NOW, HIS THOUGHTS, HIS ANGER **AREN'T** WITH CARL, WHO'S JUST ANOTHER PUPPET THAT HIS ENEMIES ARE USING. NO. CARL IS JUST AN IMPEDIMENT TO GETTING AT THOSE WHO DESTROYED HIS LIFE SO VERY LONG AGO.
AND, AS MUCH AS IT SICKENS HIM, GUNSLINGER CHANNELS HEAVEN'S ENERGY SO HE CAN...

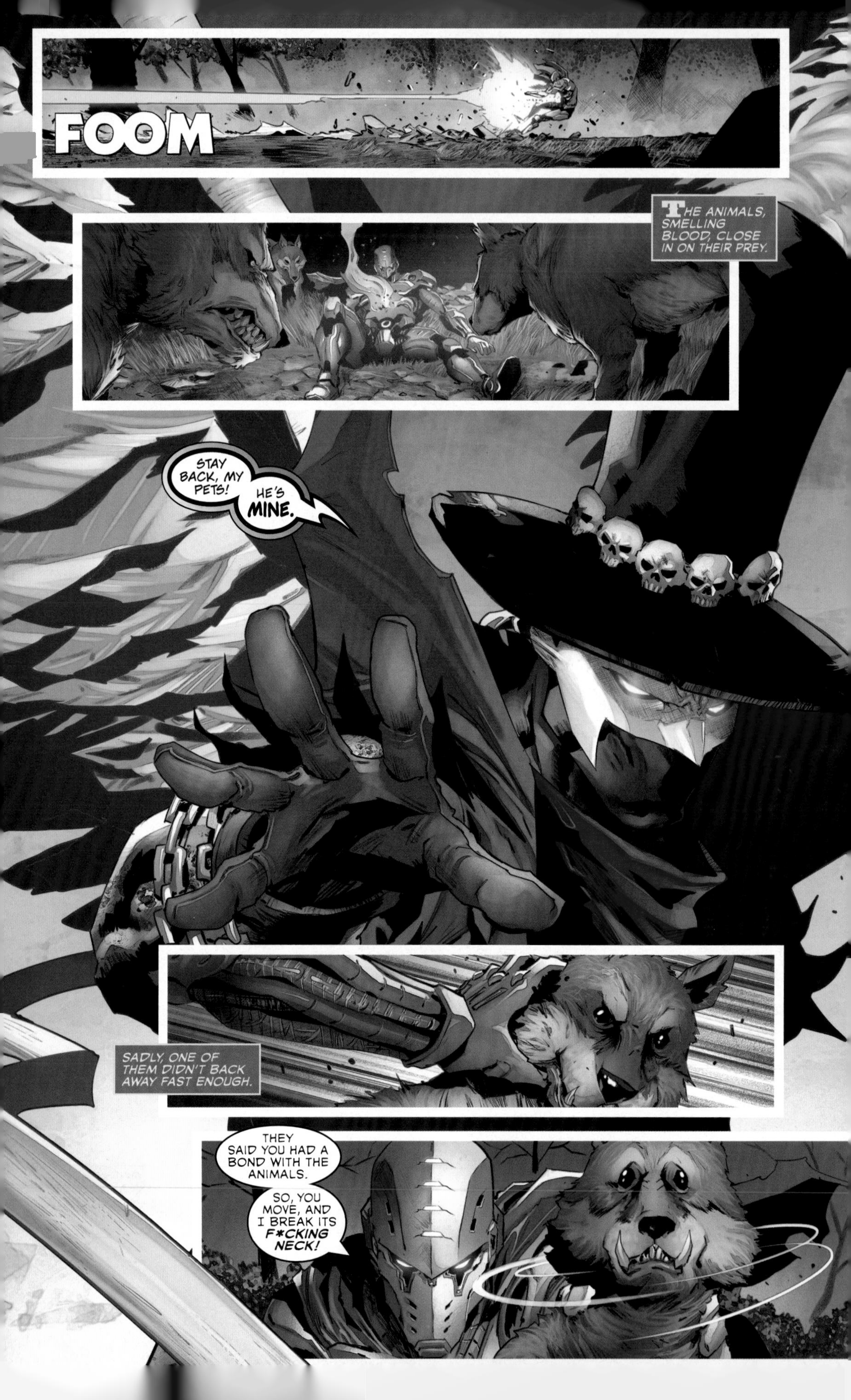
FOOM
THE ANIMALS, SMELLING BLOOD, CLOSE IN ON THEIR PREY.
STAY BACK, MY PETS!
HE'S MINE.
SADLY, ONE OF THEM DIDN'T BACK AWAY FAST ENOUGH.
THEY SAID YOU HAD A BOND WITH THE ANIMALS.
SO, YOU MOVE, AND I BREAK ITS F*CKING NECK!

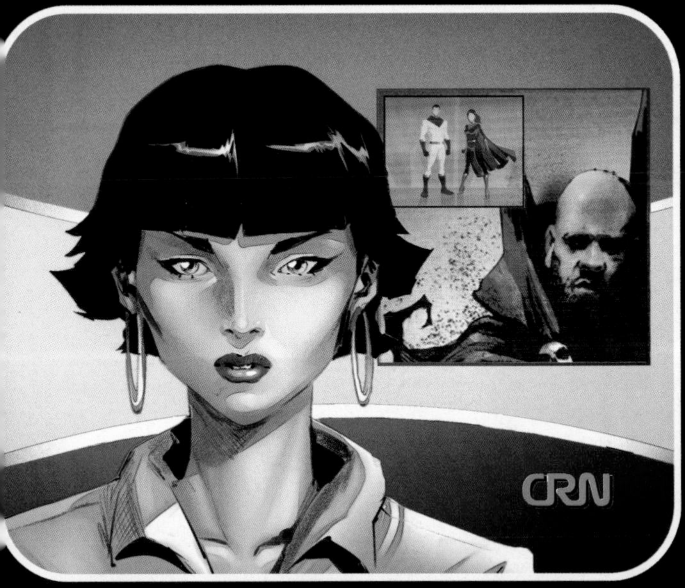
CRN

AS MORE SIGHTINGS AND INCIDENTS ARE REPORTED, CITIZENS HERE, AND AROUND THE WORLD, ARE DEMANDING ANSWERS. THE QUESTION IS, WHY HAS THE PAST YEAR SEEN SUCH AN EXPLOSIVE INCREASE IN THE NUMBER OF EXTRA-ORDINARILY POWERFUL COSTUMED BEINGS? WHEN ASKED, GOVERNMENT OFFICIALS, AND THE PENTAGON, CONTINUE TO SAY THAT THEY ARE *"CURRENTLY INVESTIGATING ALL CREDIBLE LEADS"* INTO THE CAUSATION, AND WHEREABOUTS, OF THESE COSTUMED PLAYERS.

THE GROWING DISTRUST TOWARD POLITICAL AND MILITARY LEADERS CAN BE TRACED TO THE APPEARANCE OF THE FIRST OF THESE COSTUMED PERSONS. THAT WAS, AS YOU MAY RECALL, A MAN CALLED AL SIMMONS. OFFICIAL INFORMATION INDICATES THAT SIMMONS DIED YEARS AGO IN THE LINE OF DUTY. SOMEHOW, THOUGH, HE REAPPEARED, ALIVE AND WELL.

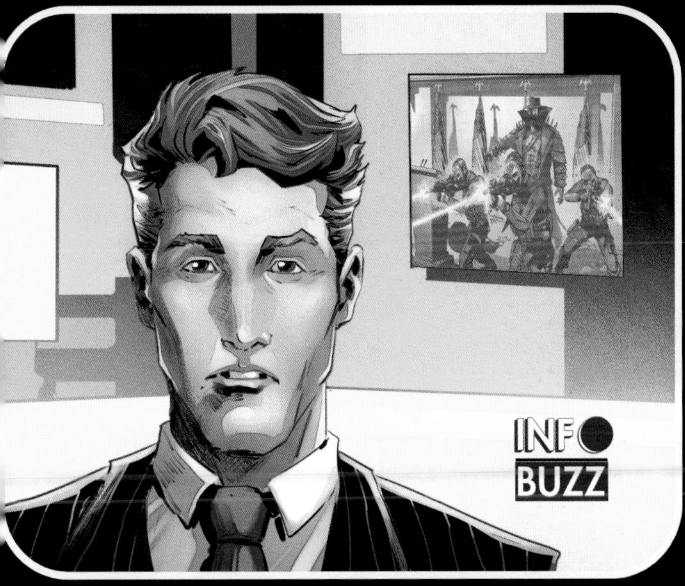
INFO
BUZZ

PARTISAN BICKERING ***CONTINUES*** AS ***BOTH*** SIDES OF THE AISLE ARE BLAMING THE ***OTHER*** FOR A *"LACK OF TRANSPARENCY."* OUR ***OWN*** REPORTERS, QUESTIONING THE DEPARTMENT OF DEFENSE FOR ***ANY*** INSIGHT AS TO WHETHER WE SHOULD BE CONCERNED, HAVE BEEN CONTINUALLY ***REBUFFED.***

AND YET A ***REASONABLE*** PERSON MUST ***WONDER*** ABOUT THOSE WHO SEEM TO BE HEROES, AND POTENTIAL ***VILLAINS.*** WHAT IS THE LIKELIHOOD OF A STAKING OUT OF AS-YET ***UNKNOWABLE*** TERRITORY OR INFLUENCE?

AND TO MAKE MATTERS ***MORE*** UNCLEAR, ***NO ONE*** SEEMS TO KNOW IF OUR OFFICIALS ARE TRYING TO STOP, OR ***RECRUIT,*** THESE BEINGS. WE RECALL A RECENT ***ASSASSINATION*** OF AN ELECTED OFFICIAL DURING A CAMPAIGN SPEECH. THE ***MANNER*** OF THE KILLING, CAUGHT ON CAMERA, DEFIES EASY ***EXPLANATION.***

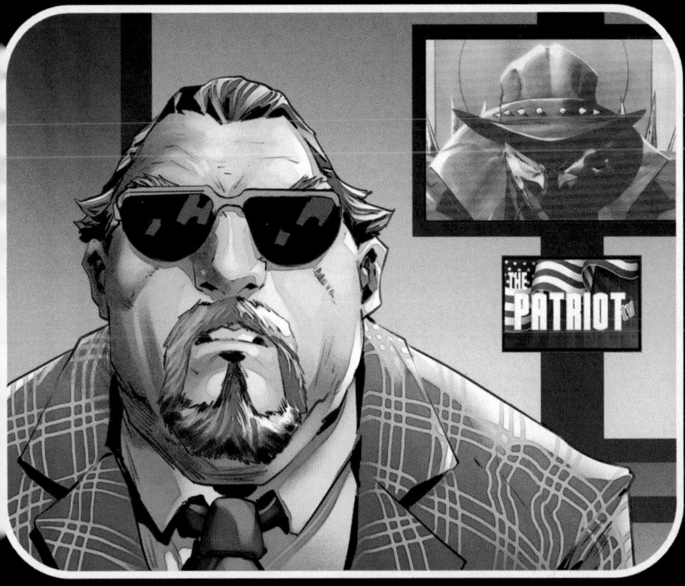
THE
PATRIOT

I TOLD YOU, DIDN'T I??
I ***HATE*** BEING RIGHT ***ALL*** THE TIME-- BUT I SAW THIS COMING ***YEARS*** AGO.

OF COURSE THEY AREN'T GOING TO TELL US ANYTHING, THEY THINK WE'RE TOO STUPID TO UNDERSTAND THE IMPACT OF THEIR ***GAMES.*** THE DEEP STATE HAS BEEN PLANNING THIS SINCE THEY KILLED ***J.F.K...*** ONLY NOW THEY ARE USING ***SUPER-POWERED*** SOLDIERS INSTEAD OF THE ***C.I.A...!!!***

I'M ***TELLING*** YOU, MAKE SURE YOU'VE GOT ENOUGH FOOD, TOILET PAPER AND A METHANE-POWERED ***GENERATOR*** BECAUSE IT WON'T BE LONG BEFORE OUR MILITARY ***JOINS FORCES*** WITH THESE "HEROES" TO CHANGE THE VERY ***WAY WE LIVE!!*** THEY DEMAND HIGHER TAXES FROM US AND SHOVE THEIR LIBERAL AGENDA DOWN OUR ***THROATS*** WHILE OUR KIDS ARE OFF BUYING LEGAL ***POT*** AT THE ***CORNER STORE.*** THIS MAY SOUND CRAZY... BUT I'M THINKING ABOUT CROSSING ILLEGALLY INTO ***MEXICO*** TO GET ***AWAY*** FROM THIS ***TIGHT-COSTUMED TYRANNY!!!!***

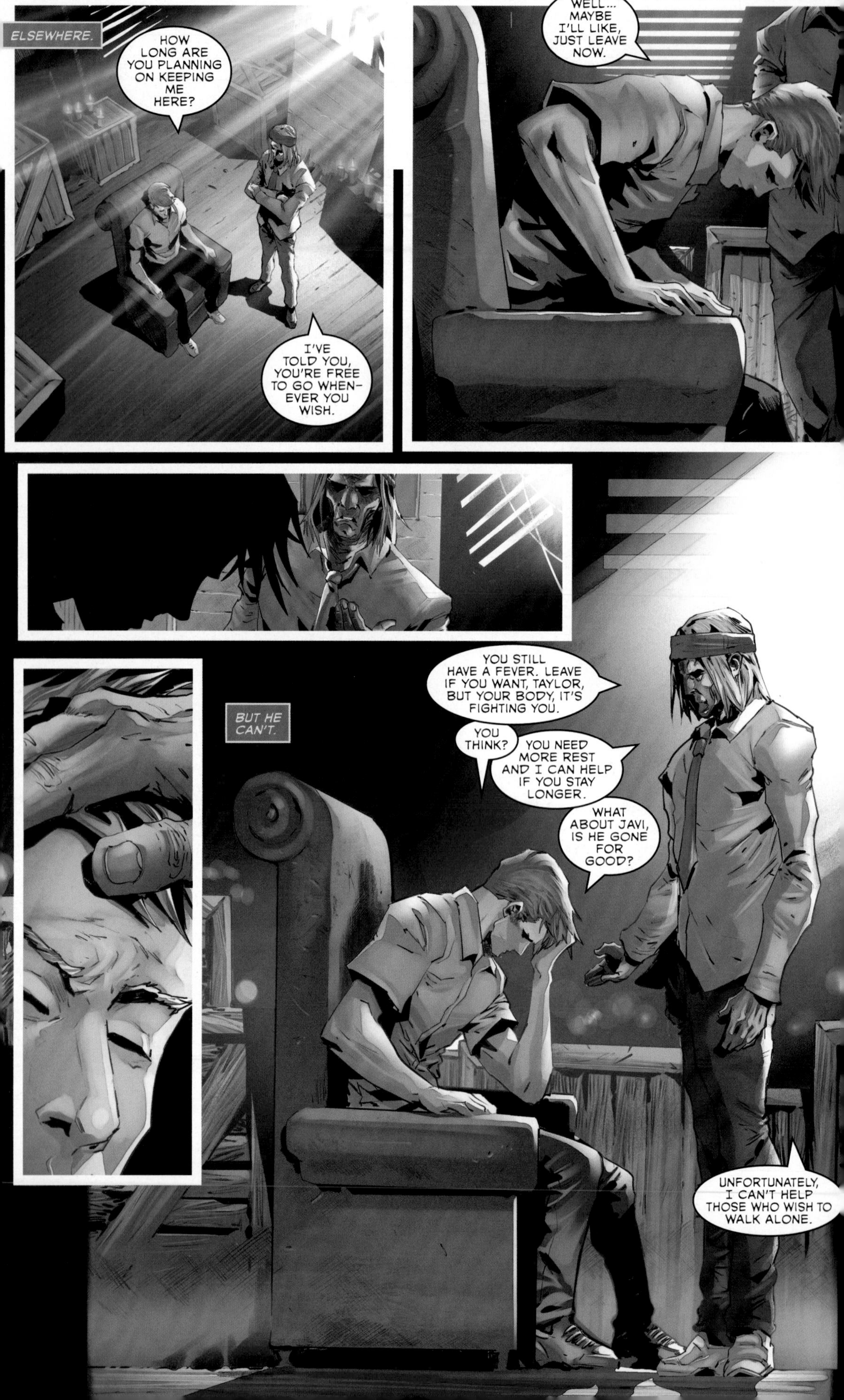
ELSEWHERE.
HOW LONG ARE YOU PLANNING ON KEEPING ME HERE?
I'VE TOLD YOU, YOU'RE FREE TO GO WHEN-EVER YOU WISH.
WELL... MAYBE I'LL LIKE, JUST LEAVE NOW.
BUT HE CAN'T.
YOU STILL HAVE A FEVER. LEAVE IF YOU WANT, TAYLOR, BUT YOUR BODY, IT'S FIGHTING YOU.
YOU THINK?
YOU NEED MORE REST AND I CAN HELP IF YOU STAY LONGER.
WHAT ABOUT JAVI, IS HE GONE FOR GOOD?
UNFORTUNATELY, I CAN'T HELP THOSE WHO WISH TO WALK ALONE.

YOU *HEAR* WHAT I SAID?!

WITH A WAVE, HE SENDS THE OTHER WOLVES AWAY.

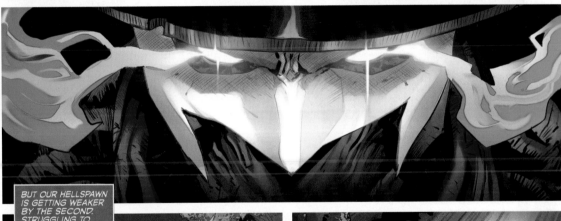

BUT OUR HELLSPAWN IS GETTING WEAKER BY THE SECOND. STRUGGLING TO HOST SUPERNATURAL POWERS FROM BOTH HEAVEN AND HELL.

HE NEEDS TO ACT QUICK.

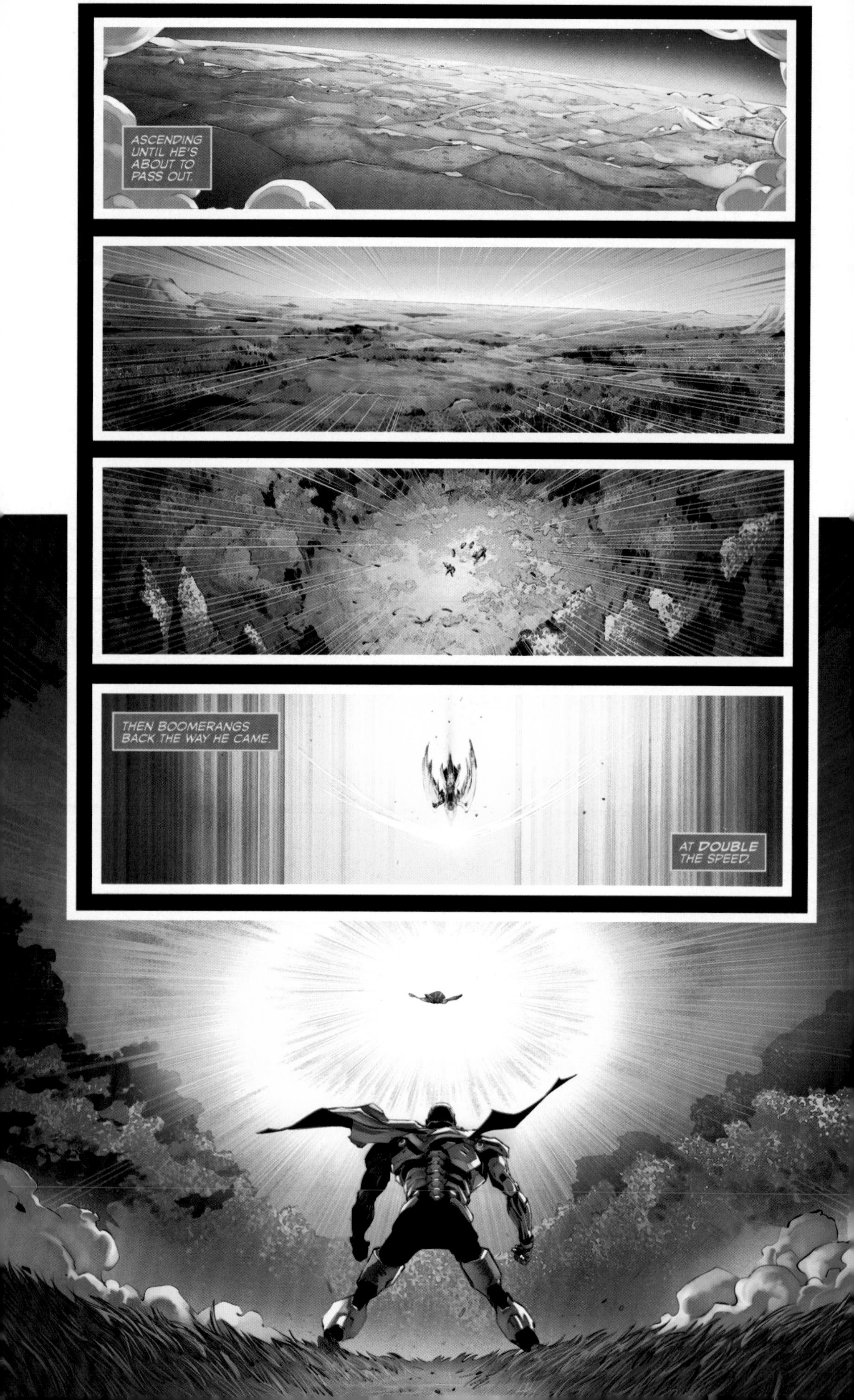
ASCENDING UNTIL HE'S ABOUT TO PASS OUT.
THEN BOOMERANGS BACK THE WAY HE CAME.
AT DOUBLE THE SPEED.

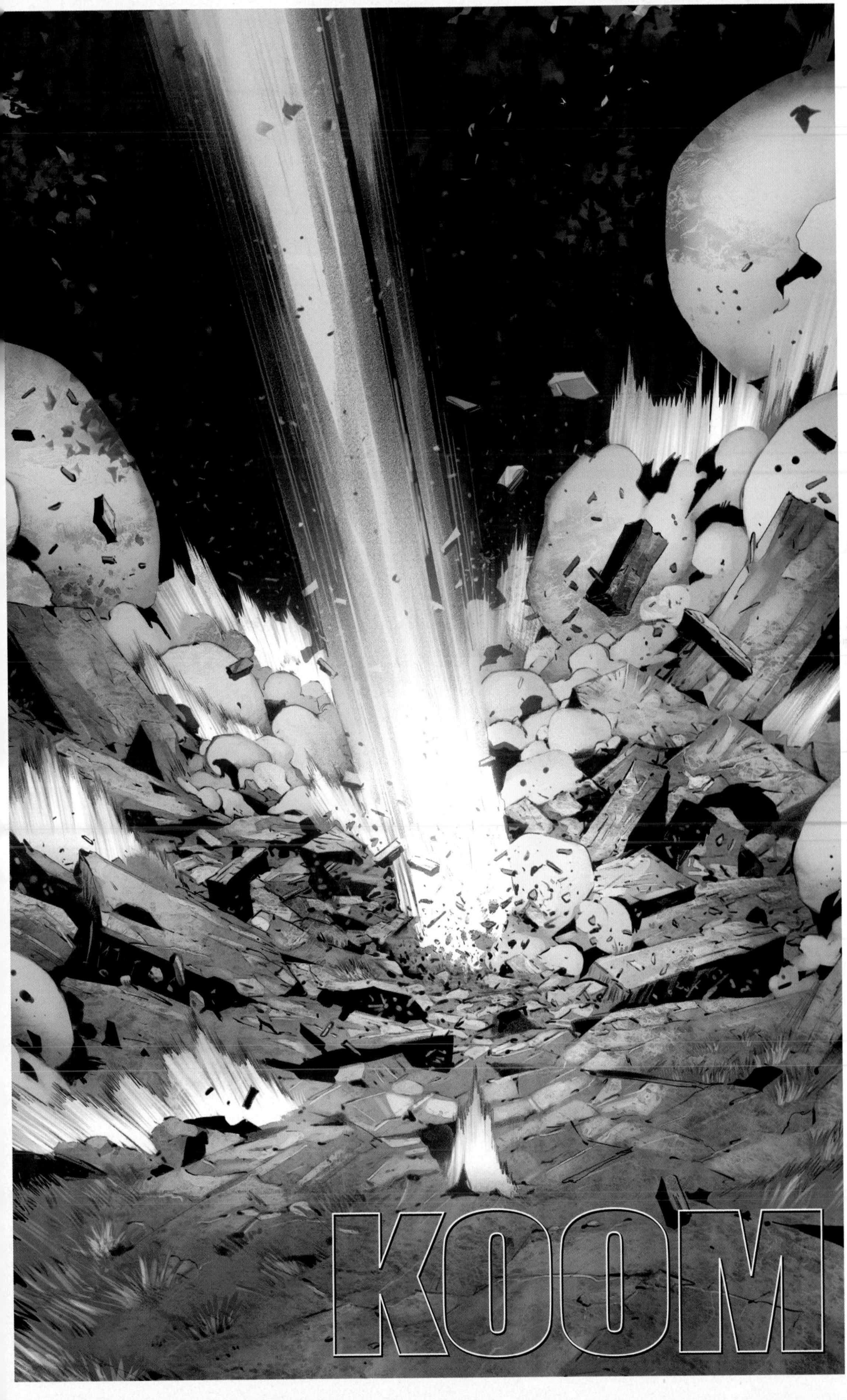
KOOM

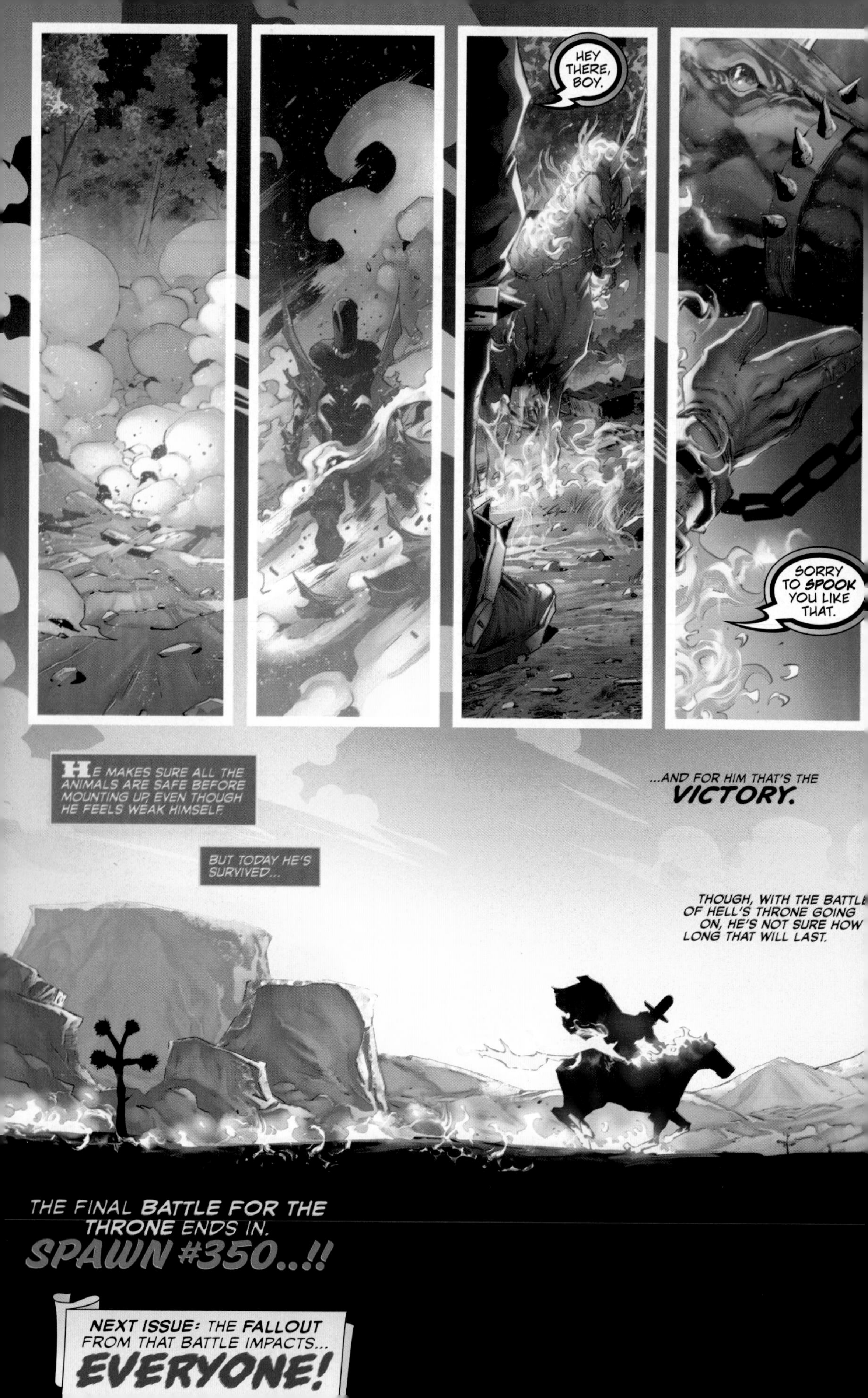
HEY THERE, BOY.
SORRY TO SPOOK YOU LIKE THAT.
HE MAKES SURE ALL THE ANIMALS ARE SAFE BEFORE MOUNTING UP, EVEN THOUGH HE FEELS WEAK HIMSELF.
BUT TODAY HE'S SURVIVED...
...AND FOR HIM THAT'S THE VICTORY.
THOUGH, WITH THE BATTLE OF HELL'S THRONE GOING ON, HE'S NOT SURE HOW LONG THAT WILL LAST.
THE FINAL BATTLE FOR THE THRONE ENDS IN. SPAWN #350..!!
NEXT ISSUE: THE FALLOUT FROM THAT BATTLE IMPACTS... EVERYONE!

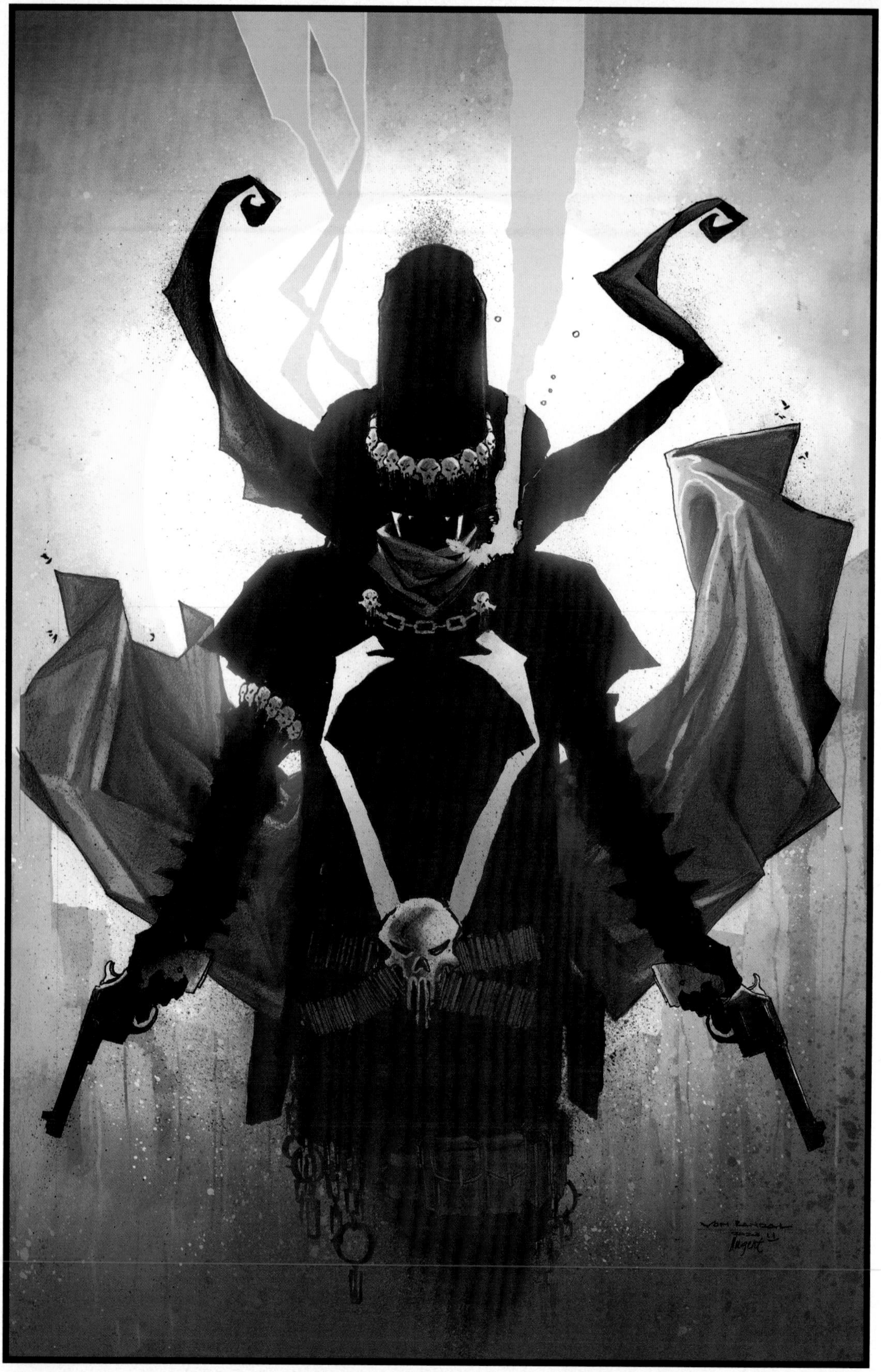

GUNSLINGER SPAWN #29 COVER 'A' BY VON RANDAL

MOTEL
APPLE VALLEY
QUEEN BEDS
CABLE TV HBO
LARGE FAMILY ROOMS
NO VACANCY
IT'S BEEN WEEKS SINCE 'THE CHANGE,' WHEN EVERY-ONE ENDOWED DIRECTLY BY HEAVEN AND HELL WITH SUPERNATURAL POWERS...
...SUDDENLY ALL BECAME MORTAL.
ALTERING THEIR STRATEGIES ON HOW TO SURVIVE.

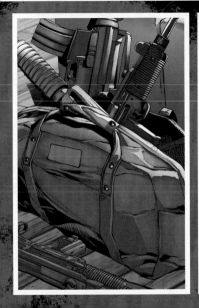

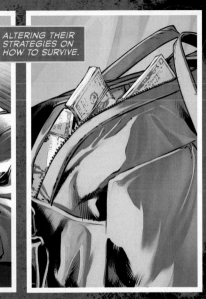

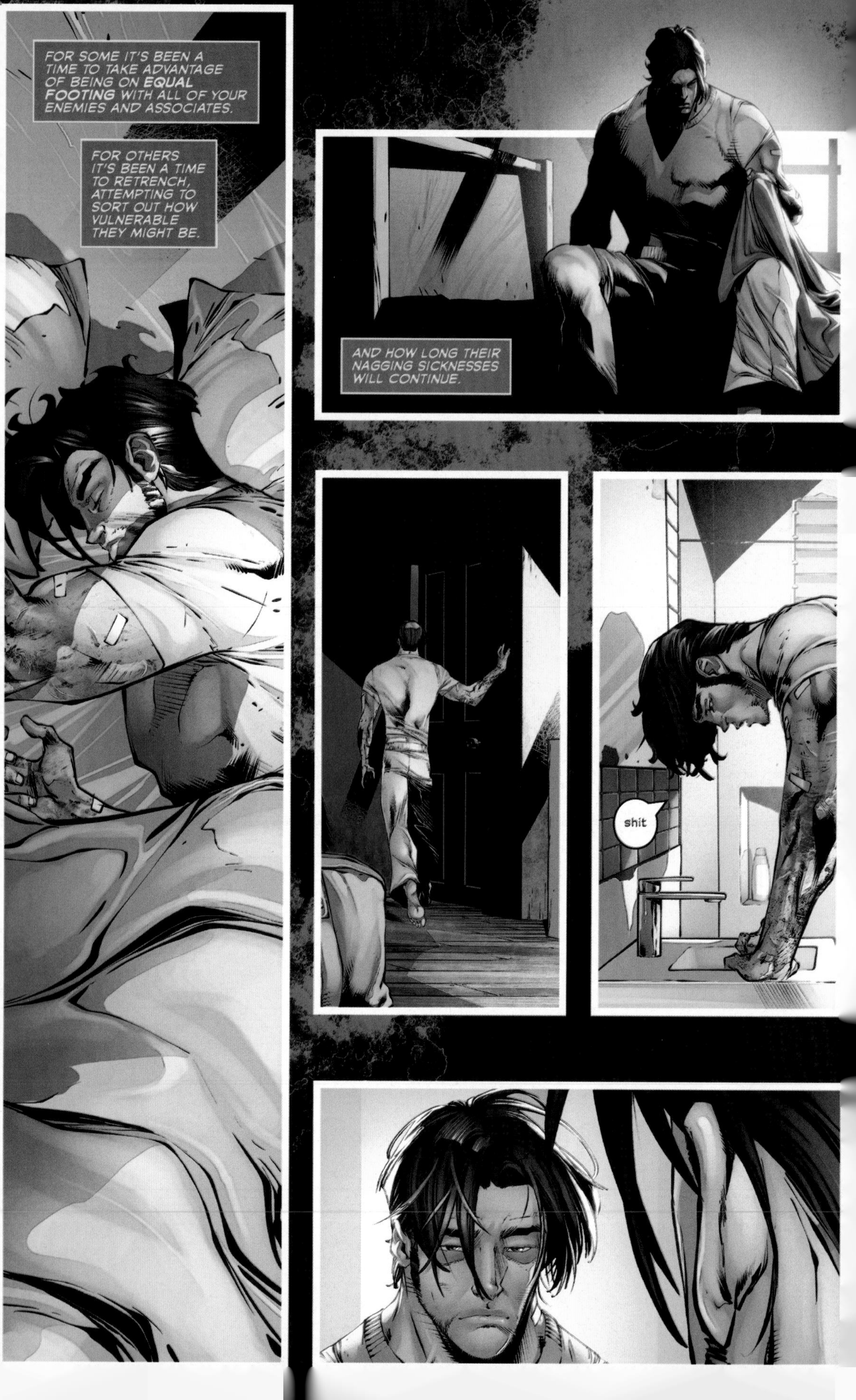
FOR SOME IT'S BEEN A TIME TO TAKE ADVANTAGE OF BEING ON **EQUAL FOOTING** WITH ALL OF YOUR ENEMIES AND ASSOCIATES.
FOR OTHERS IT'S BEEN A TIME TO RETRENCH, ATTEMPTING TO SORT OUT HOW VULNERABLE THEY MIGHT BE.
AND HOW LONG THEIR NAGGING SICKNESSES WILL CONTINUE.
shit

ESPECIALLY WHEN THAT SICKNESS IS COMBINED WITH OTHER MORE SEVERE CONDITIONS.

This... is taking too long.

MAKING HIS ENTIRE BODY FELL LIKE...

SCRATCH
SCRATCH

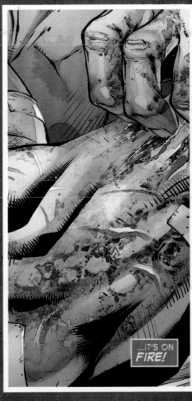

...IT'S ON FIRE!

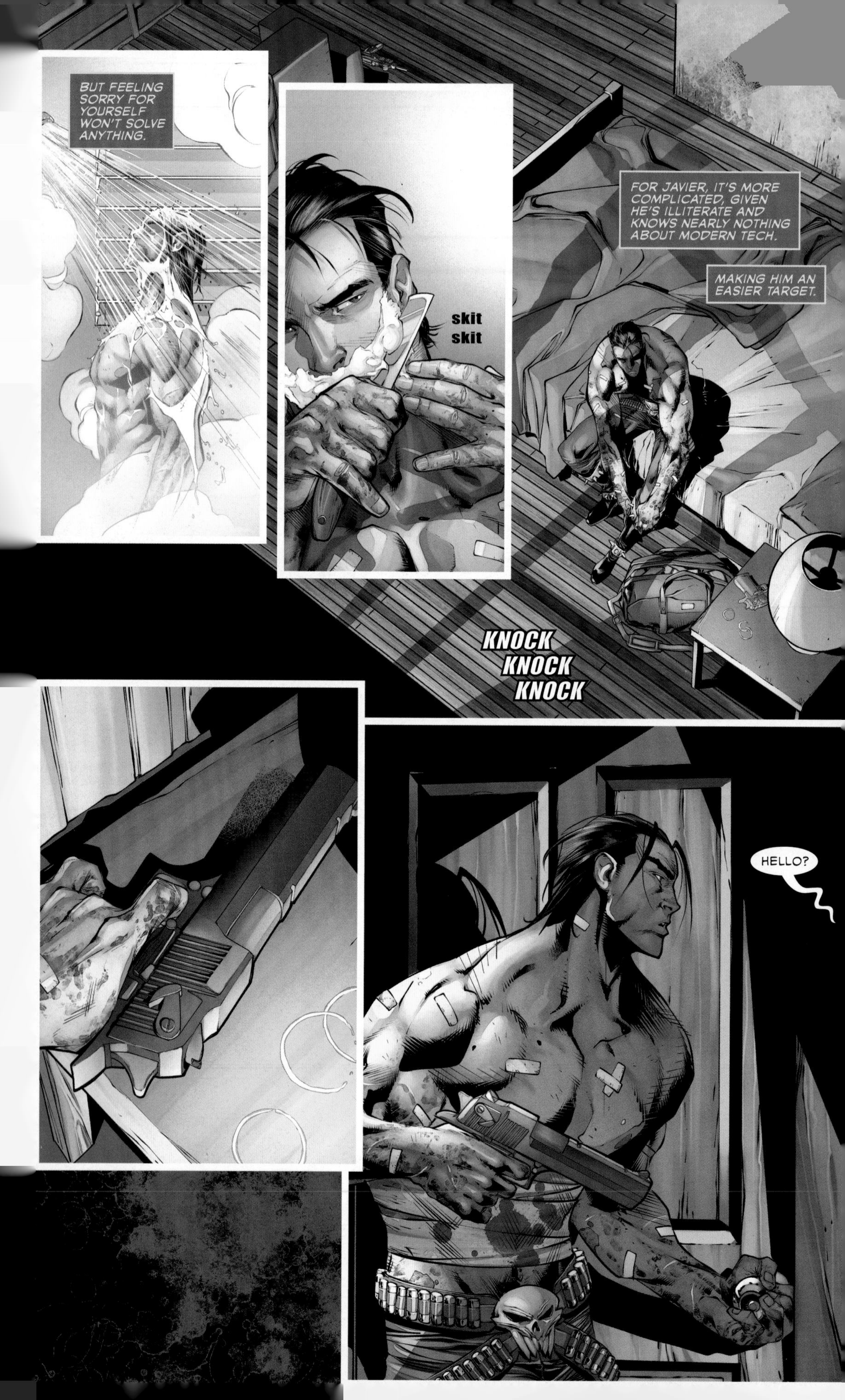
BUT FEELING SORRY FOR YOURSELF WON'T SOLVE ANYTHING.
skit
skit
FOR JAVIER, IT'S MORE COMPLICATED, GIVEN HE'S ILLITERATE AND KNOWS NEARLY NOTHING ABOUT MODERN TECH.
MAKING HIM AN EASIER TARGET.
KNOCK
KNOCK
KNOCK
HELLO?

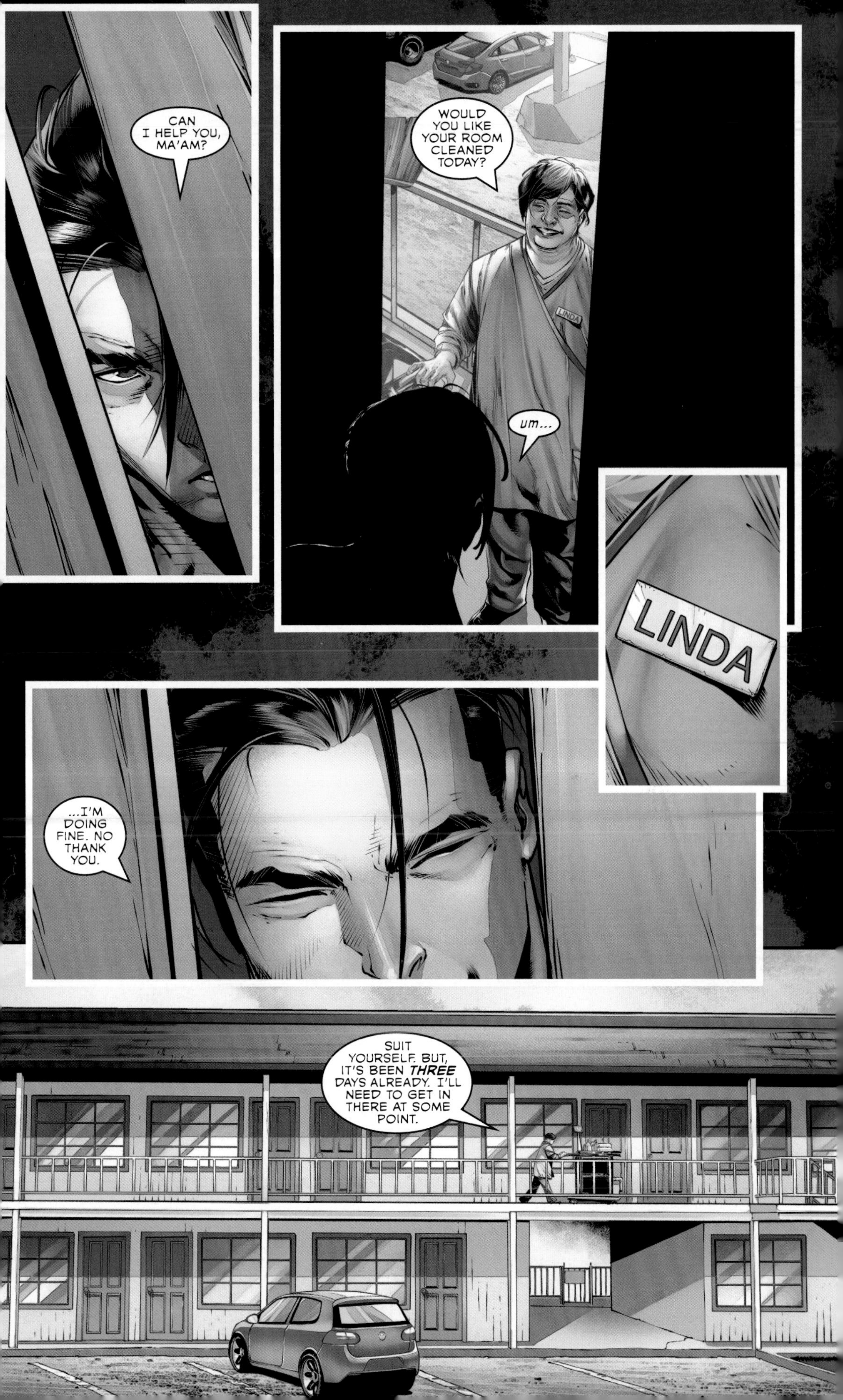
CAN I HELP YOU, MA'AM?
WOULD YOU LIKE YOUR ROOM CLEANED TODAY?
LINDA
UM...
LINDA
...I'M DOING FINE. NO THANK YOU.
SUIT YOURSELF. BUT, IT'S BEEN *THREE* DAYS ALREADY. I'LL NEED TO GET IN THERE AT SOME POINT.

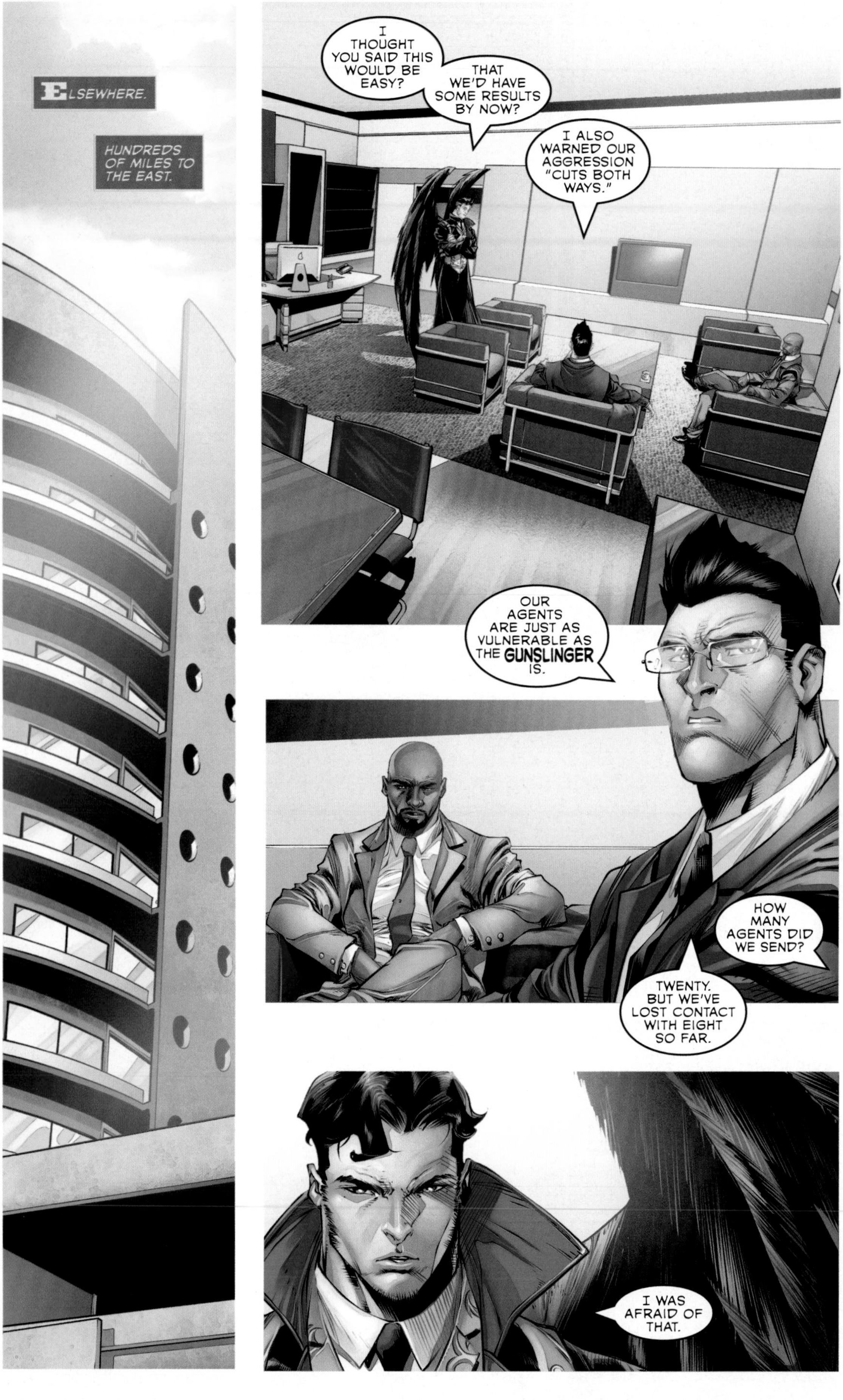
ELSEWHERE.
HUNDREDS OF MILES TO THE EAST.
I THOUGHT YOU SAID THIS WOULD BE EASY?
THAT WE'D HAVE SOME RESULTS BY NOW?
I ALSO WARNED OUR AGGRESSION "CUTS BOTH WAYS."
OUR AGENTS ARE JUST AS VULNERABLE AS THE GUNSLINGER IS.
HOW MANY AGENTS DID WE SEND?
TWENTY. BUT WE'VE LOST CONTACT WITH EIGHT SO FAR.
I WAS AFRAID OF THAT.

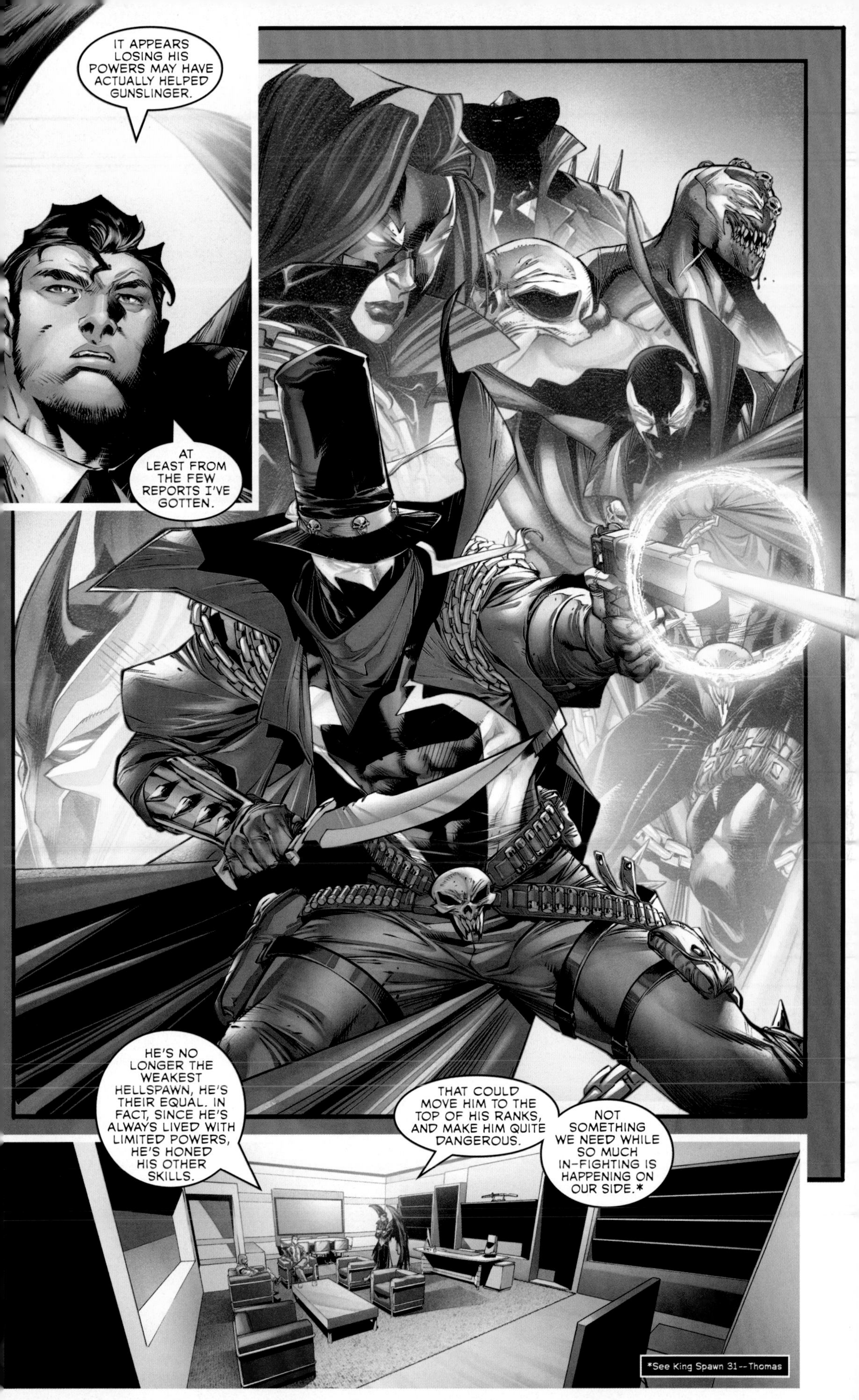
IT APPEARS LOSING HIS POWERS MAY HAVE ACTUALLY HELPED GUNSLINGER.
AT LEAST FROM THE FEW REPORTS I'VE GOTTEN.
HE'S NO LONGER THE WEAKEST HELLSPAWN, HE'S THEIR EQUAL. IN FACT, SINCE HE'S ALWAYS LIVED WITH LIMITED POWERS, HE'S HONED HIS OTHER SKILLS.
THAT COULD MOVE HIM TO THE TOP OF HIS RANKS, AND MAKE HIM QUITE DANGEROUS.
NOT SOMETHING WE NEED WHILE SO MUCH IN-FIGHTING IS HAPPENING ON OUR SIDE.*
*See King Spawn 31--Thomas

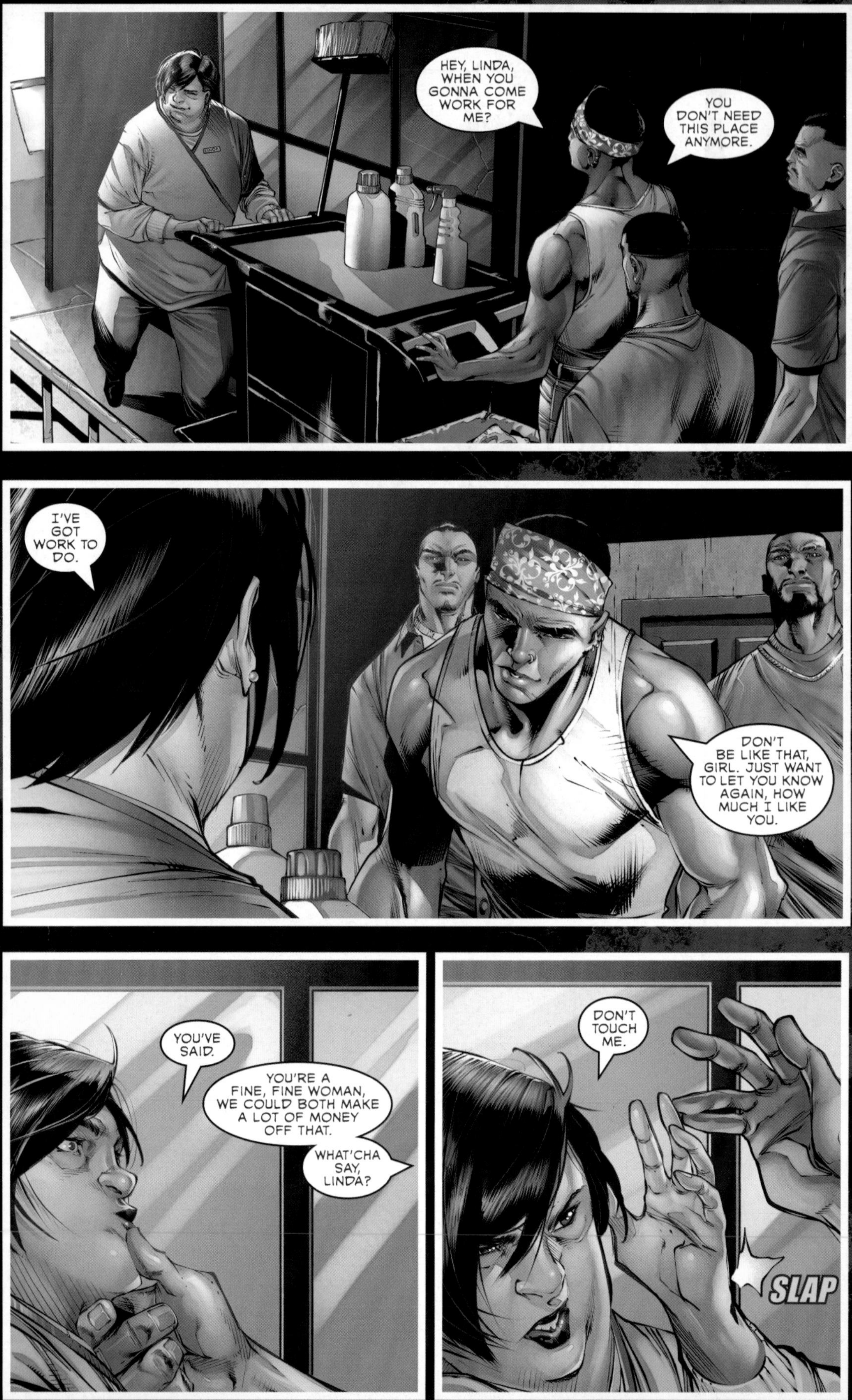
HEY, LINDA, WHEN YOU GONNA COME WORK FOR ME?
YOU DON'T NEED THIS PLACE ANYMORE.
I'VE GOT WORK TO DO.
DON'T BE LIKE THAT, GIRL. JUST WANT TO LET YOU KNOW AGAIN, HOW MUCH I LIKE YOU.
YOU'VE SAID.
YOU'RE A FINE, FINE WOMAN, WE COULD BOTH MAKE A LOT OF MONEY OFF THAT.
WHAT'CHA SAY, LINDA?
DON'T TOUCH ME.
SLAP

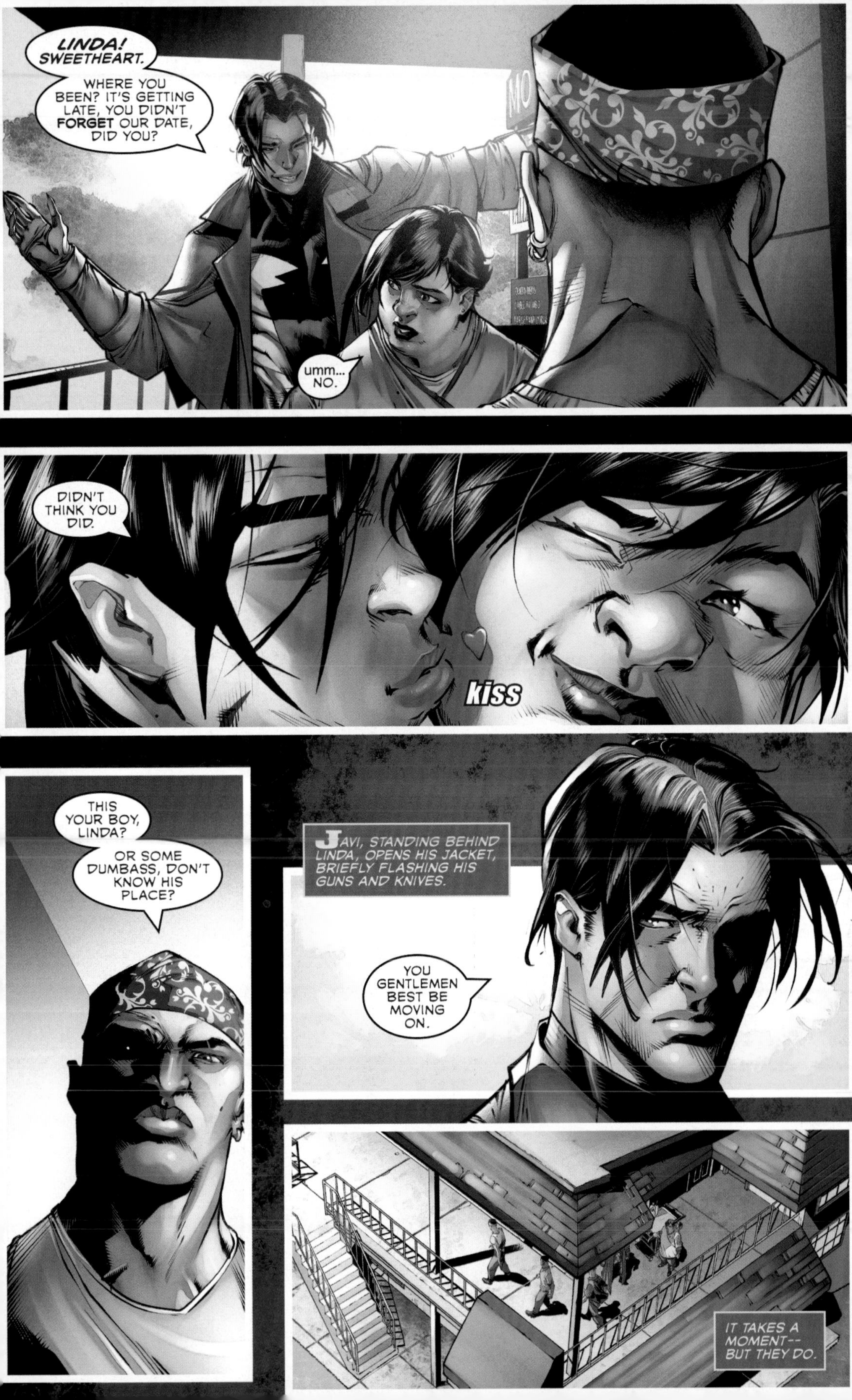

LINDA! SWEETHEART.
WHERE YOU BEEN? IT'S GETTING LATE, YOU DIDN'T FORGET OUR DATE, DID YOU?
umm... NO.
DIDN'T THINK YOU DID.
kiss
THIS YOUR BOY, LINDA?
OR SOME DUMBASS, DON'T KNOW HIS PLACE?
JAVI, STANDING BEHIND LINDA, OPENS HIS JACKET, BRIEFLY FLASHING HIS GUNS AND KNIVES.
YOU GENTLEMEN BEST BE MOVING ON.
IT TAKES A MOMENT-- BUT THEY DO.

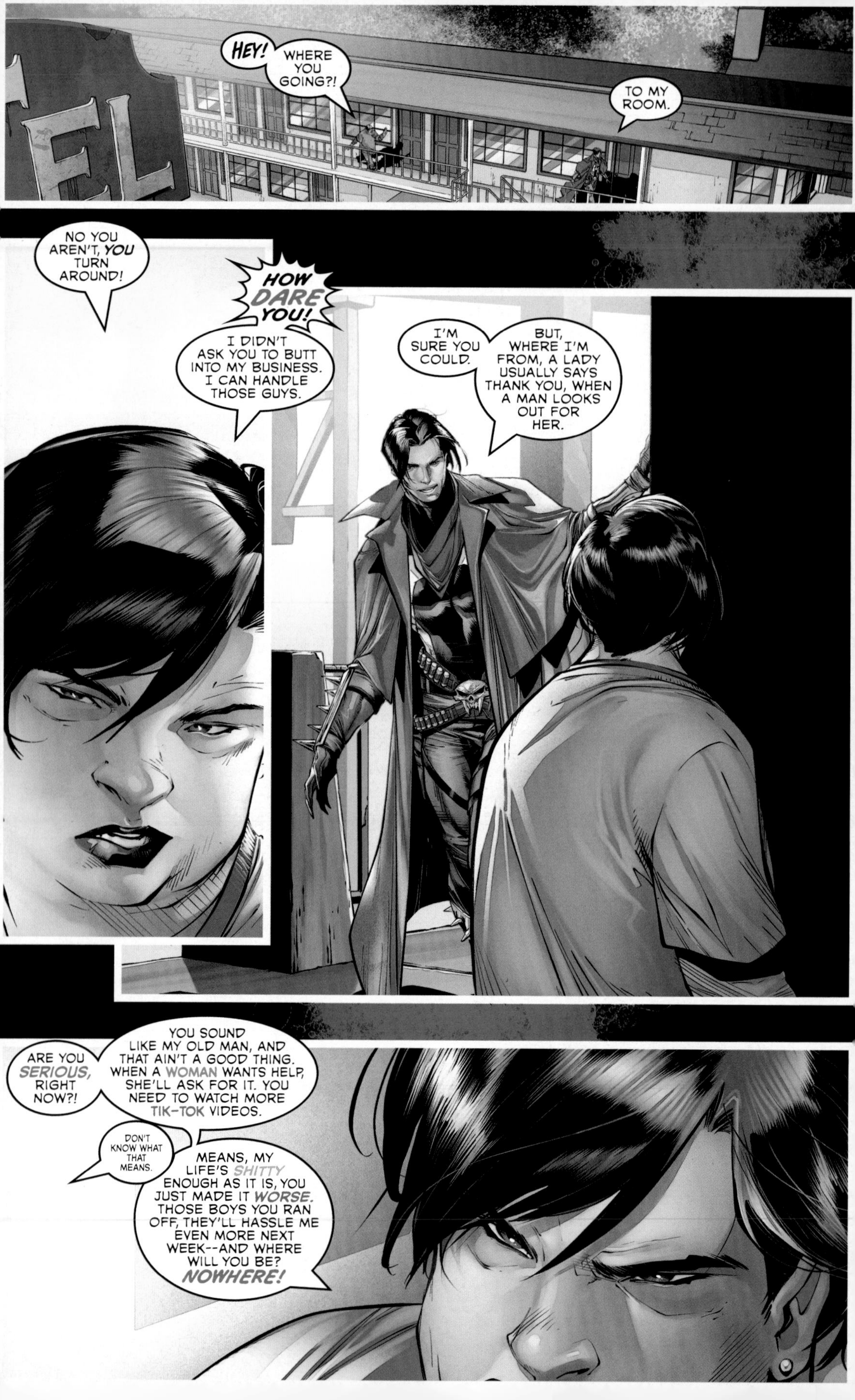

HEY!
WHERE YOU GOING?!
TO MY ROOM.
NO YOU AREN'T, YOU TURN AROUND!
HOW DARE YOU!
I DIDN'T ASK YOU TO BUTT INTO MY BUSINESS. I CAN HANDLE THOSE GUYS.
I'M SURE YOU COULD.
BUT, WHERE I'M FROM, A LADY USUALLY SAYS THANK YOU, WHEN A MAN LOOKS OUT FOR HER.
ARE YOU SERIOUS, RIGHT NOW?!
YOU SOUND LIKE MY OLD MAN, AND THAT AIN'T A GOOD THING. WHEN A WOMAN WANTS HELP, SHE'LL ASK FOR IT. YOU NEED TO WATCH MORE TIK-TOK VIDEOS.
DON'T KNOW WHAT THAT MEANS.
MEANS, MY LIFE'S SHITTY ENOUGH AS IT IS, YOU JUST MADE IT WORSE. THOSE BOYS YOU RAN OFF, THEY'LL HASSLE ME EVEN MORE NEXT WEEK--AND WHERE WILL YOU BE? NOWHERE!

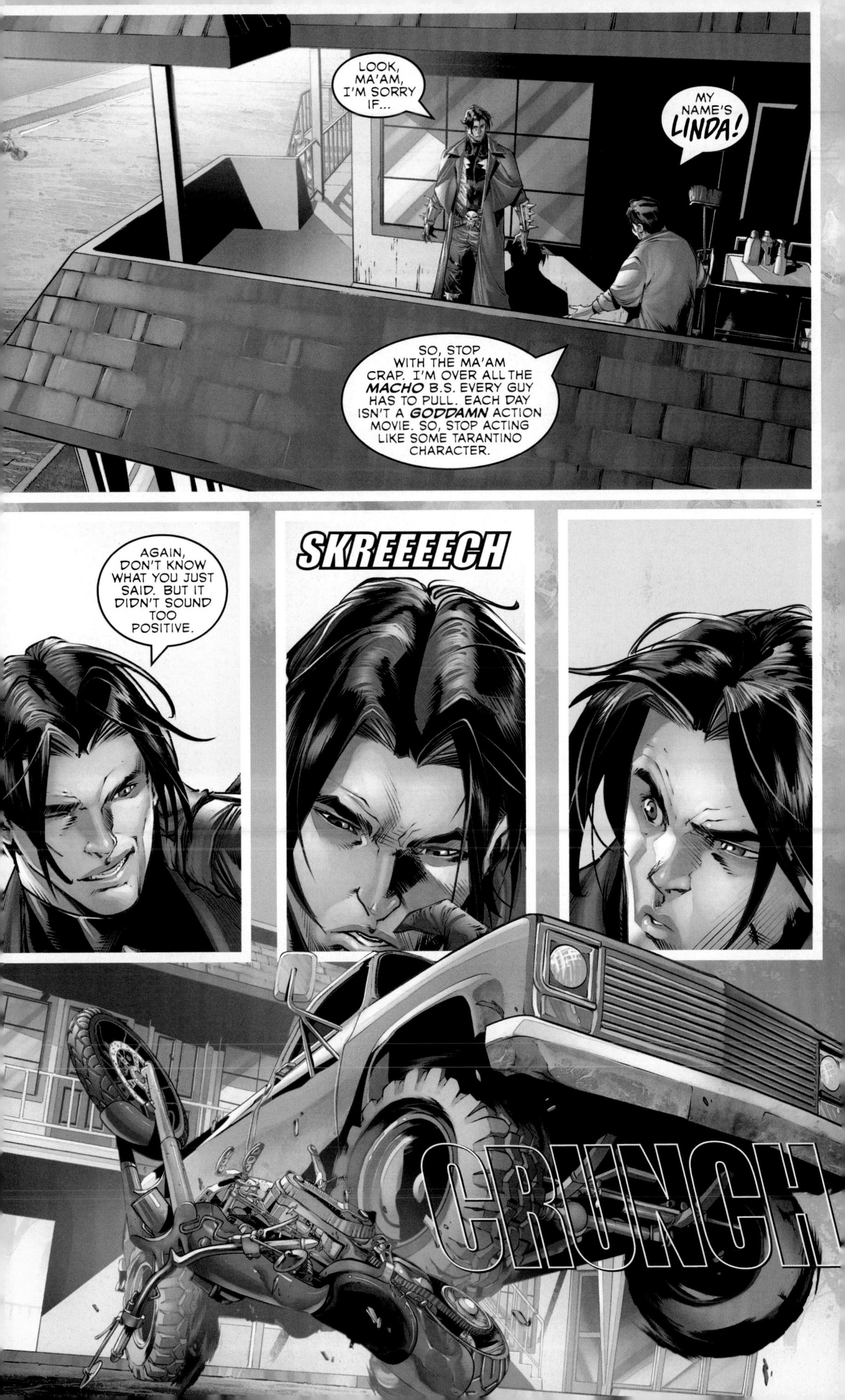

LOOK, MA'AM, I'M SORRY IF...
MY NAME'S LINDA!
SO, STOP WITH THE MA'AM CRAP. I'M OVER ALL THE MACHO B.S. EVERY GUY HAS TO PULL. EACH DAY ISN'T A GODDAMN ACTION MOVIE. SO, STOP ACTING LIKE SOME TARANTINO CHARACTER.
AGAIN, DON'T KNOW WHAT YOU JUST SAID. BUT IT DIDN'T SOUND TOO POSITIVE.
SKREEEECH
CRUNCH

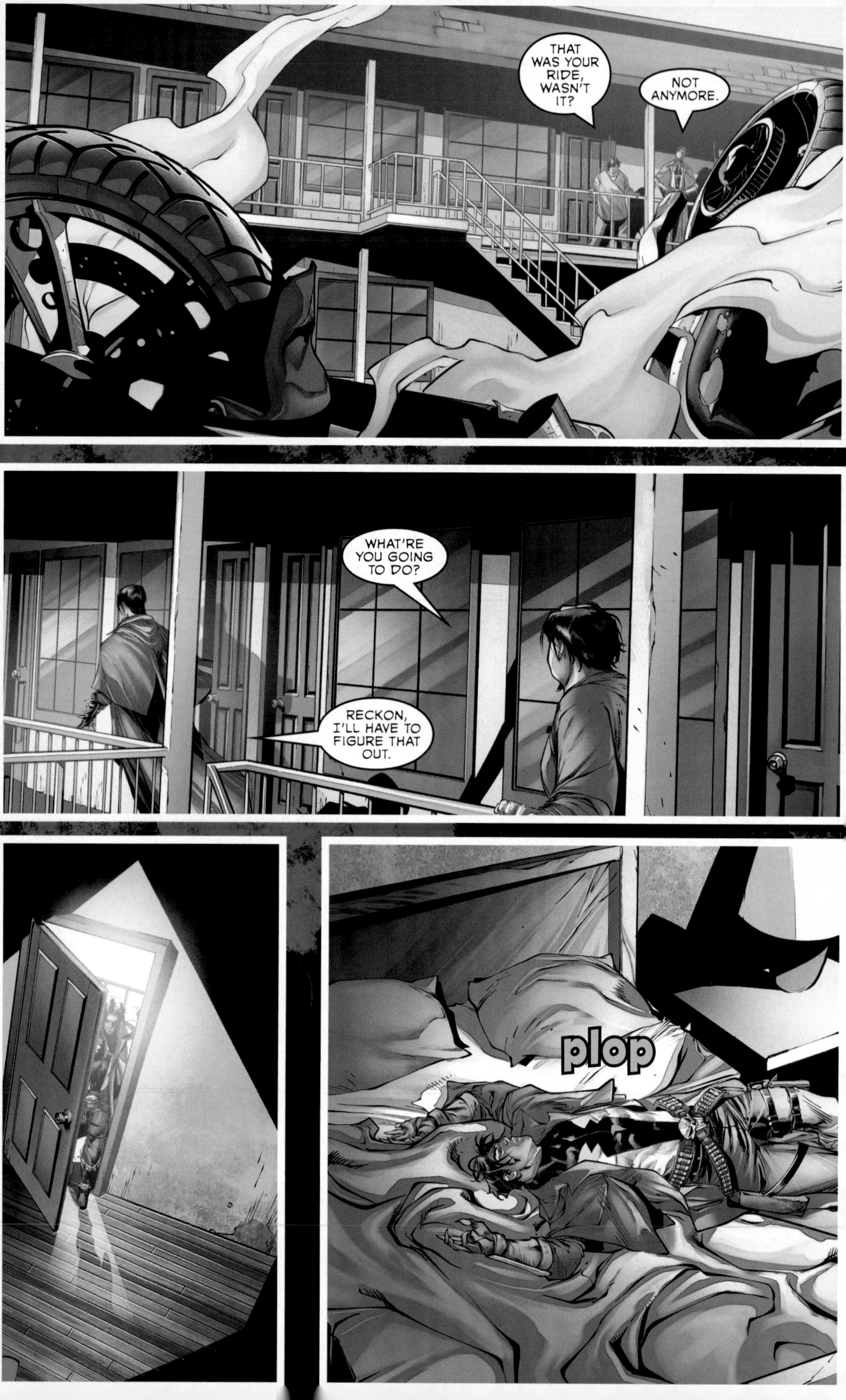
THAT WAS YOUR RIDE, WASN'T IT?
NOT ANYMORE.
WHAT'RE YOU GOING TO DO?
RECKON, I'LL HAVE TO FIGURE THAT OUT.
plop

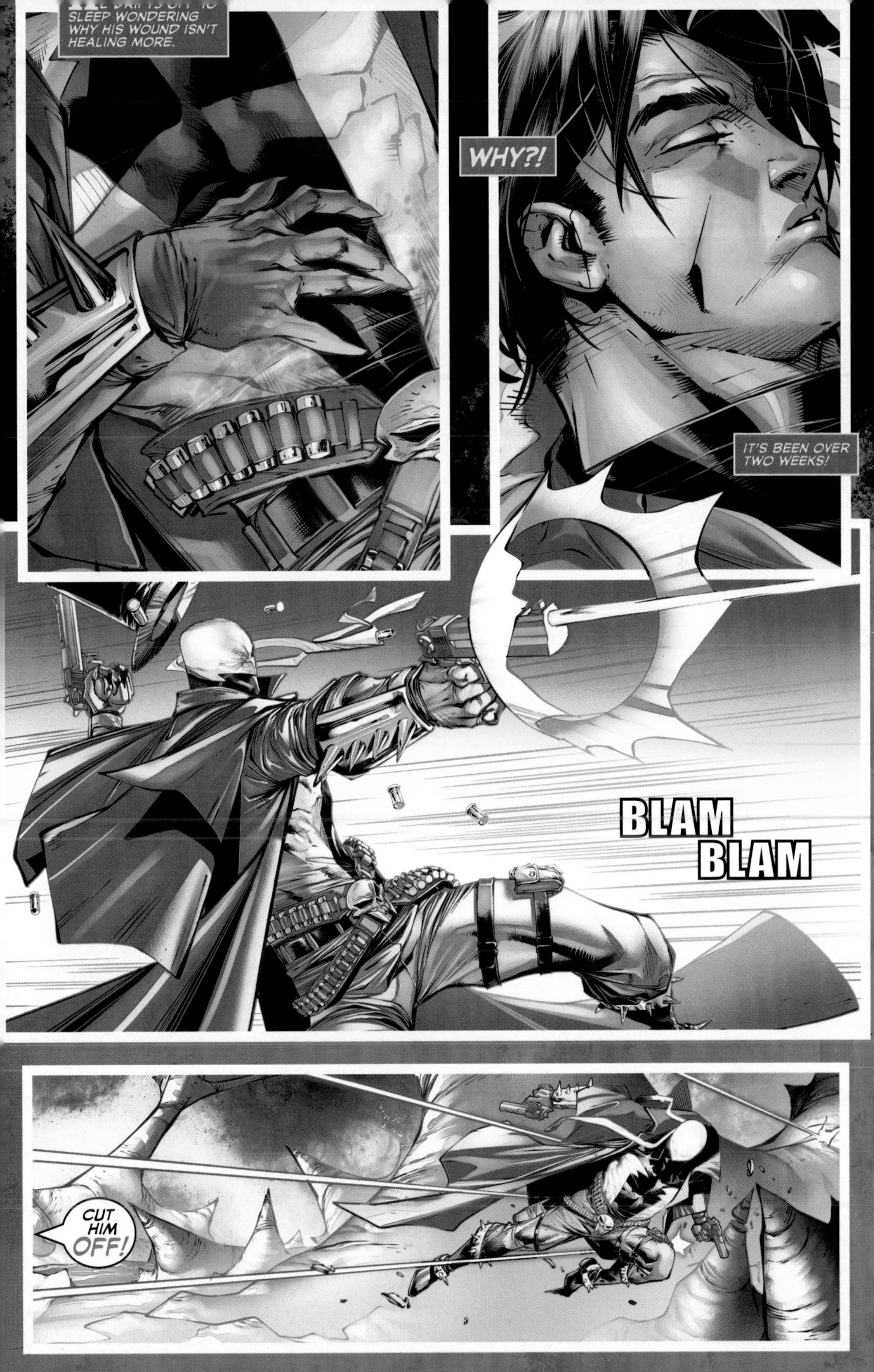
SLEEP WONDERING WHY HIS WOUND ISN'T HEALING MORE.
WHY?!
IT'S BEEN OVER TWO WEEKS!
BLAM BLAM
CUT HIM OFF!

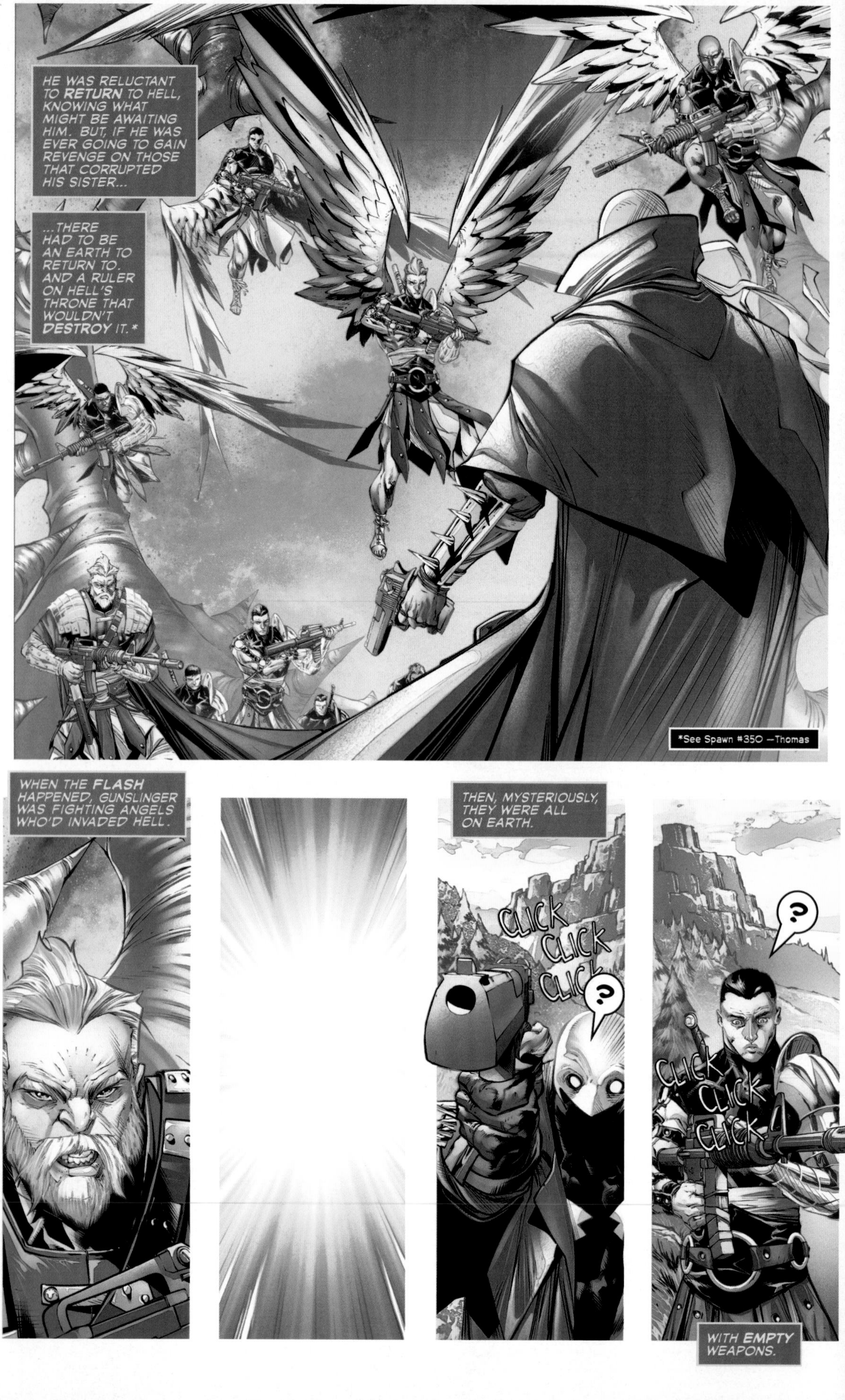
HE WAS RELUCTANT TO RETURN TO HELL, KNOWING WHAT MIGHT BE AWAITING HIM. BUT, IF HE WAS EVER GOING TO GAIN REVENGE ON THOSE THAT CORRUPTED HIS SISTER...
...THERE HAD TO BE AN EARTH TO RETURN TO. AND A RULER ON HELL'S THRONE THAT WOULDN'T DESTROY IT.*
*See Spawn #350 —Thomas
WHEN THE FLASH HAPPENED, GUNSLINGER WAS FIGHTING ANGELS WHO'D INVADED HELL.
THEN, MYSTERIOUSLY, THEY WERE ALL ON EARTH.
CLICK CLICK CLICK
?
?
CLICK CLICK CLICK
WITH EMPTY WEAPONS.

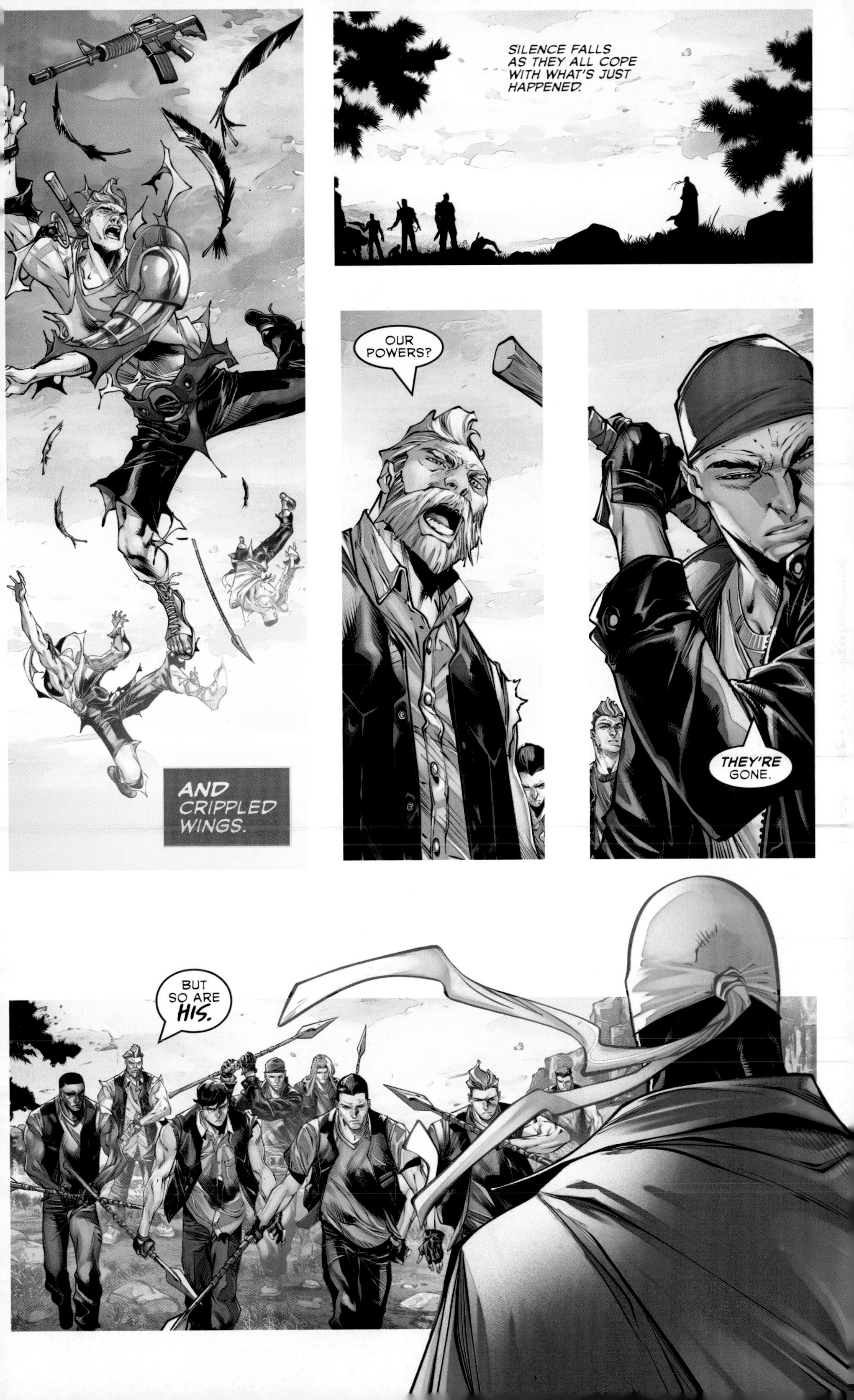
AND CRIPPLED WINGS.
SILENCE FALLS AS THEY ALL COPE WITH WHAT'S JUST HAPPENED.
OUR POWERS?
THEY'RE GONE.
BUT SO ARE HIS.

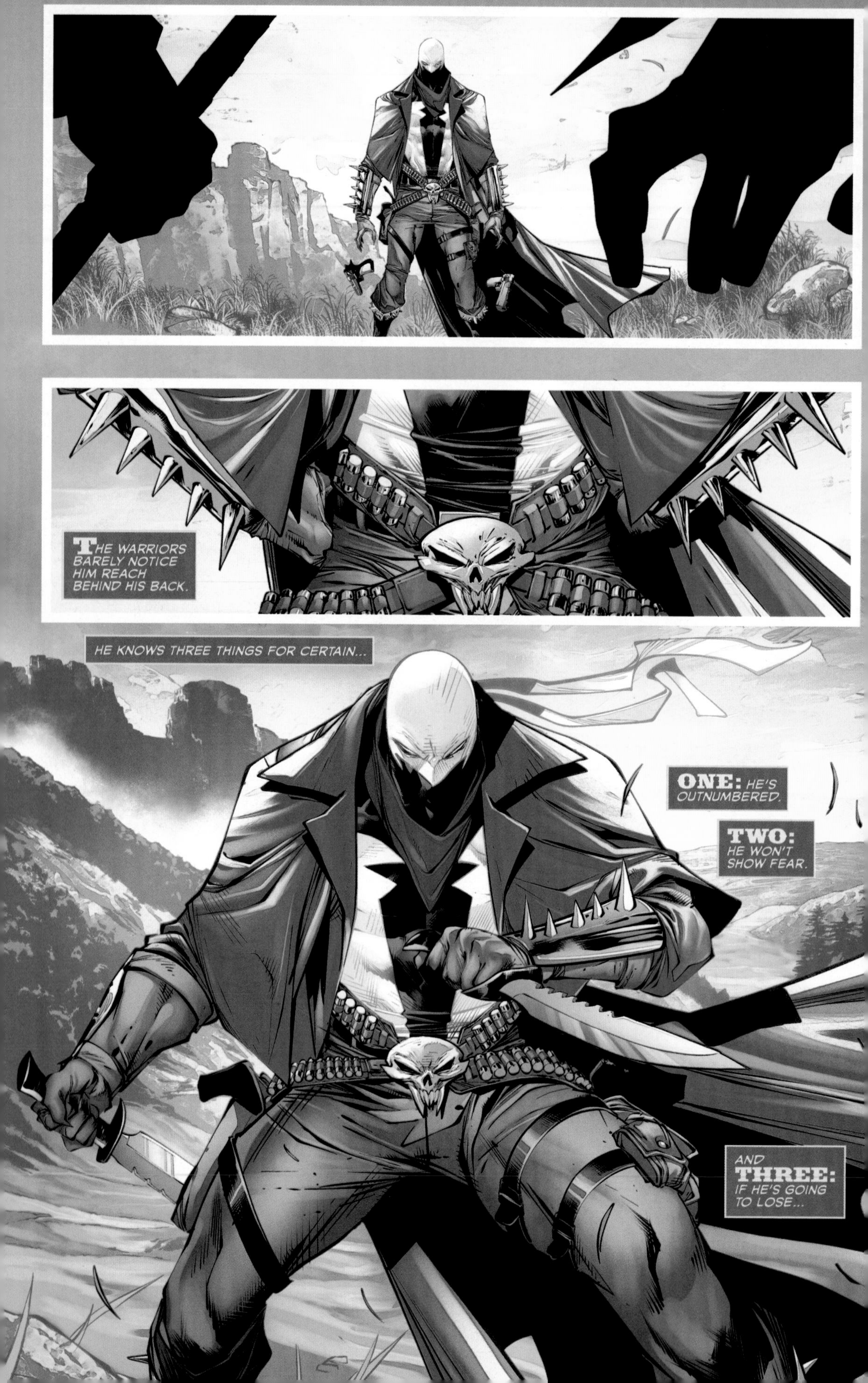
THE WARRIORS BARELY NOTICE HIM REACH BEHIND HIS BACK.
HE KNOWS THREE THINGS FOR CERTAIN...
ONE: HE'S OUTNUMBERED.
TWO: HE WON'T SHOW FEAR.
AND THREE: IF HE'S GOING TO LOSE...

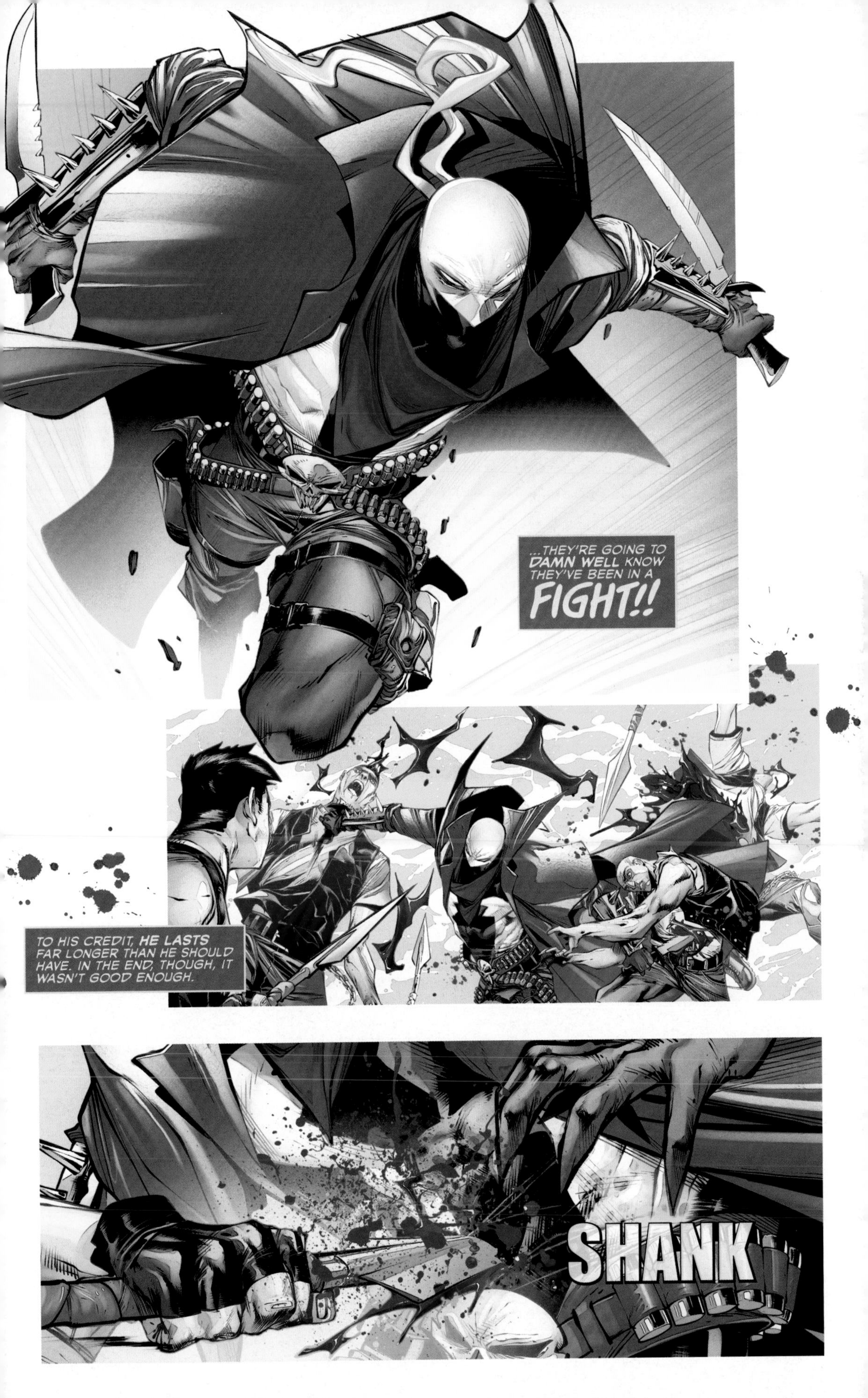
...THEY'RE GOING TO DAMN WELL KNOW THEY'VE BEEN IN A FIGHT!!
TO HIS CREDIT, HE LASTS FAR LONGER THAN HE SHOULD HAVE. IN THE END, THOUGH, IT WASN'T GOOD ENOUGH.
SHANK

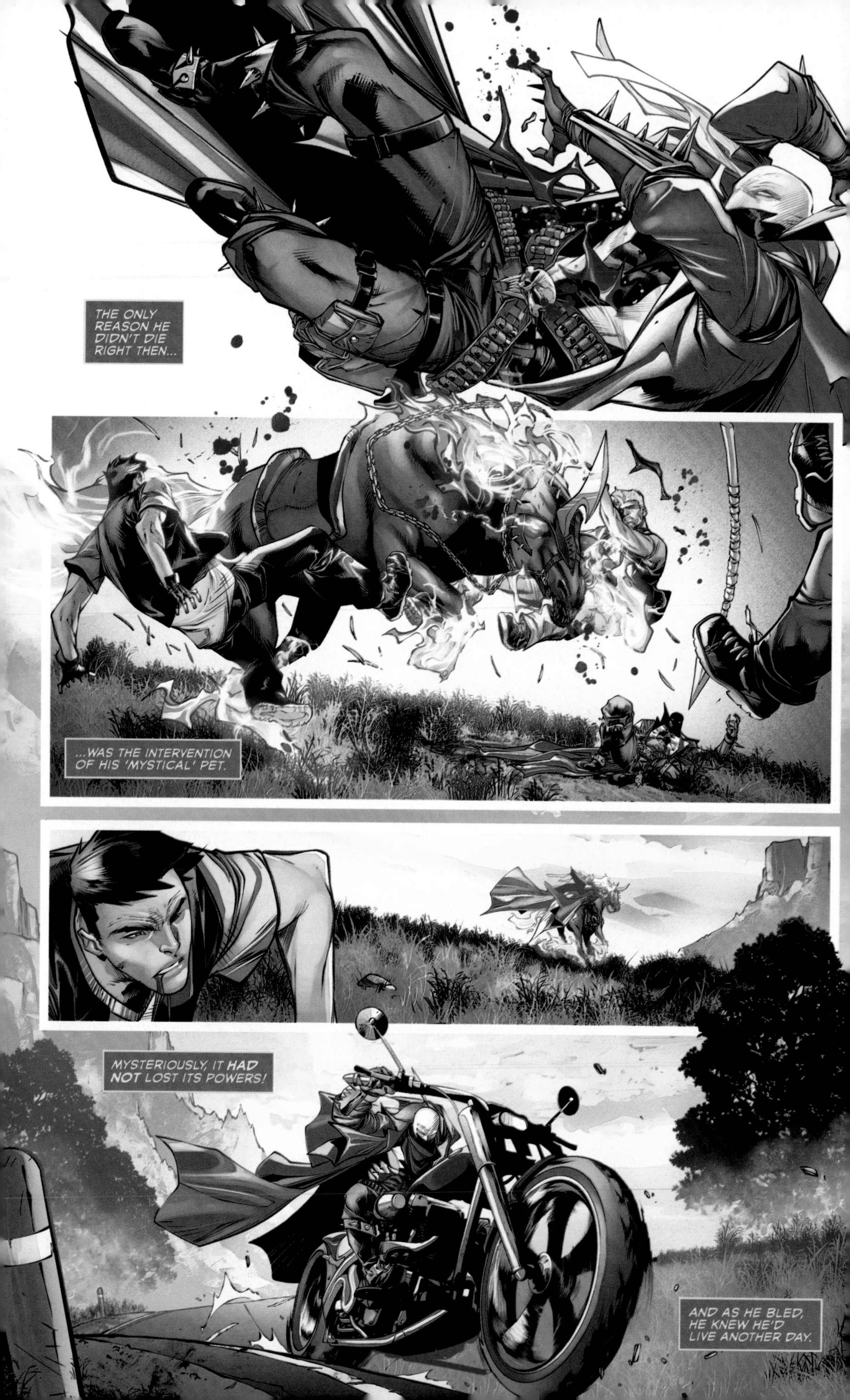
THE ONLY REASON HE DIDN'T DIE RIGHT THEN...
...WAS THE INTERVENTION OF HIS 'MYSTICAL' PET.
MYSTERIOUSLY, IT HAD NOT LOST ITS POWERS!
AND AS HE BLED, HE KNEW HE'D LIVE ANOTHER DAY.

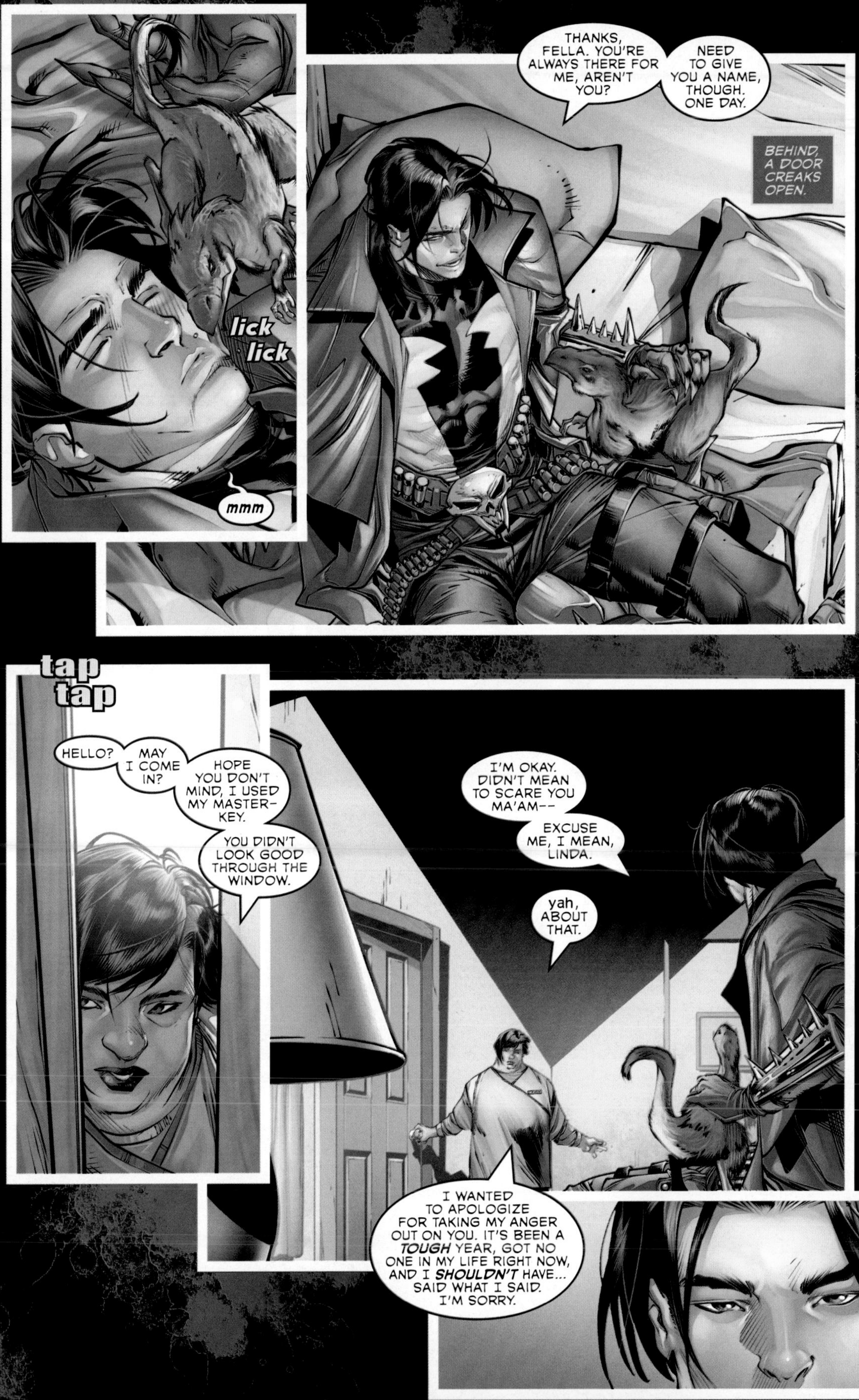
lick
lick
mmm
THANKS, FELLA. YOU'RE ALWAYS THERE FOR ME, AREN'T YOU?
NEED TO GIVE YOU A NAME, THOUGH. ONE DAY.
BEHIND, A DOOR CREAKS OPEN.
tap tap
HELLO?
MAY I COME IN?
HOPE YOU DON'T MIND, I USED MY MASTER-KEY.
YOU DIDN'T LOOK GOOD THROUGH THE WINDOW.
I'M OKAY. DIDN'T MEAN TO SCARE YOU MA'AM--
EXCUSE ME, I MEAN, LINDA.
yah, ABOUT THAT.
I WANTED TO APOLOGIZE FOR TAKING MY ANGER OUT ON YOU. IT'S BEEN A TOUGH YEAR, GOT NO ONE IN MY LIFE RIGHT NOW, AND I SHOULDN'T HAVE... SAID WHAT I SAID. I'M SORRY.

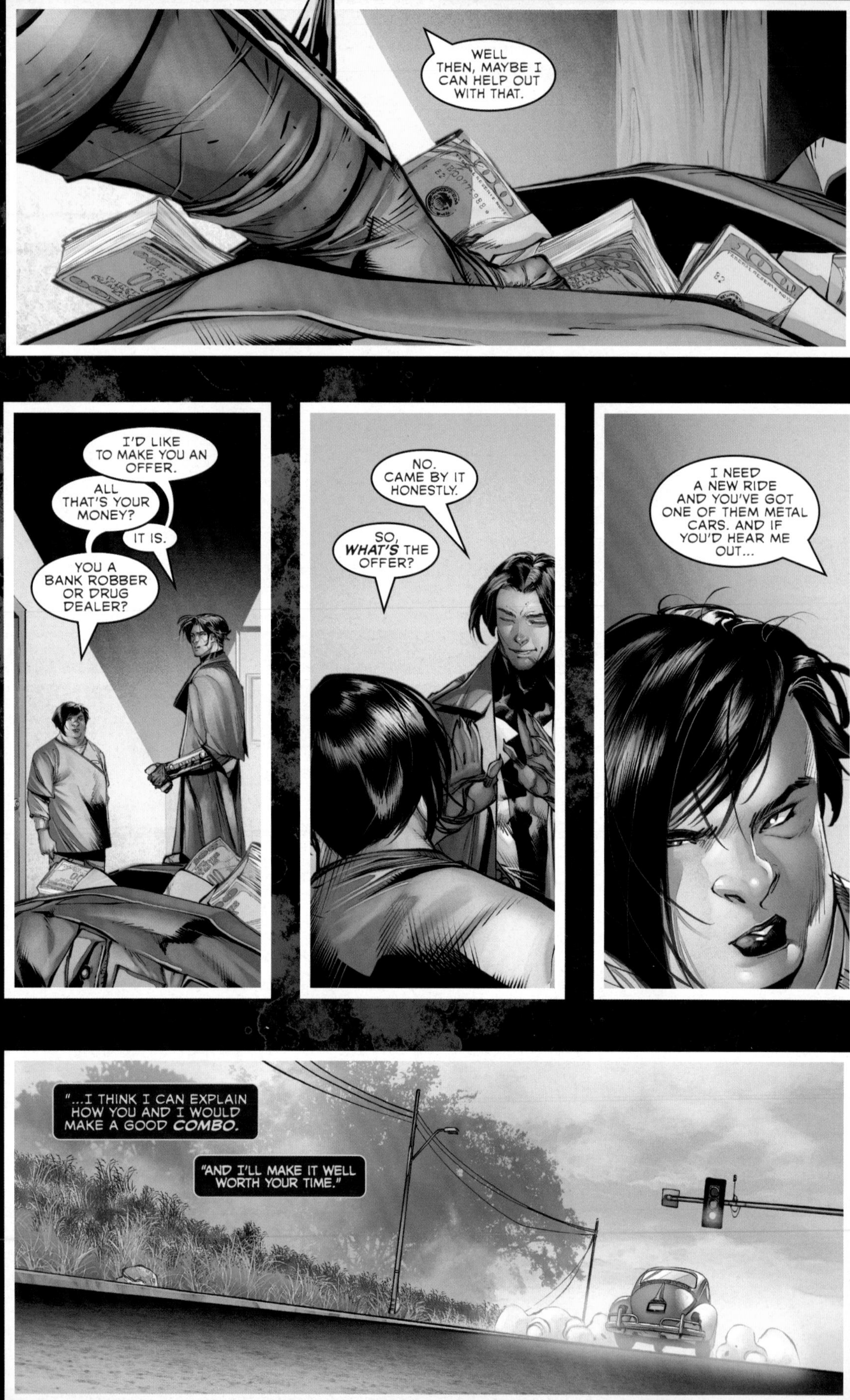
WELL THEN, MAYBE I CAN HELP OUT WITH THAT.
I'D LIKE TO MAKE YOU AN OFFER.
ALL THAT'S YOUR MONEY?
IT IS.
YOU A BANK ROBBER OR DRUG DEALER?
NO. CAME BY IT HONESTLY.
SO, WHAT'S THE OFFER?
I NEED A NEW RIDE AND YOU'VE GOT ONE OF THEM METAL CARS. AND IF YOU'D HEAR ME OUT...
"...I THINK I CAN EXPLAIN HOW YOU AND I WOULD MAKE A GOOD COMBO.
"AND I'LL MAKE IT WELL WORTH YOUR TIME."

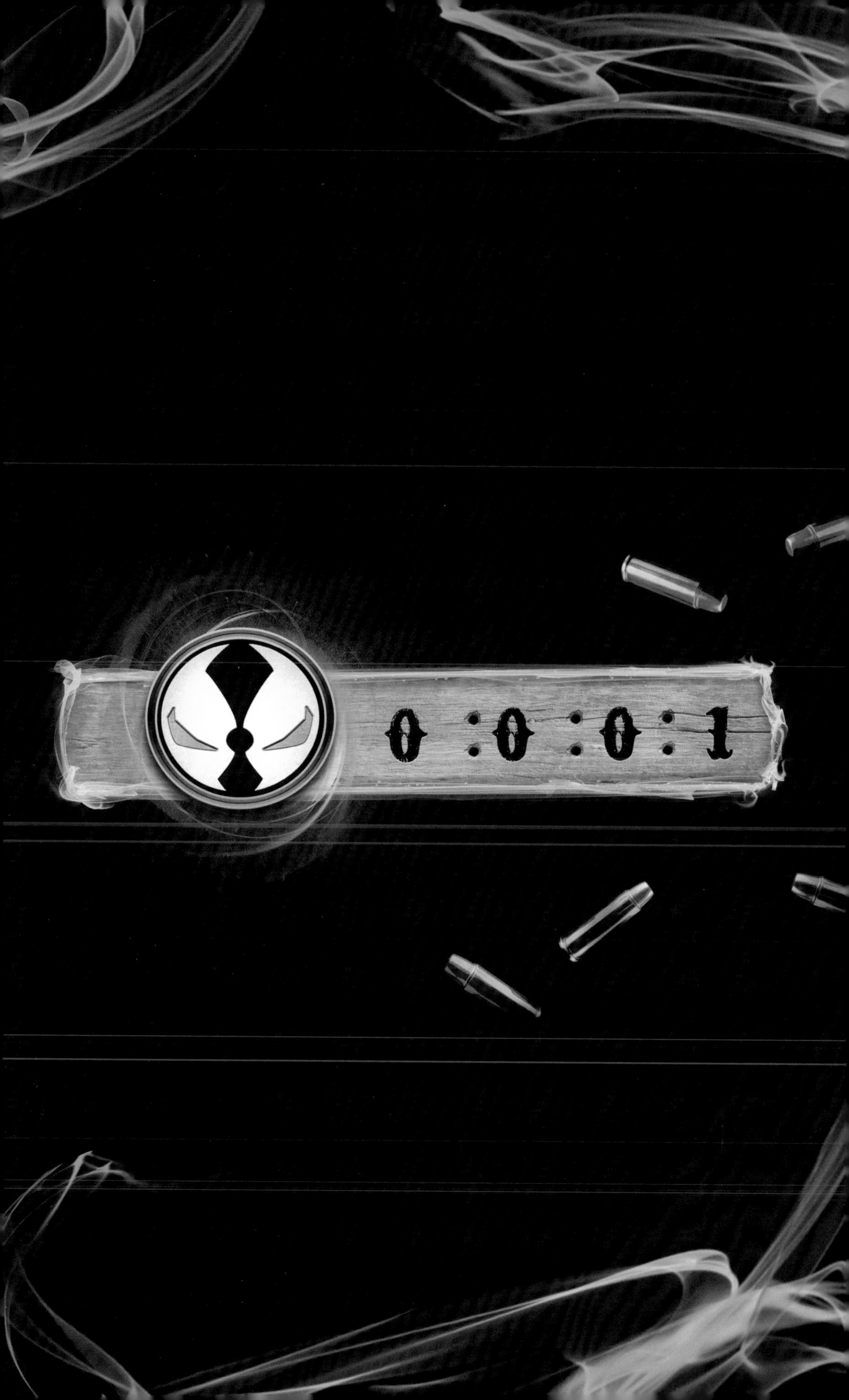
0:0:0:1

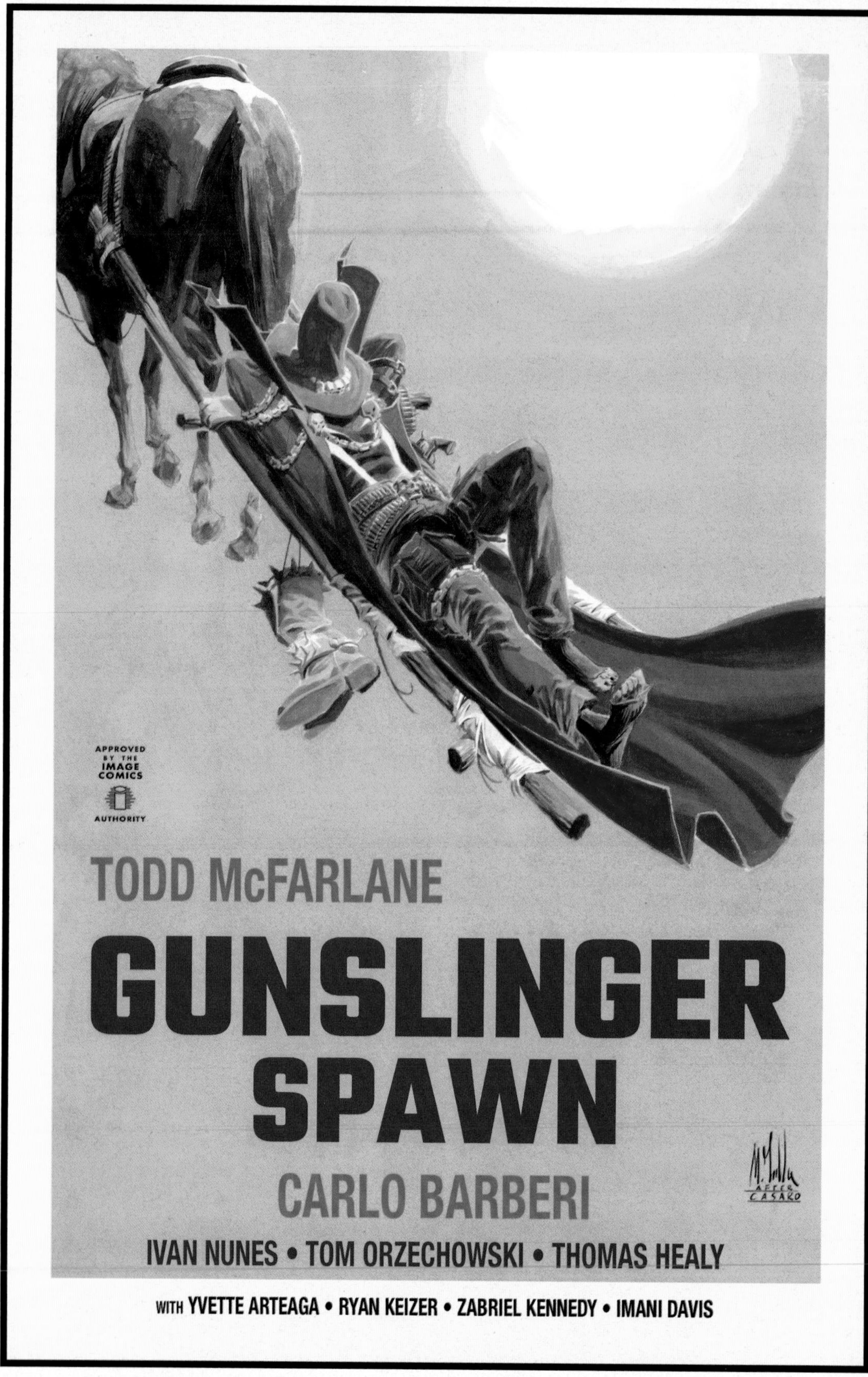
APPROVED BY THE IMAGE COMICS AUTHORITY
TODD McFARLANE
GUNSLINGER SPAWN
CARLO BARBERI
IVAN NUNES • TOM ORZECHOWSKI • THOMAS HEALY
WITH YVETTE ARTEAGA • RYAN KEIZER • ZABRIEL KENNEDY • IMANI DAVIS

GUNSLINGER SPAWN #30 COVER 'A' BY MARCO FAILLA

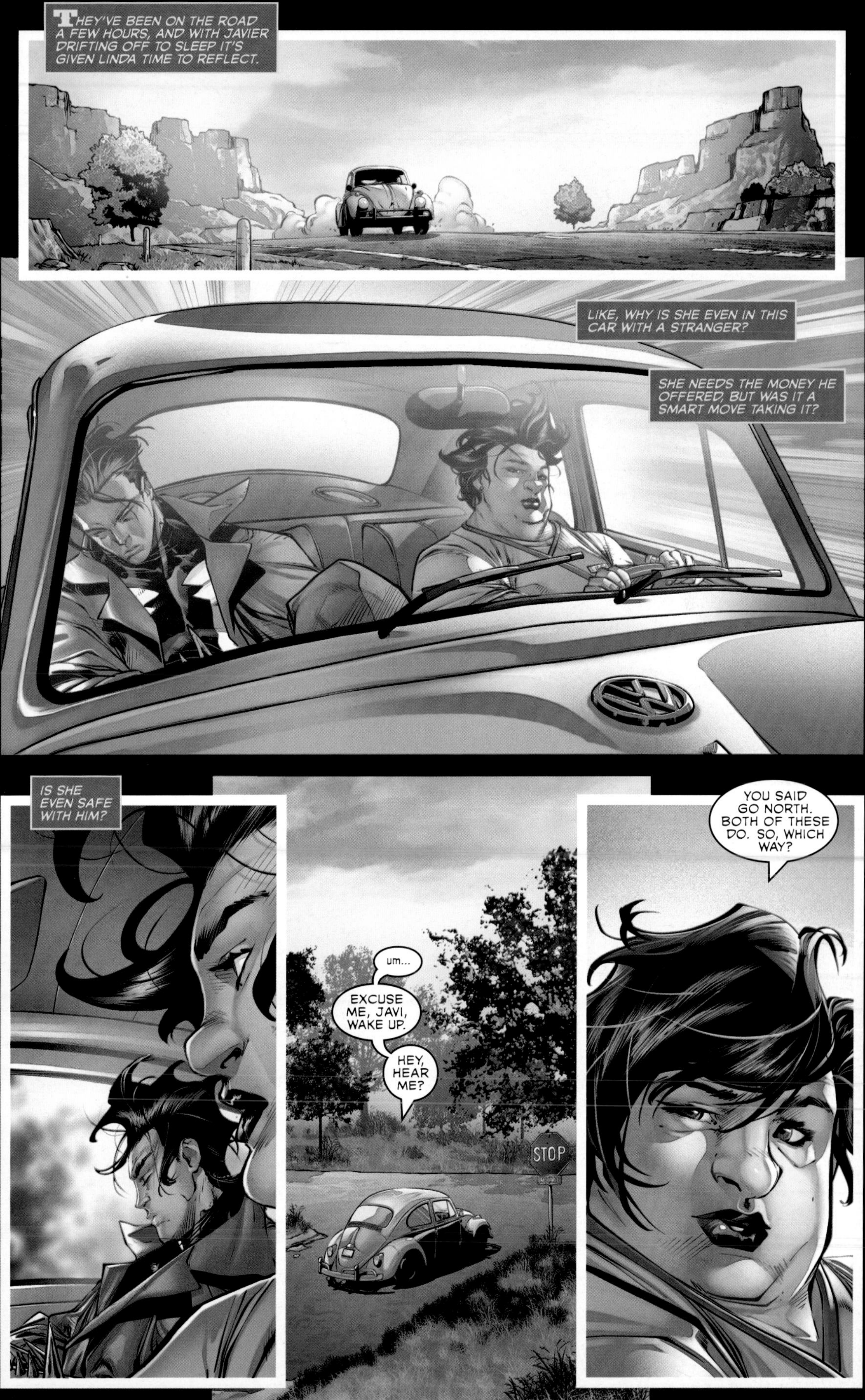
THEY'VE BEEN ON THE ROAD A FEW HOURS, AND WITH JAVIER DRIFTING OFF TO SLEEP IT'S GIVEN LINDA TIME TO REFLECT.
LIKE, WHY IS SHE EVEN IN THIS CAR WITH A STRANGER?
SHE NEEDS THE MONEY HE OFFERED, BUT WAS IT A SMART MOVE TAKING IT?
IS SHE EVEN SAFE WITH HIM?
um...
EXCUSE ME, JAVI, WAKE UP.
HEY, HEAR ME?
STOP
YOU SAID GO NORTH. BOTH OF THESE DO. SO, WHICH WAY?

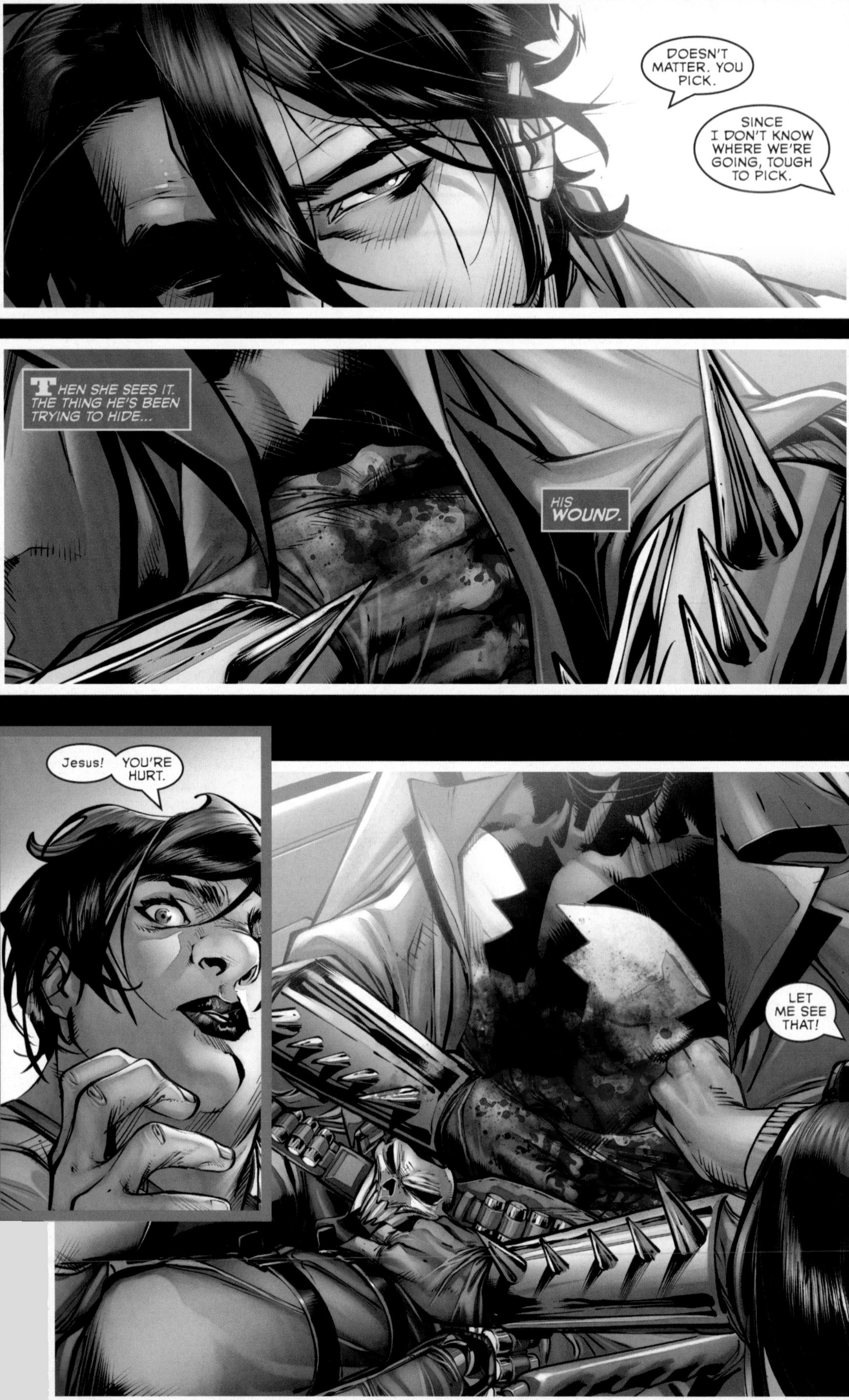
DOESN'T MATTER. YOU PICK.
SINCE I DON'T KNOW WHERE WE'RE GOING, TOUGH TO PICK.
THEN SHE SEES IT. THE THING HE'S BEEN TRYING TO HIDE...
HIS WOUND.
Jesus!
YOU'RE HURT.
LET ME SEE THAT!

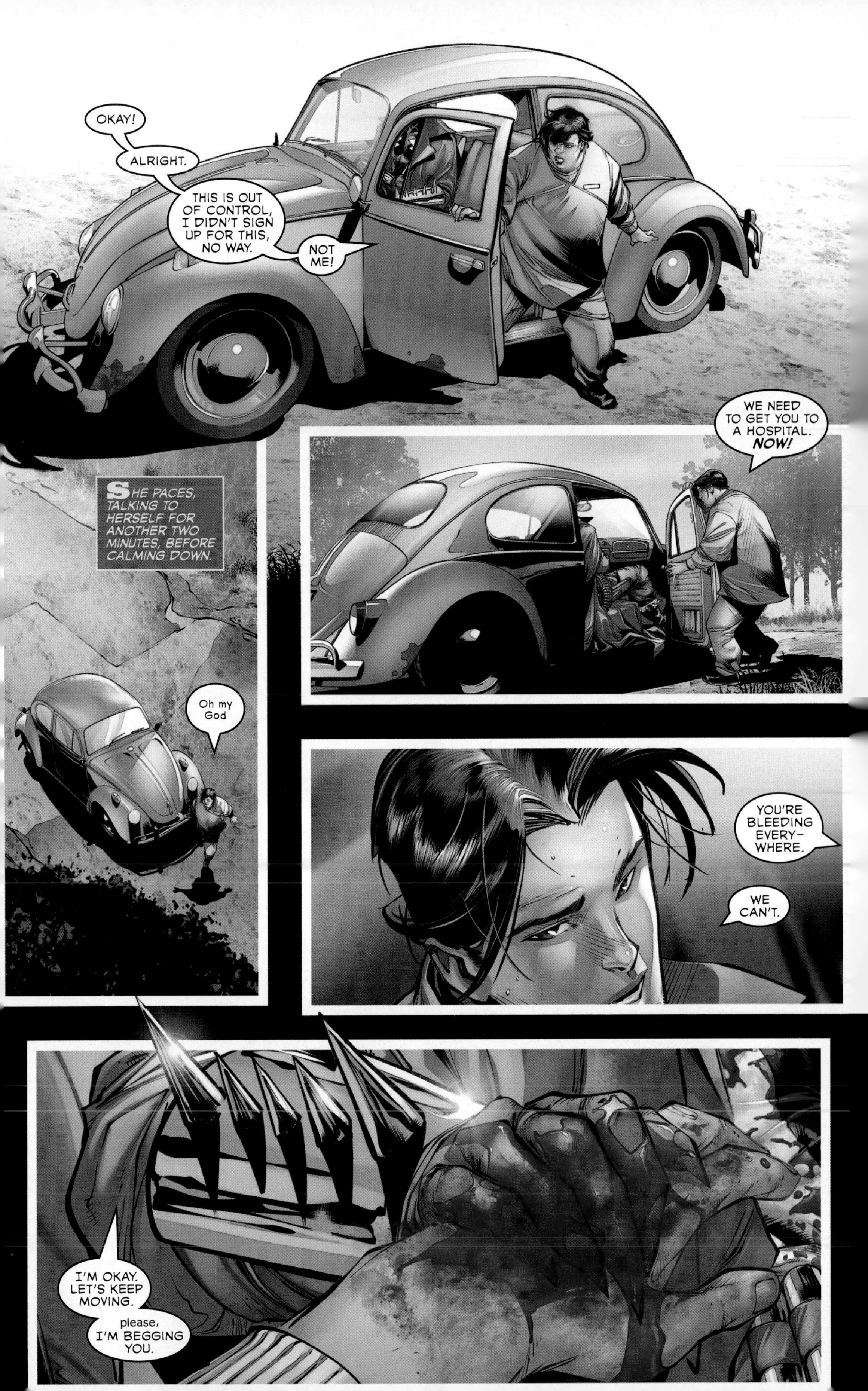
OKAY!
ALRIGHT.
THIS IS OUT OF CONTROL, I DIDN'T SIGN UP FOR THIS, NO WAY.
NOT ME!
SHE PACES, TALKING TO HERSELF FOR ANOTHER TWO MINUTES, BEFORE CALMING DOWN.
Oh my God
WE NEED TO GET YOU TO A HOSPITAL. NOW!
YOU'RE BLEEDING EVERY-WHERE.
WE CAN'T.
I'M OKAY. LET'S KEEP MOVING.
please, I'M BEGGING YOU.

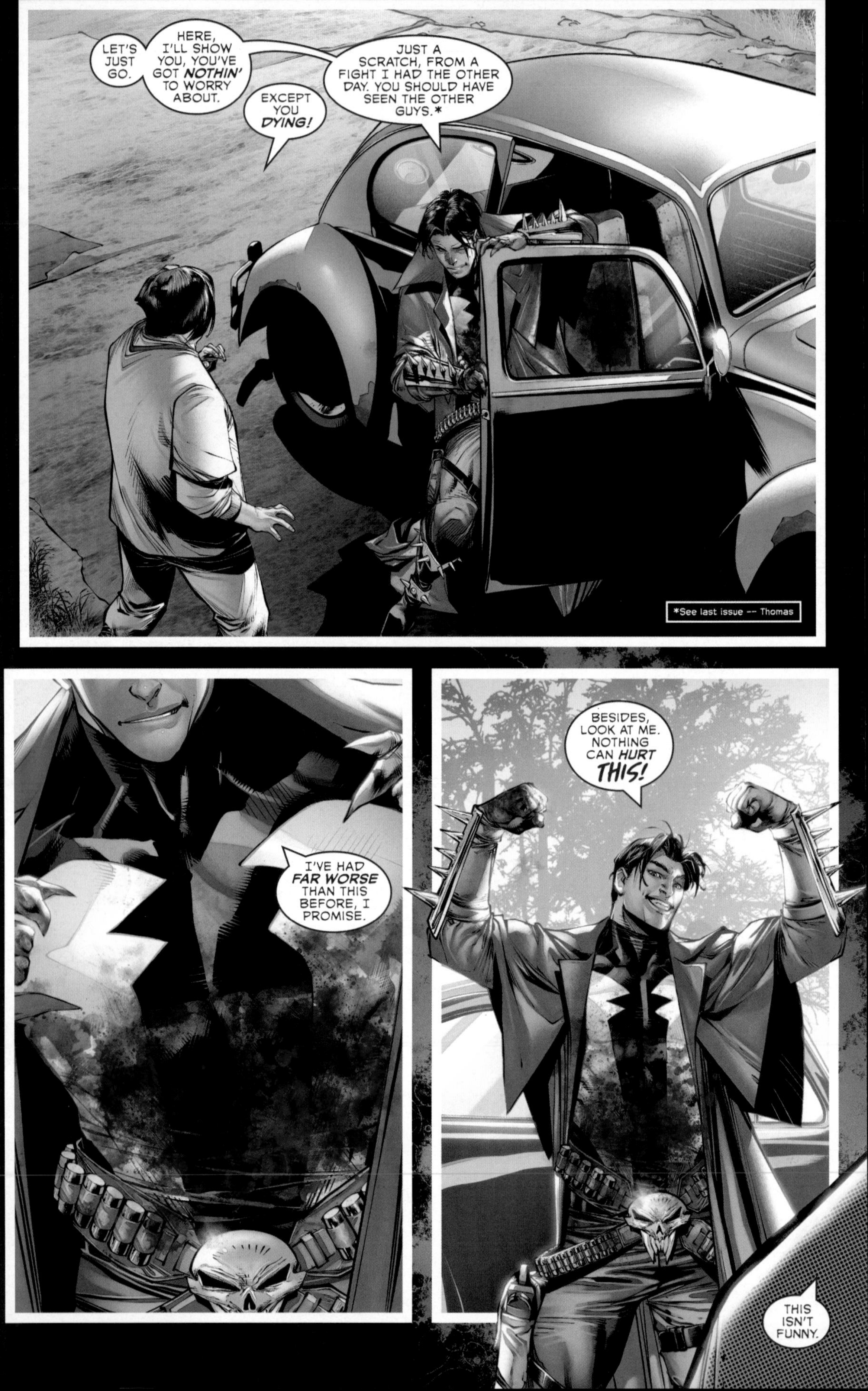
LET'S JUST GO.
HERE, I'LL SHOW YOU, YOU'VE GOT *NOTHIN'* TO WORRY ABOUT.
EXCEPT YOU *DYING!*
JUST A SCRATCH, FROM A FIGHT I HAD THE OTHER DAY. YOU SHOULD HAVE SEEN THE OTHER GUYS.*
*See last issue -- Thomas
I'VE HAD *FAR WORSE* THAN THIS BEFORE, I PROMISE.
BESIDES, LOOK AT ME. NOTHING CAN *HURT* *THIS!*
THIS ISN'T FUNNY.

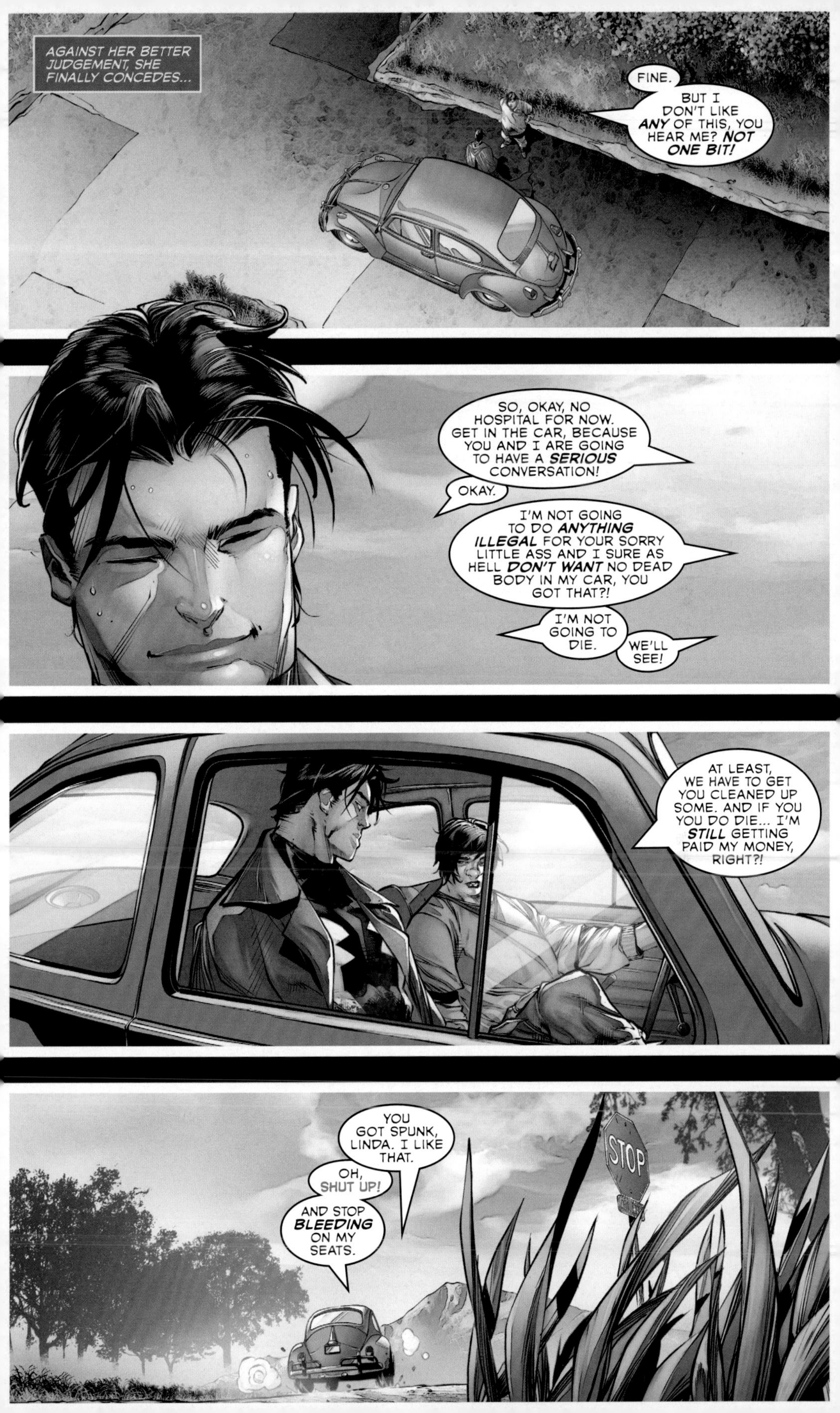
AGAINST HER BETTER JUDGEMENT, SHE FINALLY CONCEDES...
FINE.
BUT I DON'T LIKE ANY OF THIS, YOU HEAR ME? NOT ONE BIT!
SO, OKAY, NO HOSPITAL FOR NOW. GET IN THE CAR, BECAUSE YOU AND I ARE GOING TO HAVE A SERIOUS CONVERSATION!
OKAY.
I'M NOT GOING TO DO ANYTHING ILLEGAL FOR YOUR SORRY LITTLE ASS AND I SURE AS HELL DON'T WANT NO DEAD BODY IN MY CAR, YOU GOT THAT?!
I'M NOT GOING TO DIE.
WE'LL SEE!
AT LEAST, WE HAVE TO GET YOU CLEANED UP SOME. AND IF YOU YOU DO DIE... I'M STILL GETTING PAID MY MONEY, RIGHT?!
YOU GOT SPUNK, LINDA. I LIKE THAT.
OH, SHUT UP!
AND STOP BLEEDING ON MY SEATS.
STOP

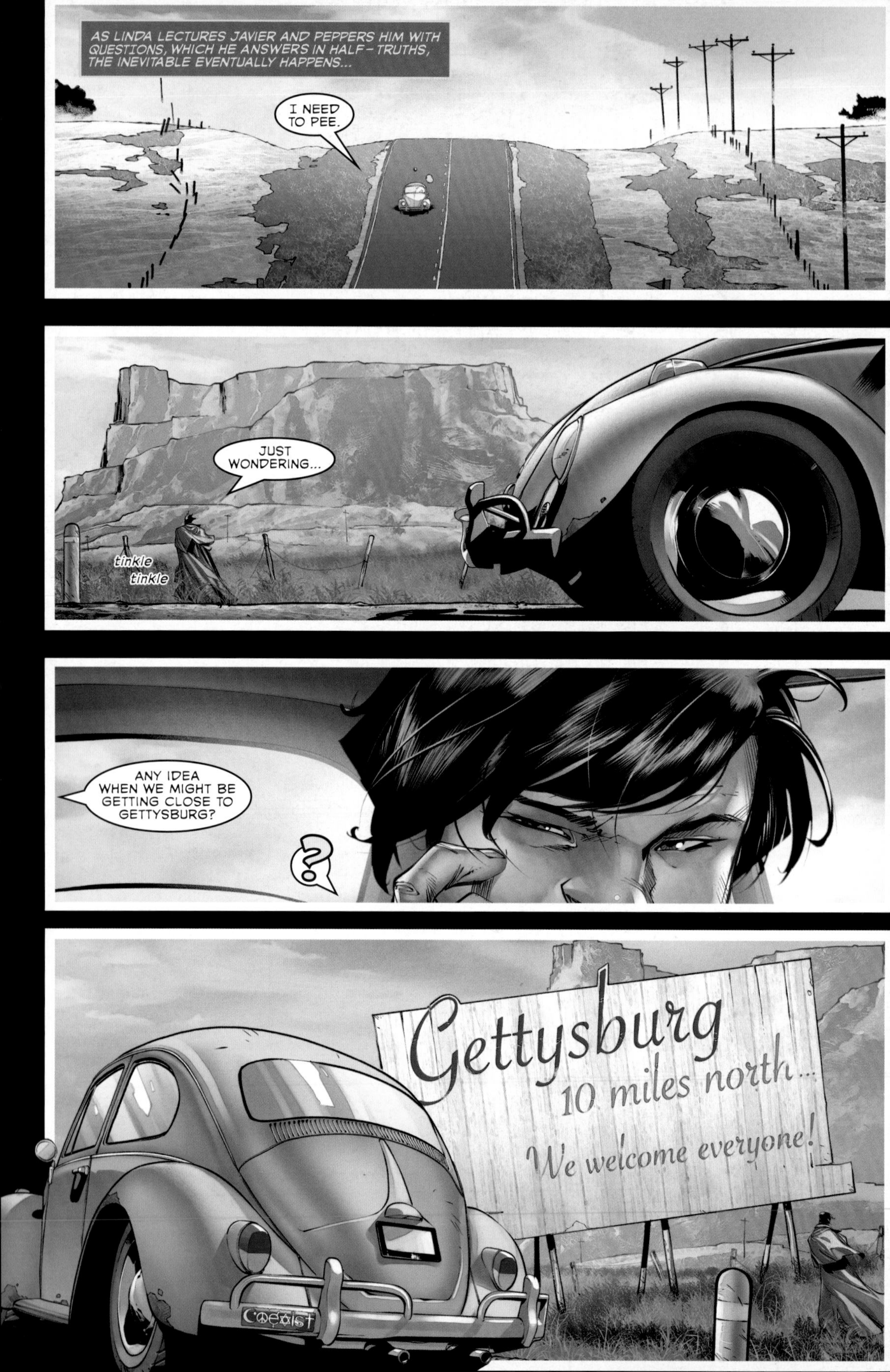
AS LINDA LECTURES JAVIER AND PEPPERS HIM WITH QUESTIONS, WHICH HE ANSWERS IN HALF-TRUTHS, THE INEVITABLE EVENTUALLY HAPPENS...
I NEED TO PEE.
JUST WONDERING...
tinkle
tinkle
ANY IDEA WHEN WE MIGHT BE GETTING CLOSE TO GETTYSBURG?
?
Gettysburg
10 miles north...
We welcome everyone!

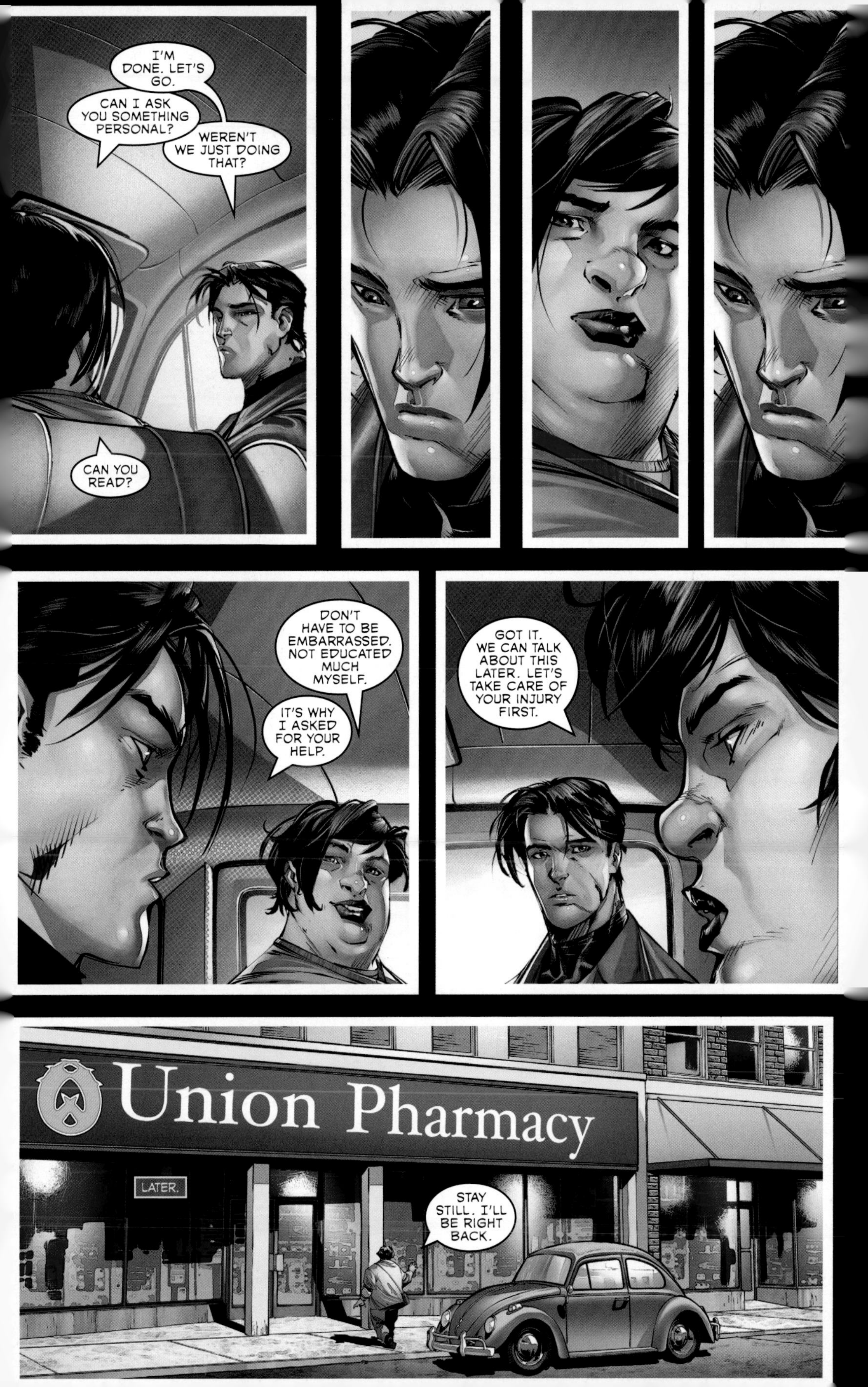

I'M DONE. LET'S GO.
CAN I ASK YOU SOMETHING PERSONAL?
WEREN'T WE JUST DOING THAT?
CAN YOU READ?
DON'T HAVE TO BE EMBARRASSED. NOT EDUCATED MUCH MYSELF.
IT'S WHY I ASKED FOR YOUR HELP.
GOT IT. WE CAN TALK ABOUT THIS LATER. LET'S TAKE CARE OF YOUR INJURY FIRST.
Union Pharmacy
LATER.
STAY STILL. I'LL BE RIGHT BACK.

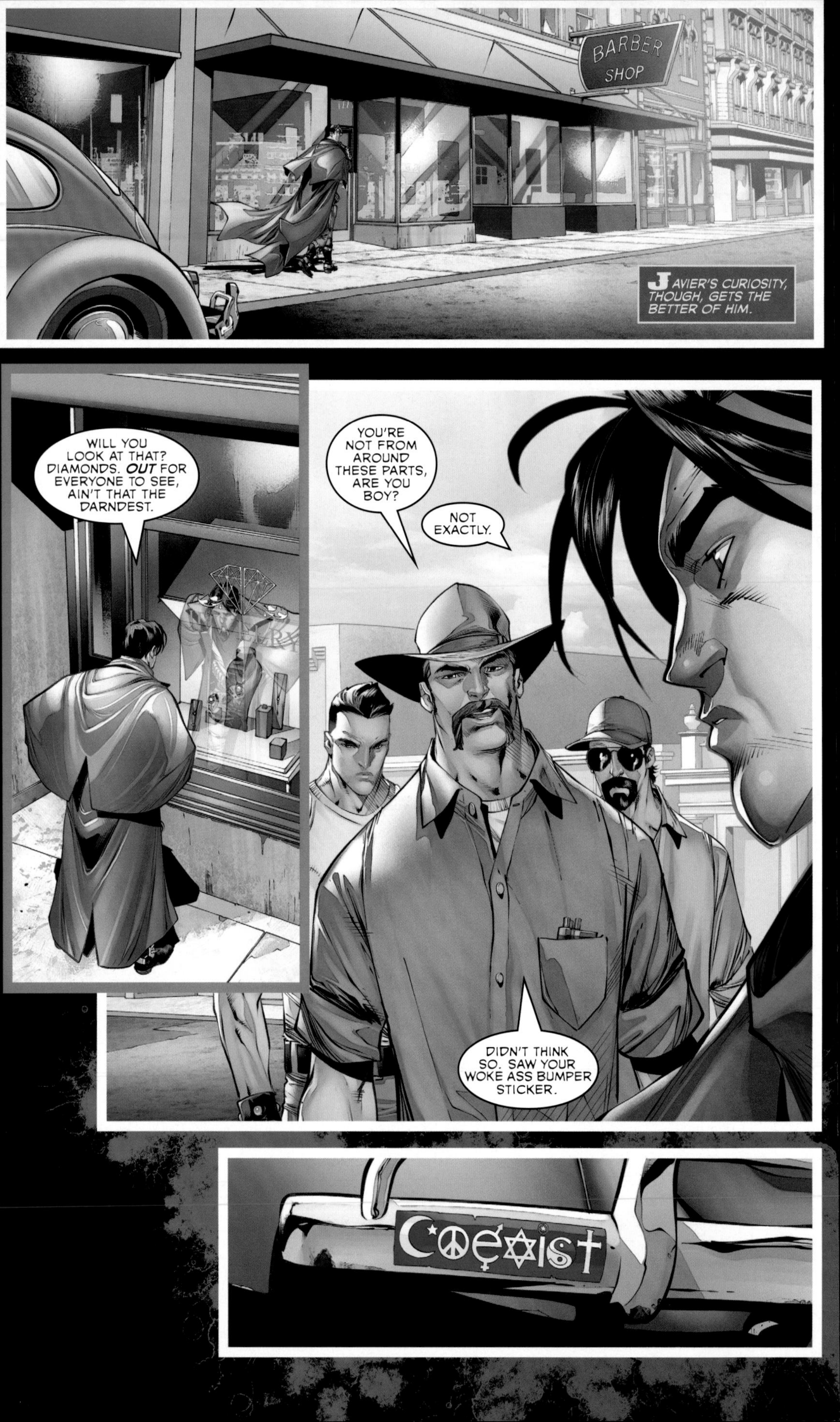
BARBER SHOP
JAVIER'S CURIOSITY, THOUGH, GETS THE BETTER OF HIM.
WILL YOU LOOK AT THAT? DIAMONDS. *OUT* FOR EVERYONE TO SEE, AIN'T THAT THE DARNDEST.
YOU'RE NOT FROM AROUND THESE PARTS, ARE YOU BOY?
NOT EXACTLY.
DIDN'T THINK SO. SAW YOUR WOKE ASS BUMPER STICKER.
COEXIST

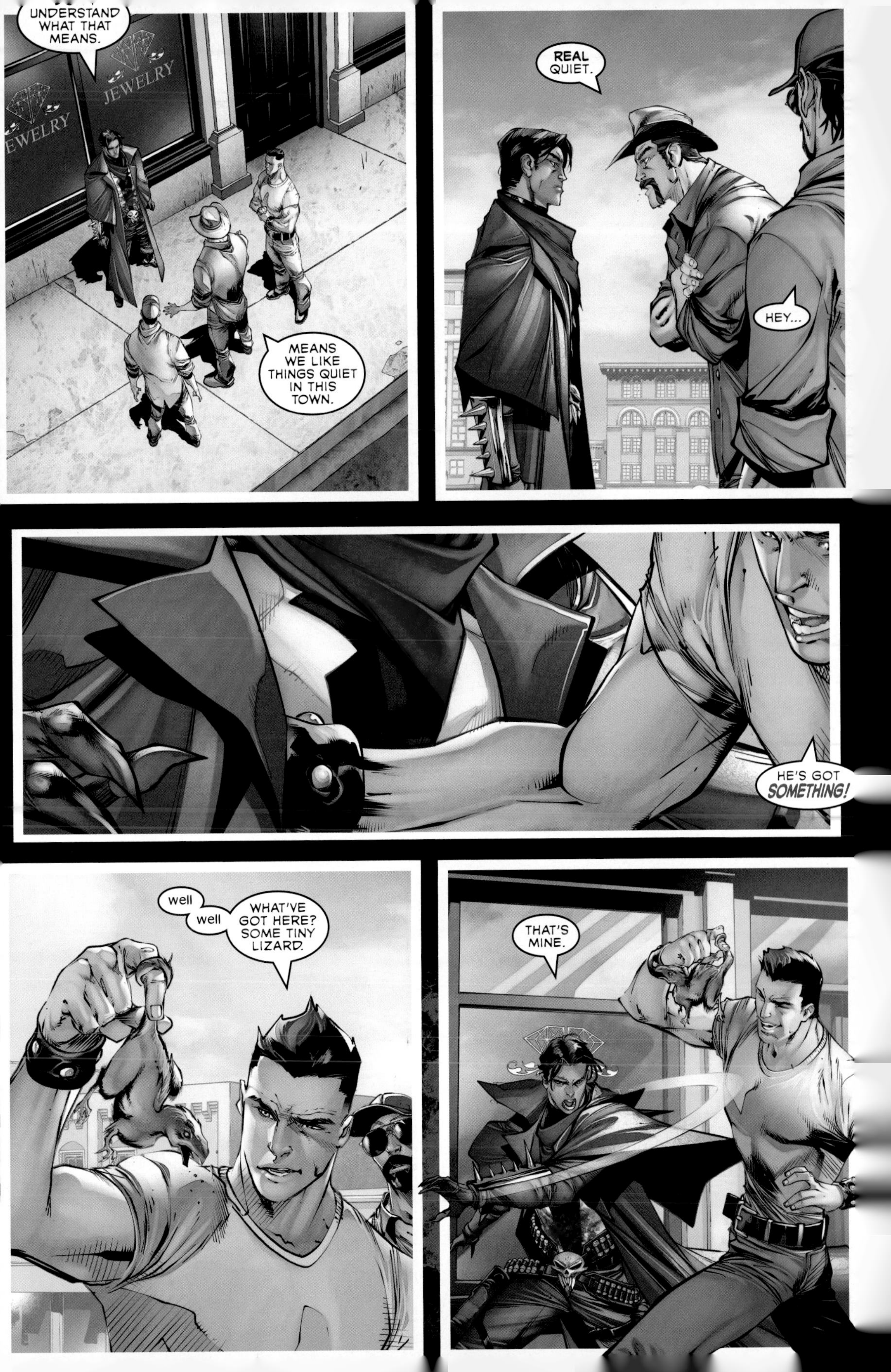
UNDERSTAND WHAT THAT MEANS.
JEWELRY
JEWELRY
MEANS WE LIKE THINGS QUIET IN THIS TOWN.
REAL QUIET.
HEY...
HE'S GOT SOMETHING!
well
well
WHAT'VE GOT HERE? SOME TINY LIZARD.
THAT'S MINE.

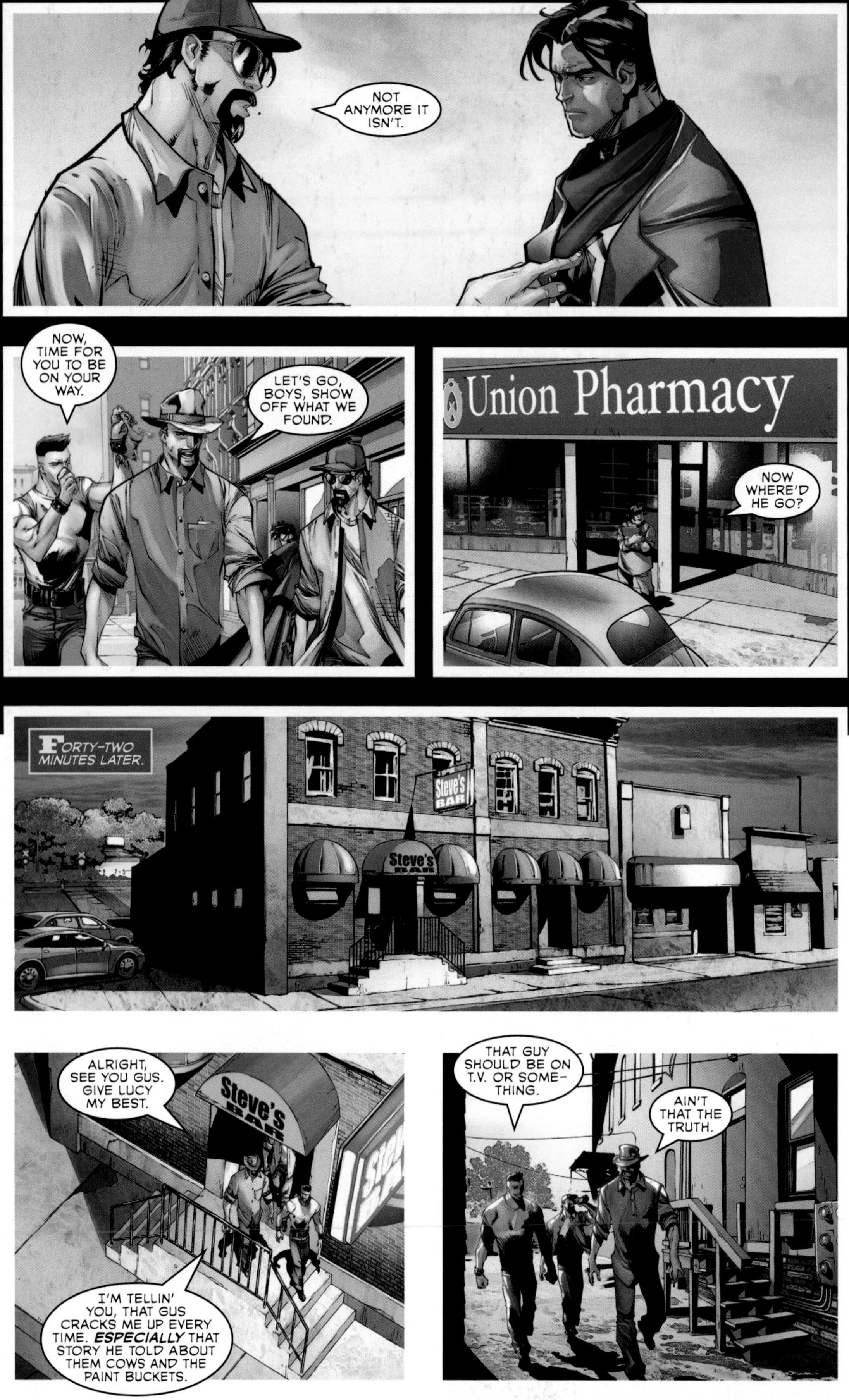
NOT ANYMORE IT ISN'T.
NOW, TIME FOR YOU TO BE ON YOUR WAY.
LET'S GO, BOYS, SHOW OFF WHAT WE FOUND.
Union Pharmacy
NOW WHERE'D HE GO?
FORTY-TWO MINUTES LATER.
Steve's BAR
Steve's BAR
ALRIGHT, SEE YOU GUS. GIVE LUCY MY BEST.
Steve's BAR
I'M TELLIN' YOU, THAT GUS CRACKS ME UP EVERY TIME. *ESPECIALLY* THAT STORY HE TOLD ABOUT THEM COWS AND THE PAINT BUCKETS.
THAT GUY SHOULD BE ON T.V. OR SOMETHING.
AIN'T THAT THE TRUTH.

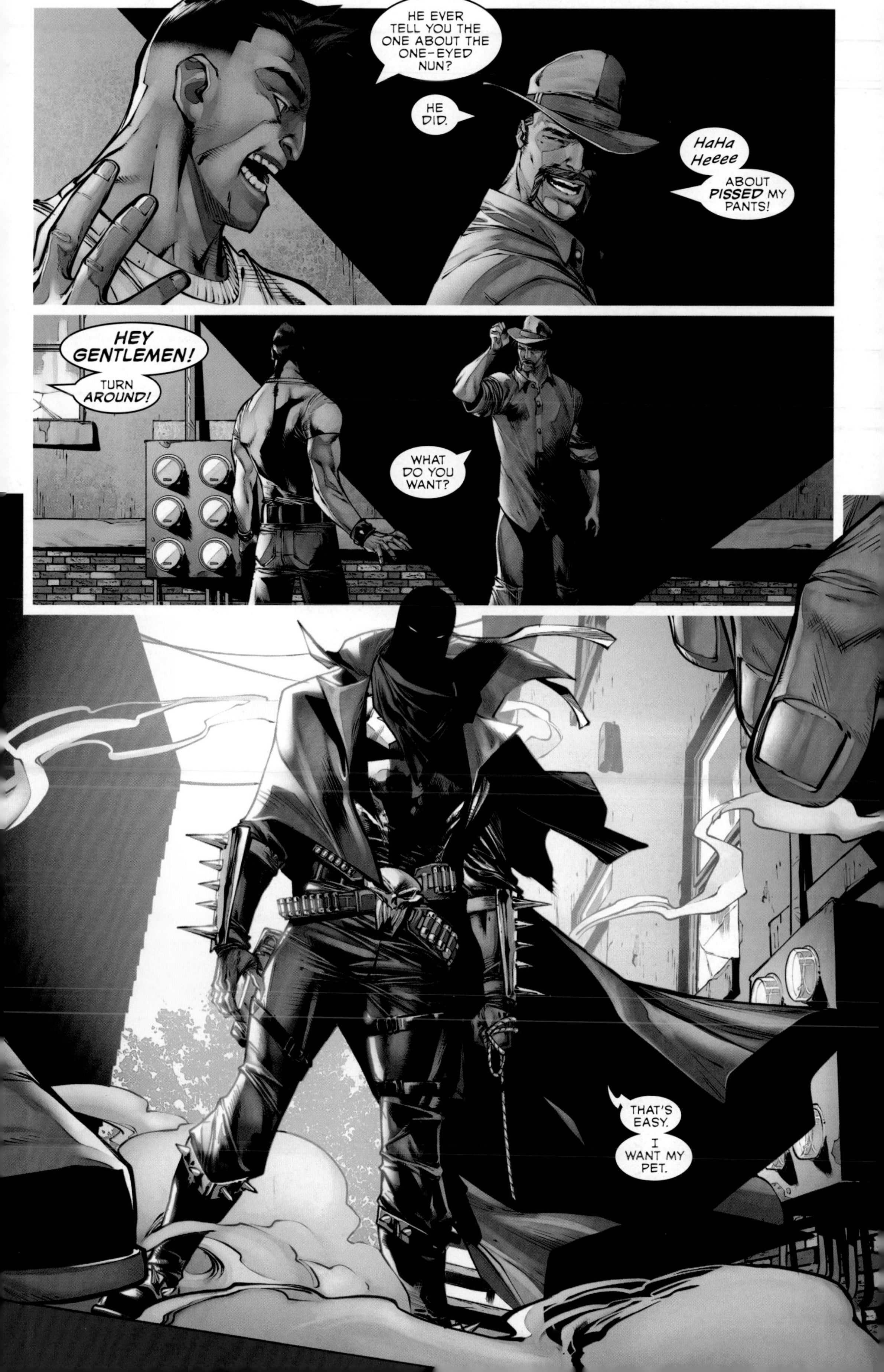
HE EVER TELL YOU THE ONE ABOUT THE ONE-EYED NUN?
HE DID.
HaHa Heeee
ABOUT PISSED MY PANTS!
HEY GENTLEMEN!
TURN AROUND!
WHAT DO YOU WANT?
THAT'S EASY.
I WANT MY PET.

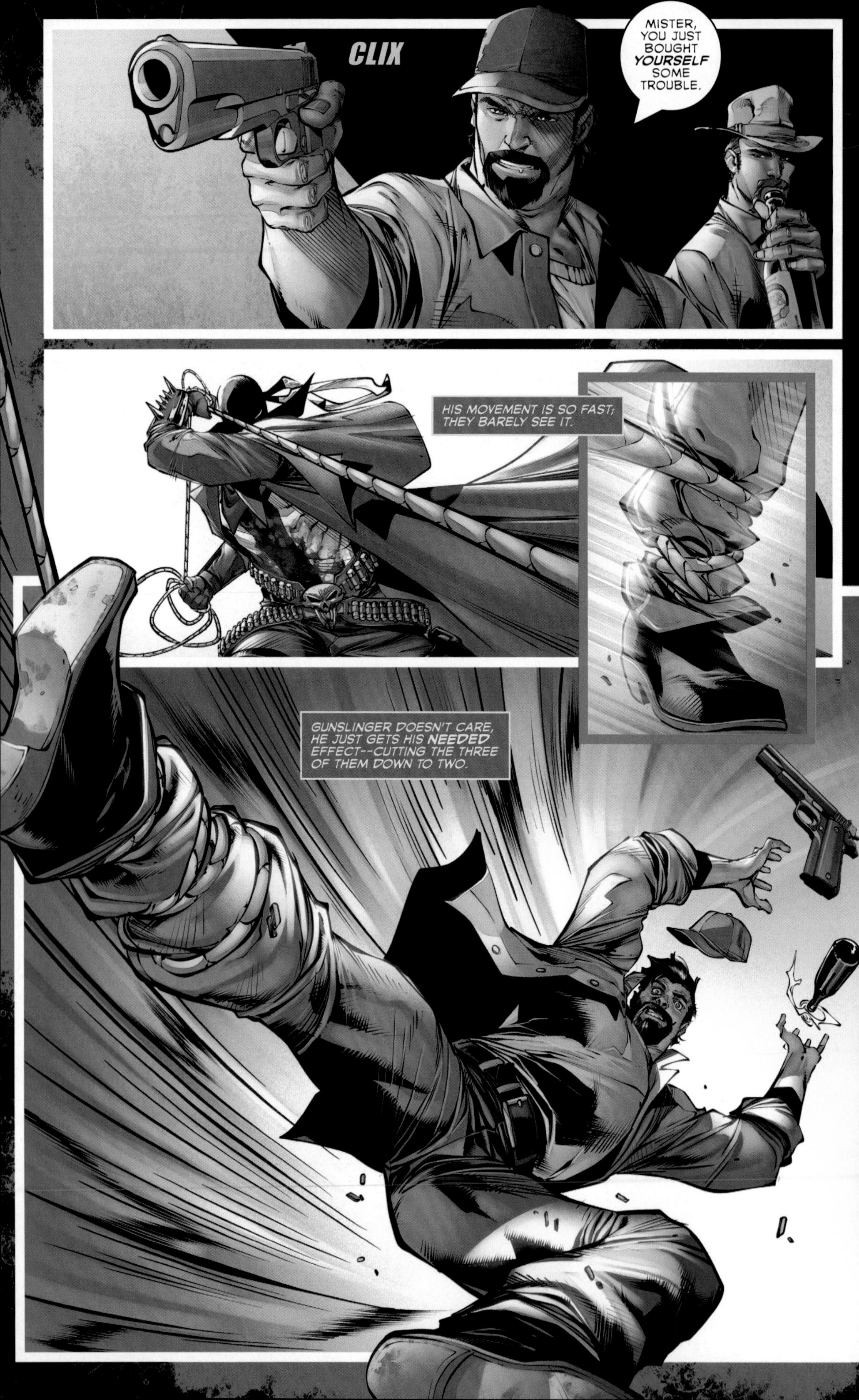
CLIX
MISTER, YOU JUST BOUGHT YOURSELF SOME TROUBLE.
HIS MOVEMENT IS SO FAST; THEY BARELY SEE IT.
GUNSLINGER DOESN'T CARE, HE JUST GETS HIS NEEDED EFFECT--CUTTING THE THREE OF THEM DOWN TO TWO.

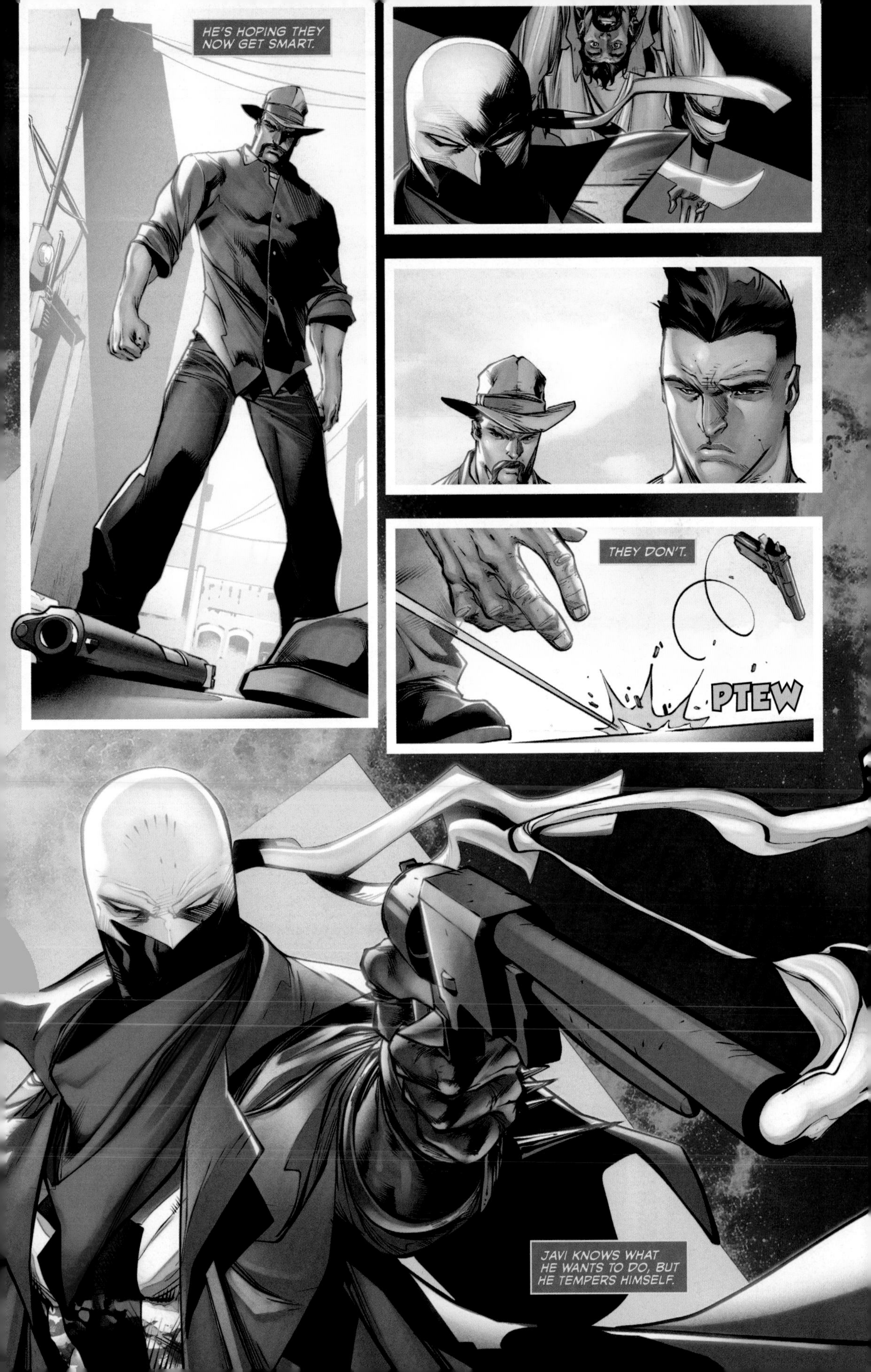
HE'S HOPING THEY NOW GET SMART.
THEY DON'T.
PTEW
JAVI KNOWS WHAT HE WANTS TO DO, BUT HE TEMPERS HIMSELF.

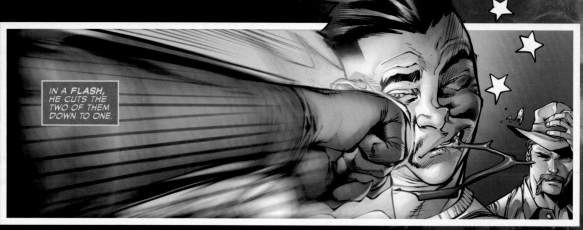

IN A FLASH, HE CUTS THE TWO OF THEM DOWN TO ONE.

YOU WANT YOUR PET?

GOT HIM RIGHT HERE. NOW, DROP YOUR GUN.

BEFORE I BREAK ITS F*CKING NECK.

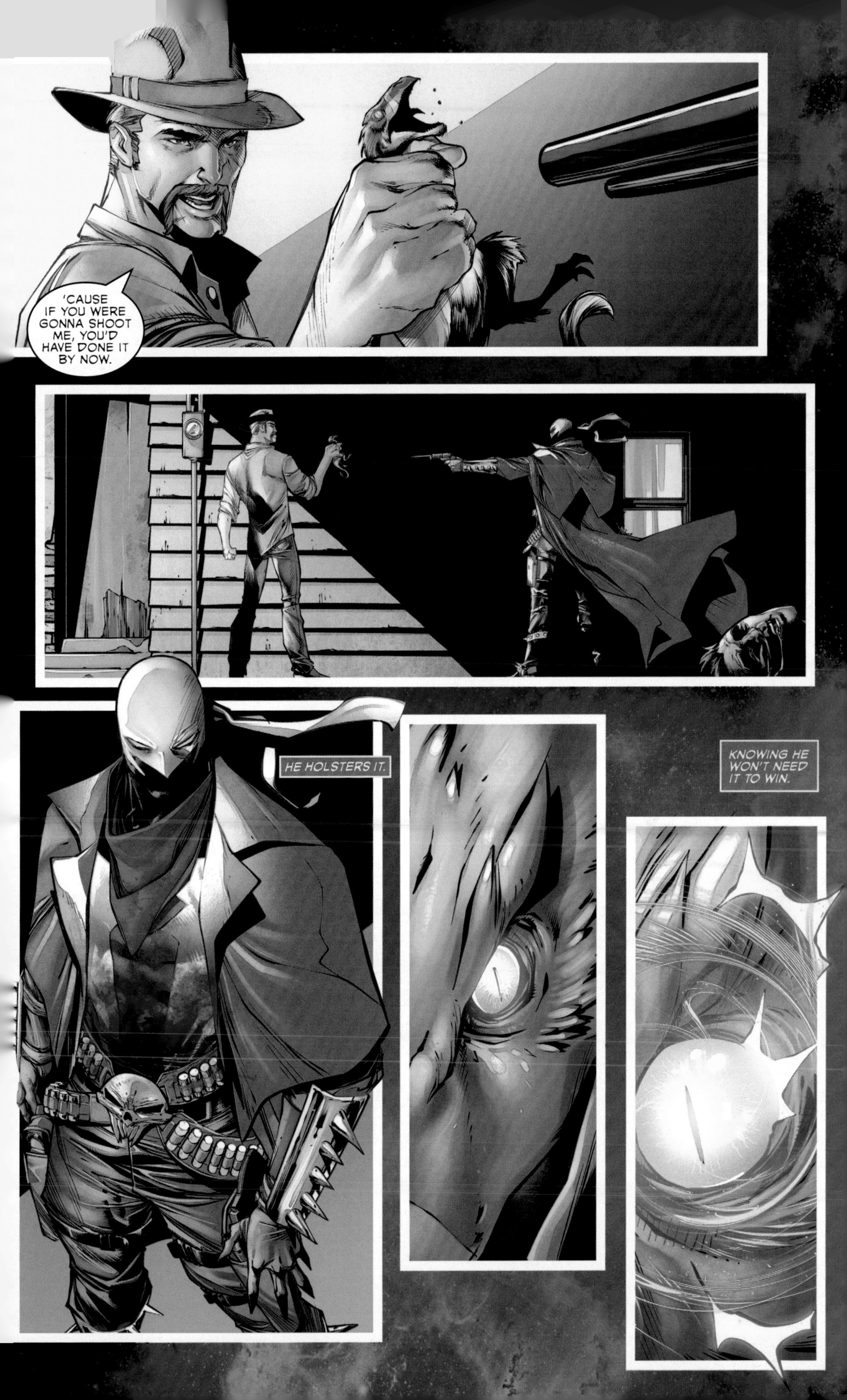
'CAUSE IF YOU WERE GONNA SHOOT ME, YOU'D HAVE DONE IT BY NOW.
HE HOLSTERS IT.
KNOWING HE WON'T NEED IT TO WIN.

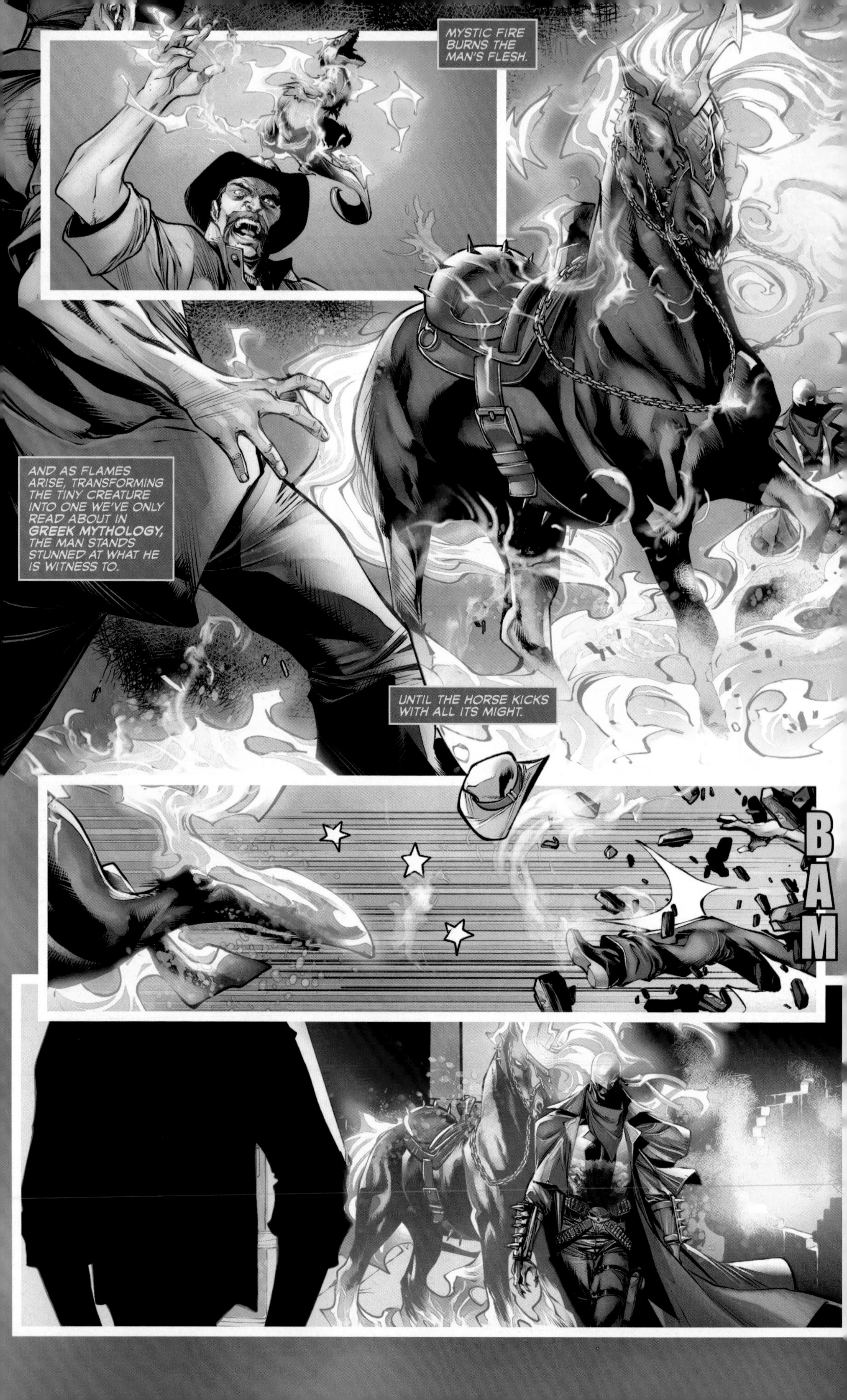
MYSTIC FIRE BURNS THE MAN'S FLESH.
AND AS FLAMES ARISE, TRANSFORMING THE TINY CREATURE INTO ONE WE'VE ONLY READ ABOUT IN **GREEK MYTHOLOGY,** THE MAN STANDS STUNNED AT WHAT HE IS WITNESS TO.
UNTIL THE HORSE KICKS WITH ALL ITS MIGHT.
BAM

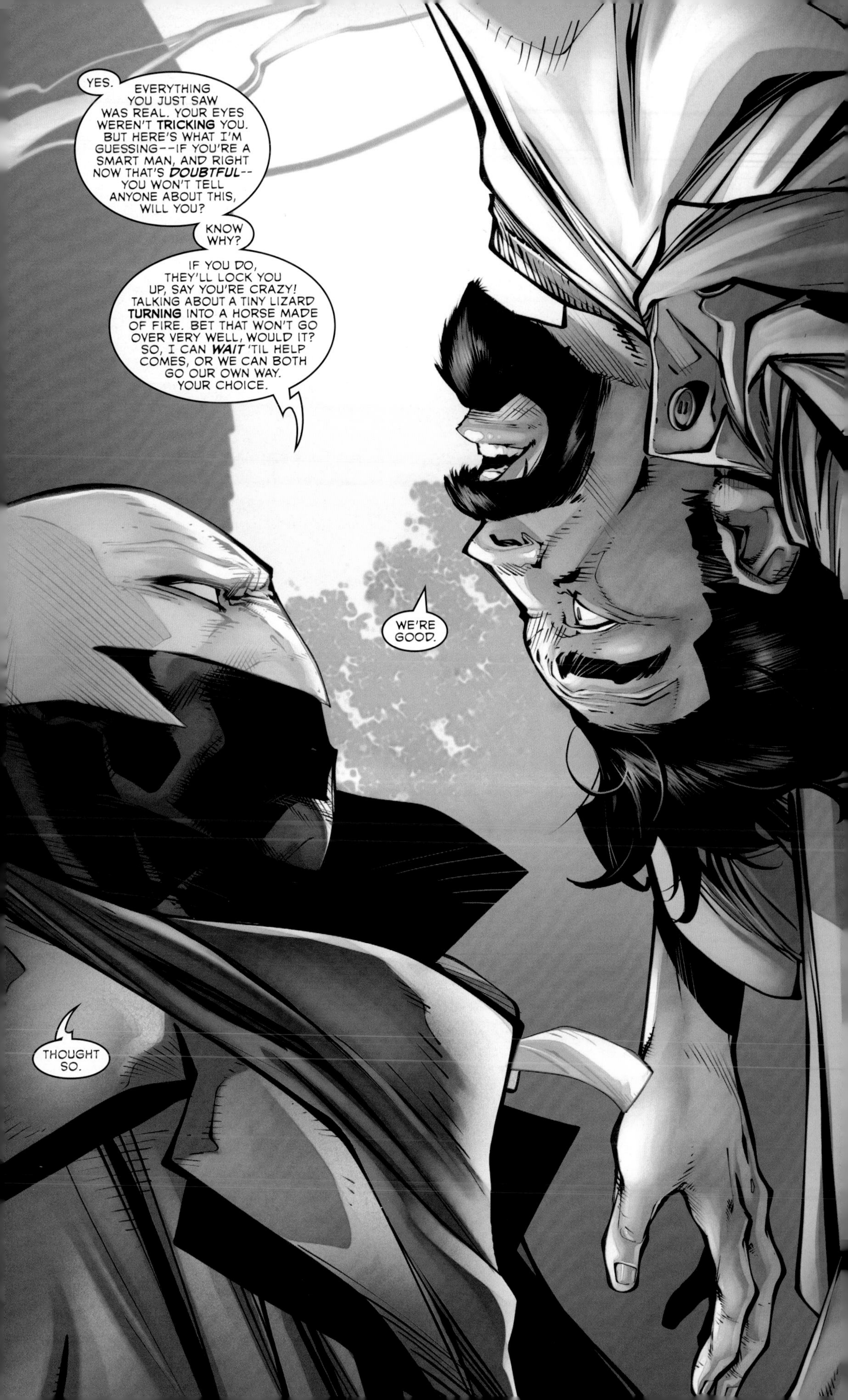
YES.
EVERYTHING YOU JUST SAW WAS REAL. YOUR EYES WEREN'T **TRICKING** YOU. BUT HERE'S WHAT I'M GUESSING--IF YOU'RE A SMART MAN, AND RIGHT NOW THAT'S ***DOUBTFUL***--YOU WON'T TELL ANYONE ABOUT THIS, WILL YOU?
KNOW WHY?
IF YOU DO, THEY'LL LOCK YOU UP, SAY YOU'RE CRAZY! TALKING ABOUT A TINY LIZARD **TURNING** INTO A HORSE MADE OF FIRE. BET THAT WON'T GO OVER VERY WELL, WOULD IT? SO, I CAN ***WAIT*** 'TIL HELP COMES, OR WE CAN BOTH GO OUR OWN WAY. YOUR CHOICE.
WE'RE GOOD.
THOUGHT SO.

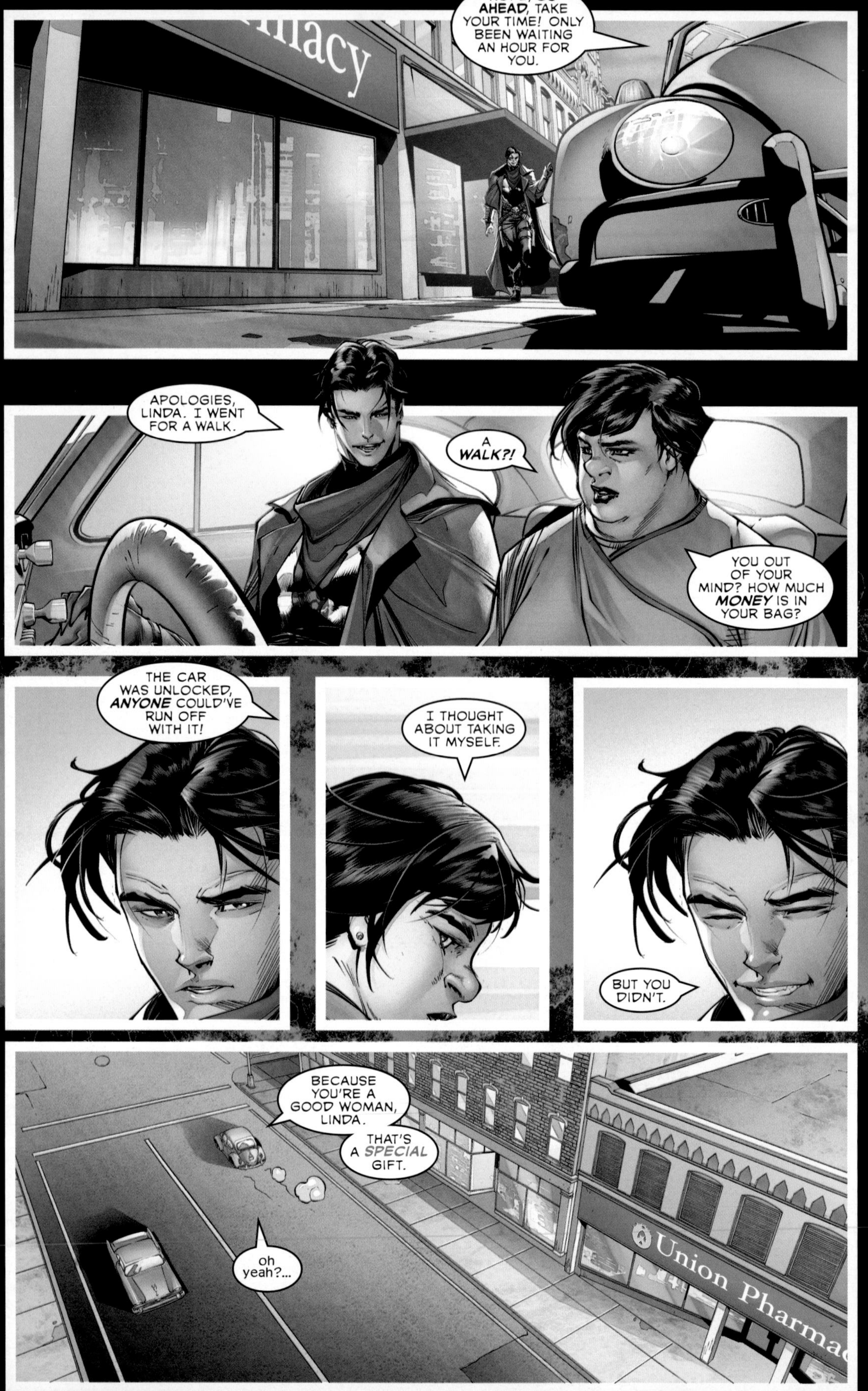
rmacy
NOPE, **GO AHEAD**, TAKE YOUR TIME! ONLY BEEN WAITING AN HOUR FOR YOU.
APOLOGIES, LINDA. I WENT FOR A WALK.
A ***WALK?!***
YOU OUT OF YOUR MIND? HOW MUCH ***MONEY*** IS IN YOUR BAG?
THE CAR WAS UNLOCKED, ***ANYONE*** COULD'VE RUN OFF WITH IT!
I THOUGHT ABOUT TAKING IT MYSELF.
BUT YOU DIDN'T.
BECAUSE YOU'RE A GOOD WOMAN, LINDA.
THAT'S A *SPECIAL* GIFT.
oh yeah?...
Union Pharma

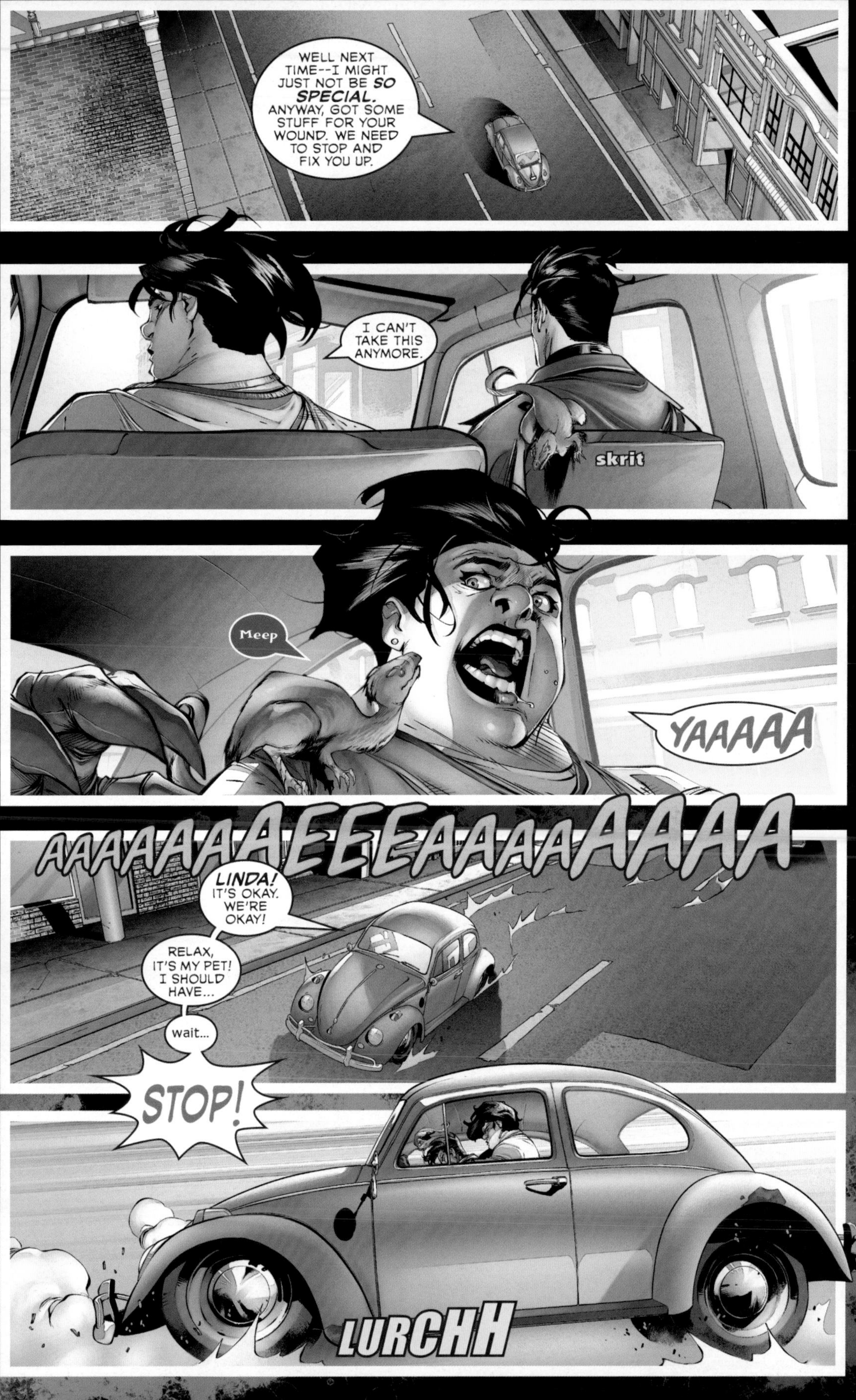

WELL NEXT TIME--I MIGHT JUST NOT BE SO SPECIAL. ANYWAY, GOT SOME STUFF FOR YOUR WOUND. WE NEED TO STOP AND FIX YOU UP.
I CAN'T TAKE THIS ANYMORE.
skrit
Meep
YAAAAA
AAAAAAAEEEAAAAAAAAA
LINDA! IT'S OKAY. WE'RE OKAY!
RELAX, IT'S MY PET! I SHOULD HAVE...
wait...
STOP!
LURCHH

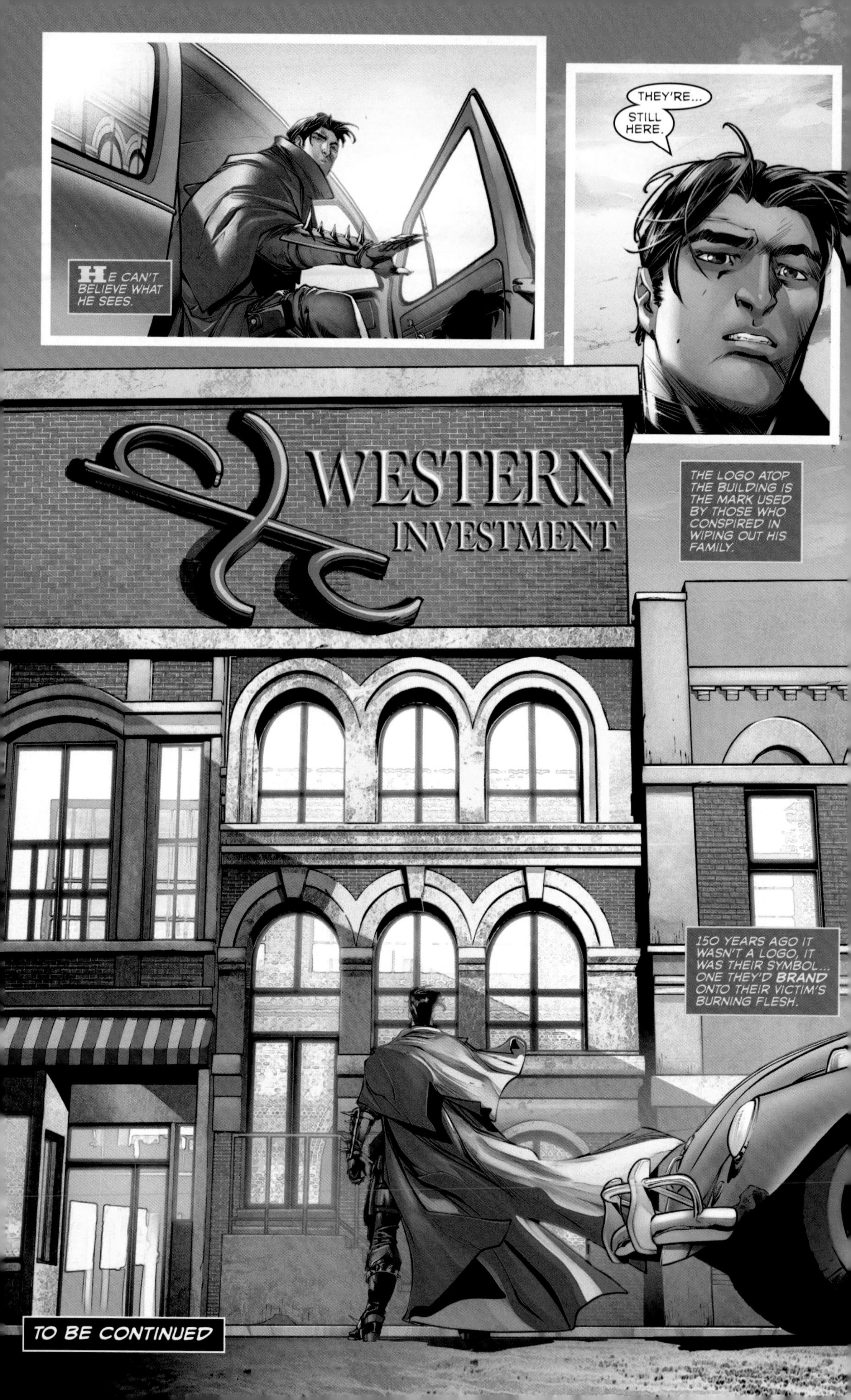
HE CAN'T BELIEVE WHAT HE SEES.
THEY'RE...
STILL HERE.
WESTERN INVESTMENT
THE LOGO ATOP THE BUILDING IS THE MARK USED BY THOSE WHO CONSPIRED IN WIPING OUT HIS FAMILY.
150 YEARS AGO IT WASN'T A LOGO, IT WAS THEIR SYMBOL... ONE THEY'D BRAND ONTO THEIR VICTIM'S BURNING FLESH.
TO BE CONTINUED

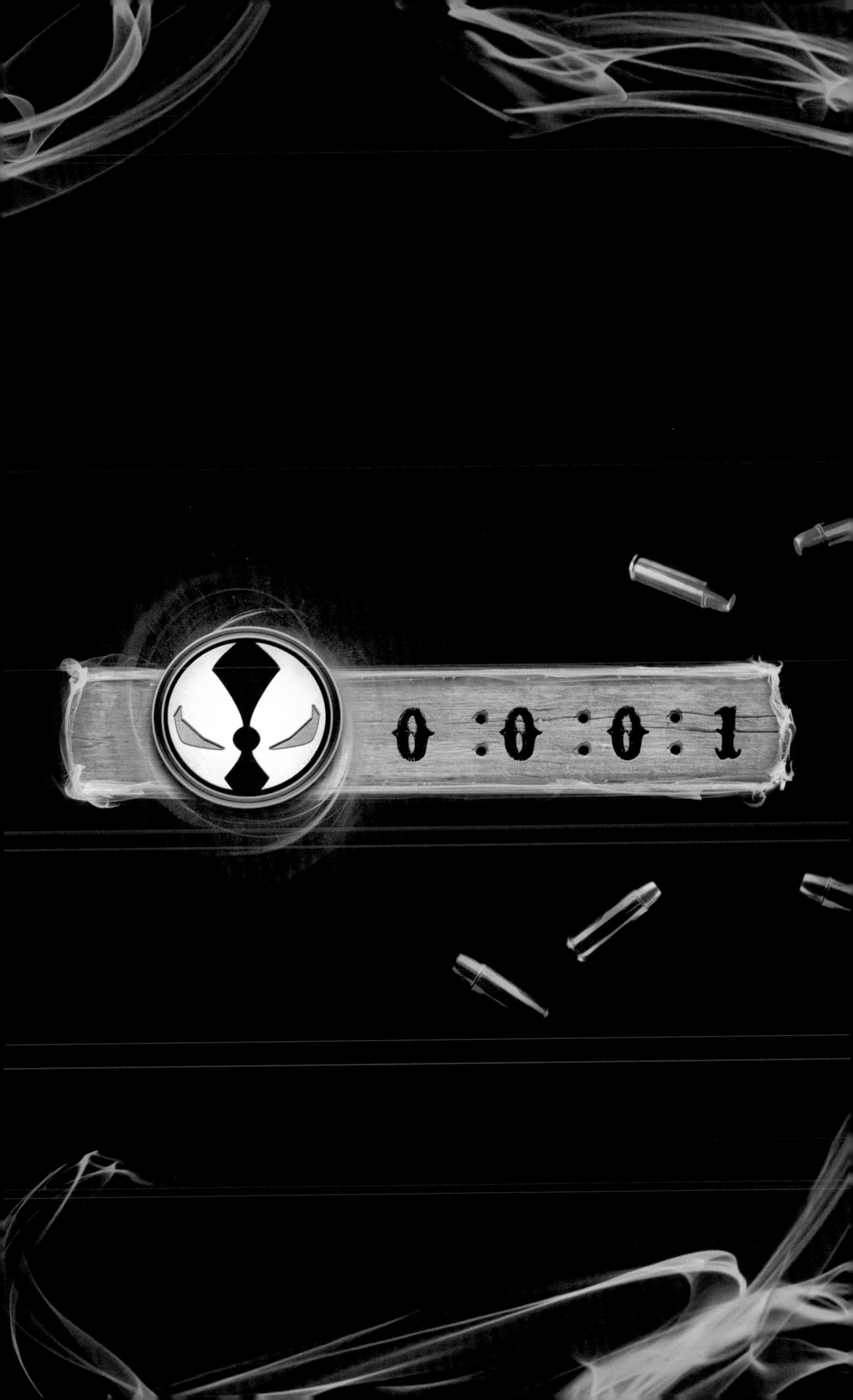
0:0:0:1

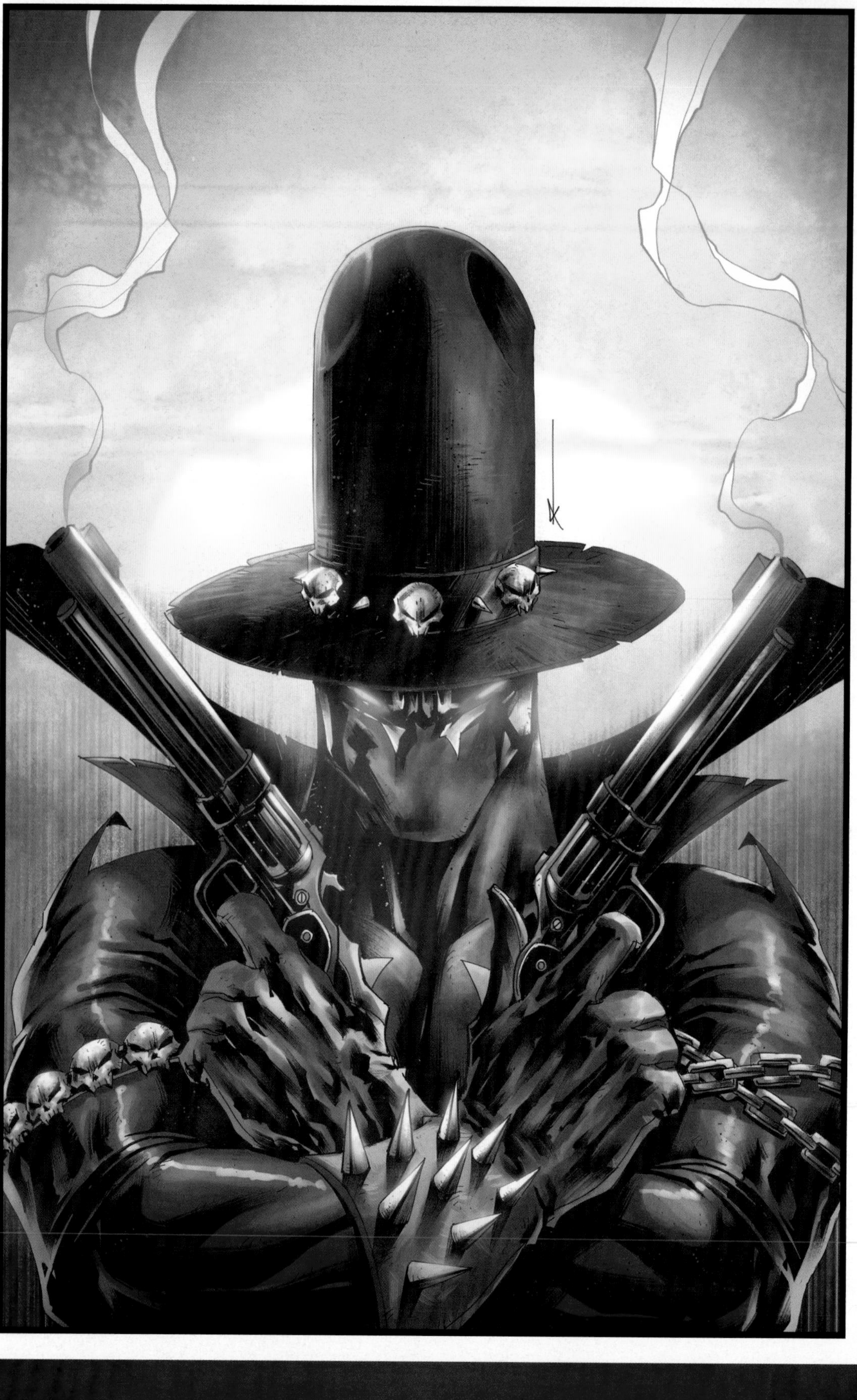

GUNSLINGER SPAWN #25 COVER 'B' BY KEVIN KEANE

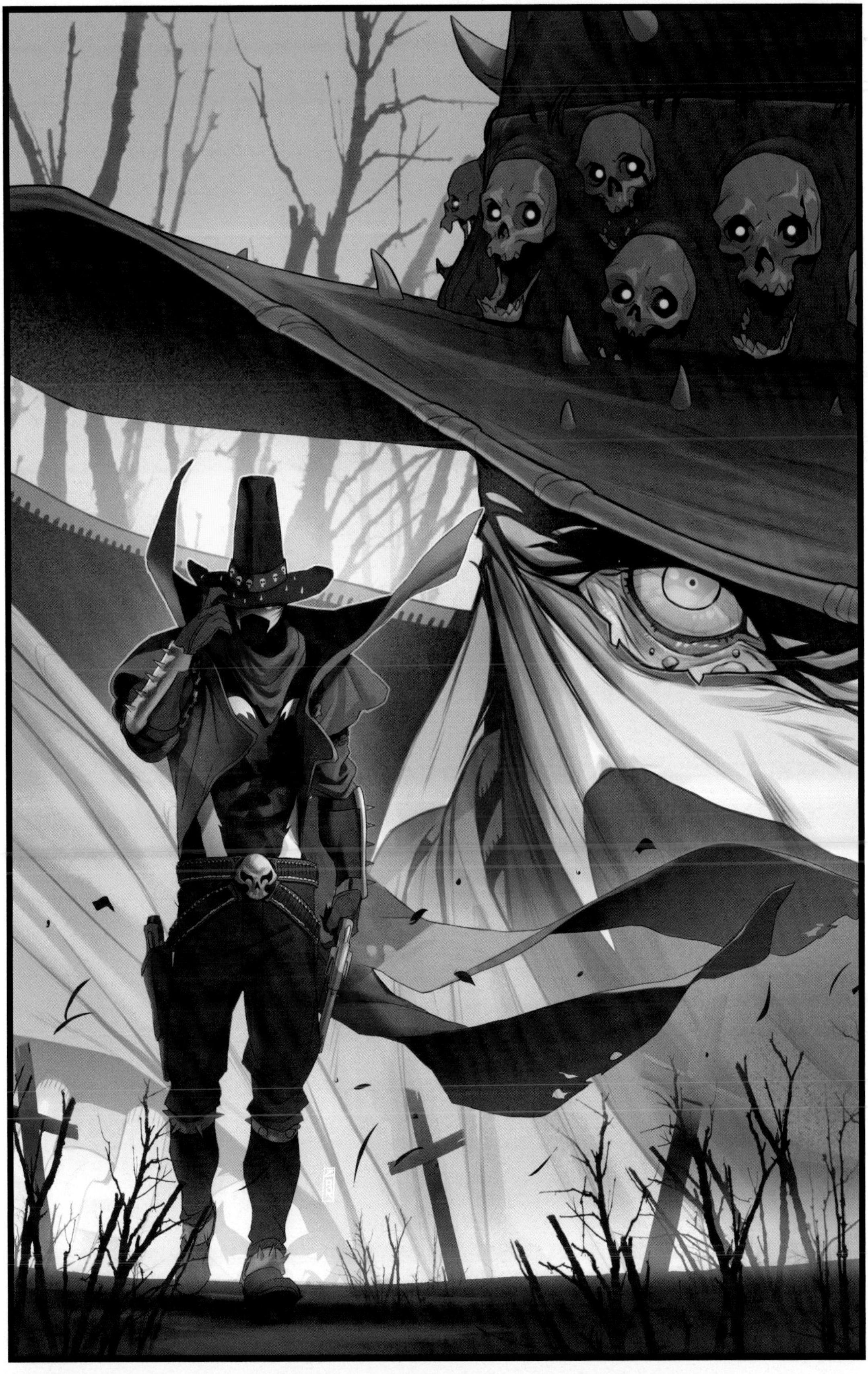

GUNSLINGER SPAWN #26 COVER 'B' BY GABRIEL GOMEZ

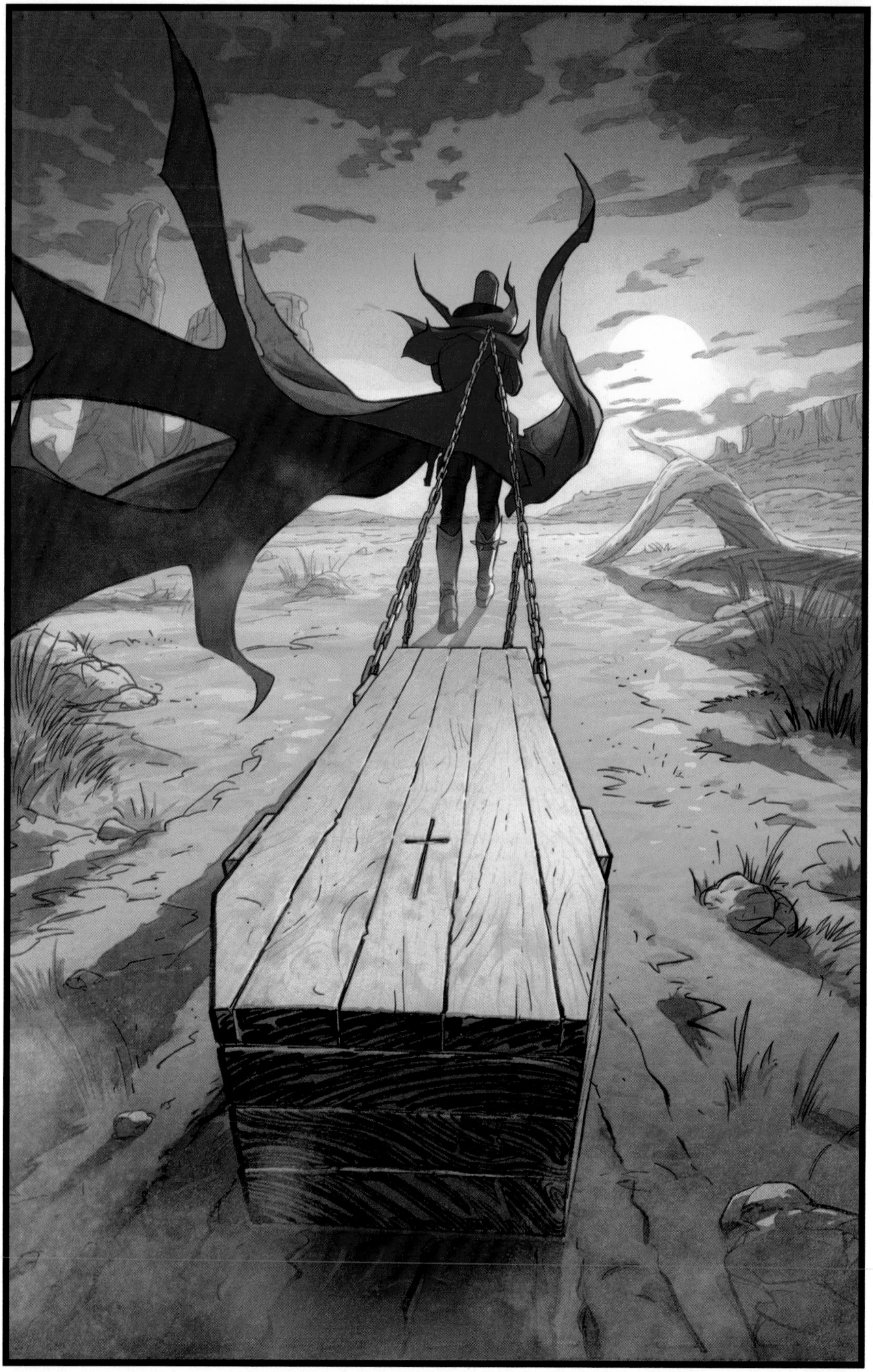

GUNSLINGER SPAWN #27 COVER 'B' BY MARCIAL TOLEDANO

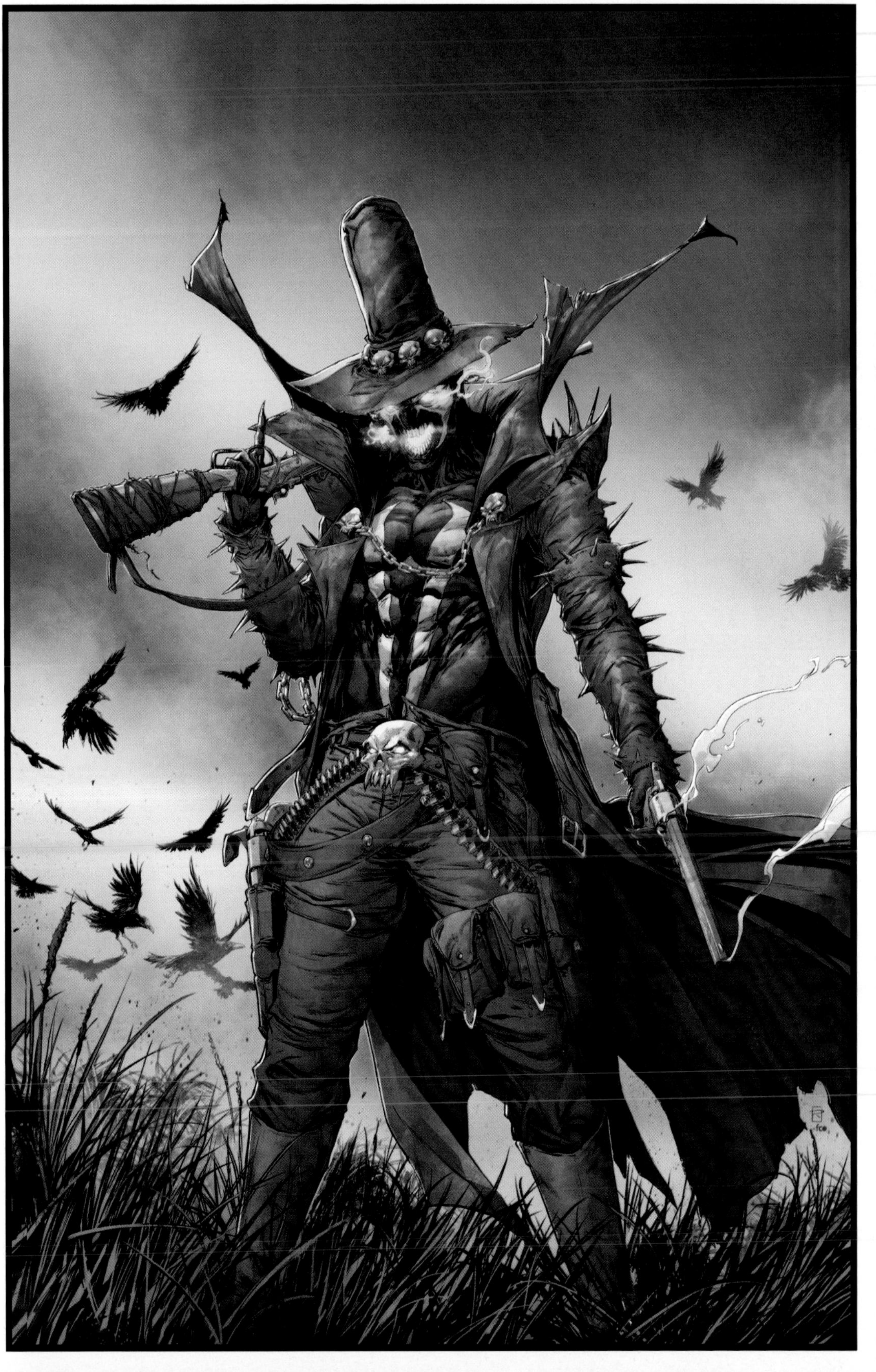

GUNSLINGER SPAWN #28 COVER 'B' BY RAYMOND GAY

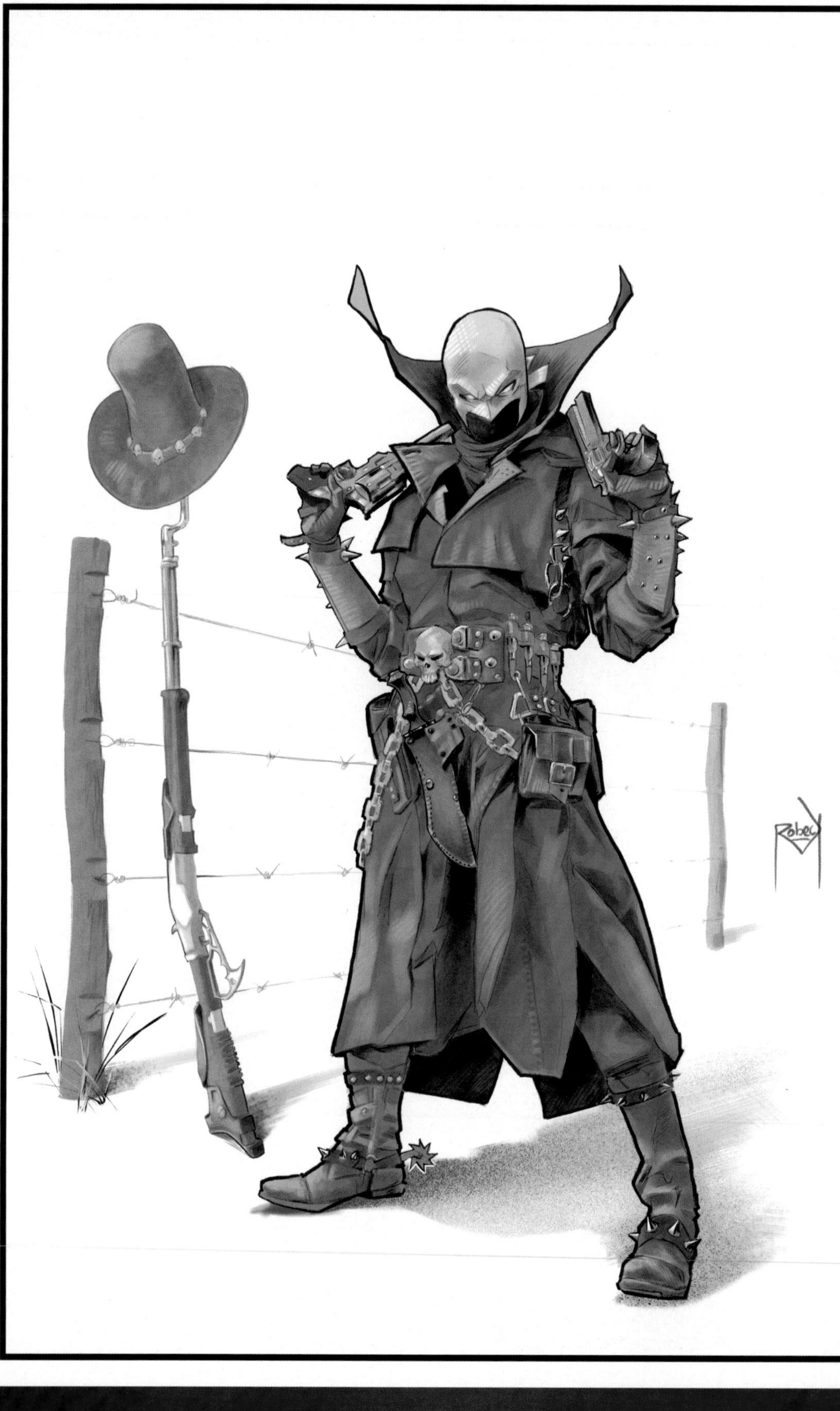
Robeck

GUNSLINGER SPAWN #29 COVER 'B' BY THADDEUS ROBECK

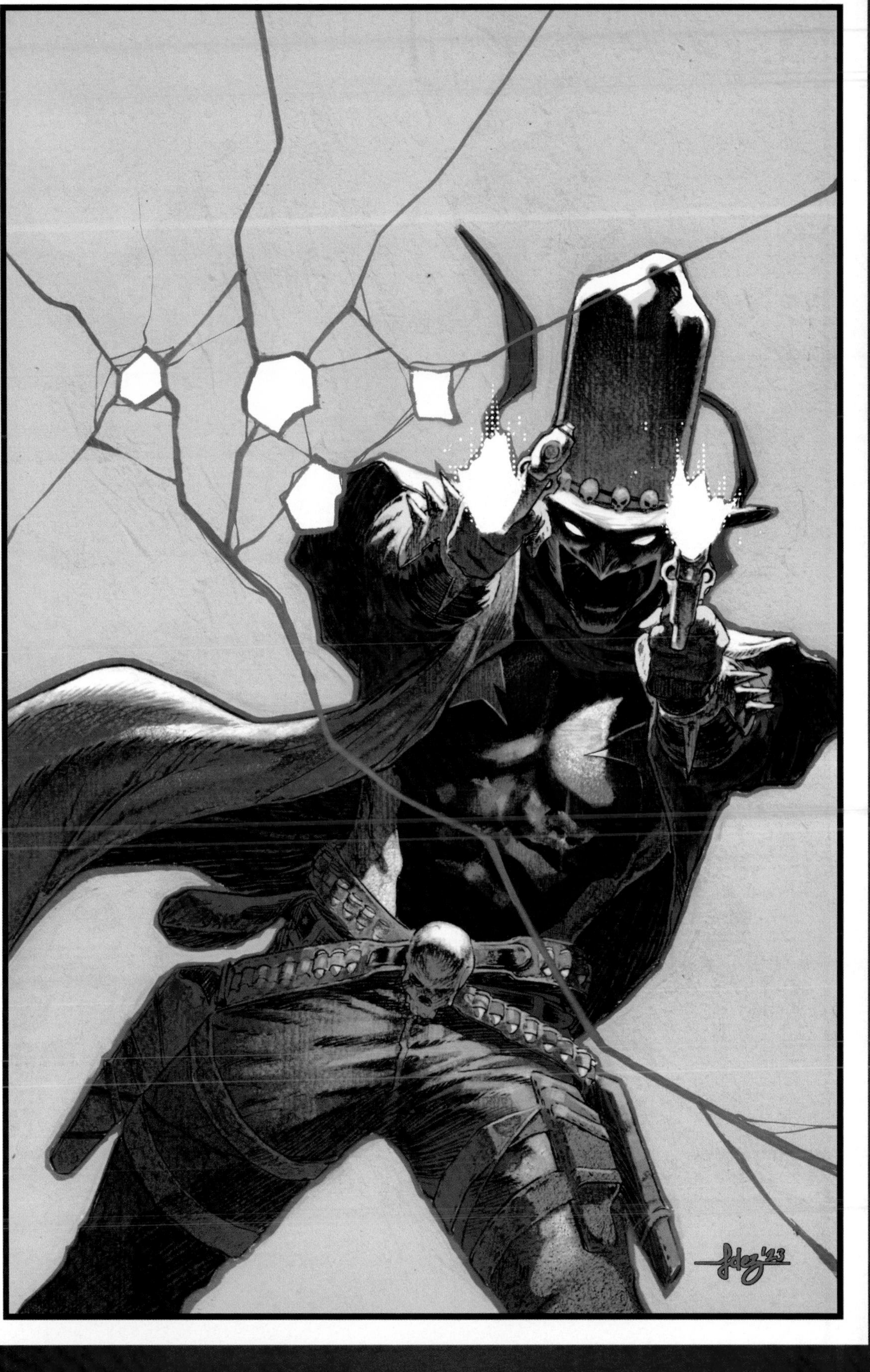
fdez '23

GUNSLINGER SPAWN #30 COVER 'B' BY JAVI FERNANDEZ

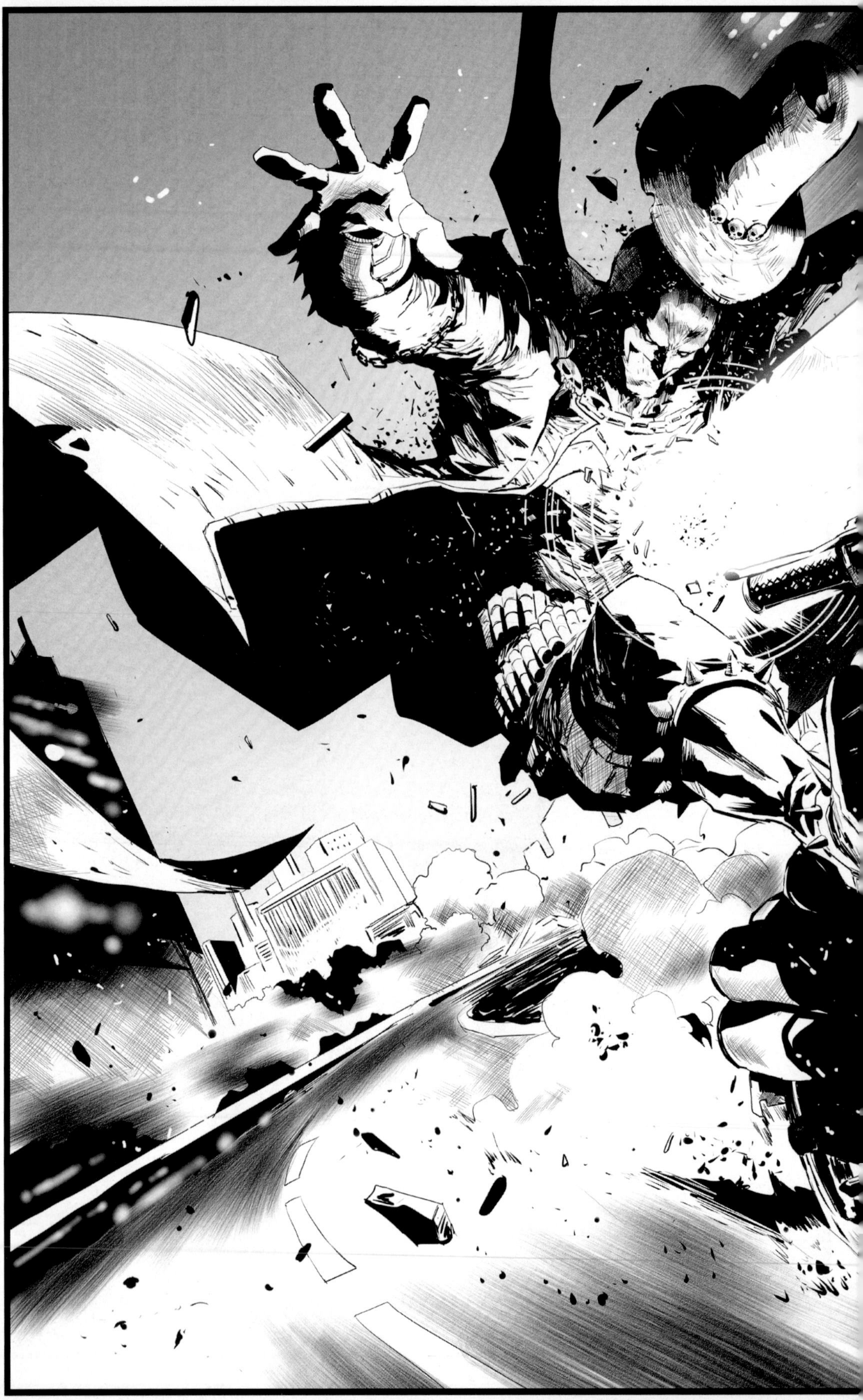

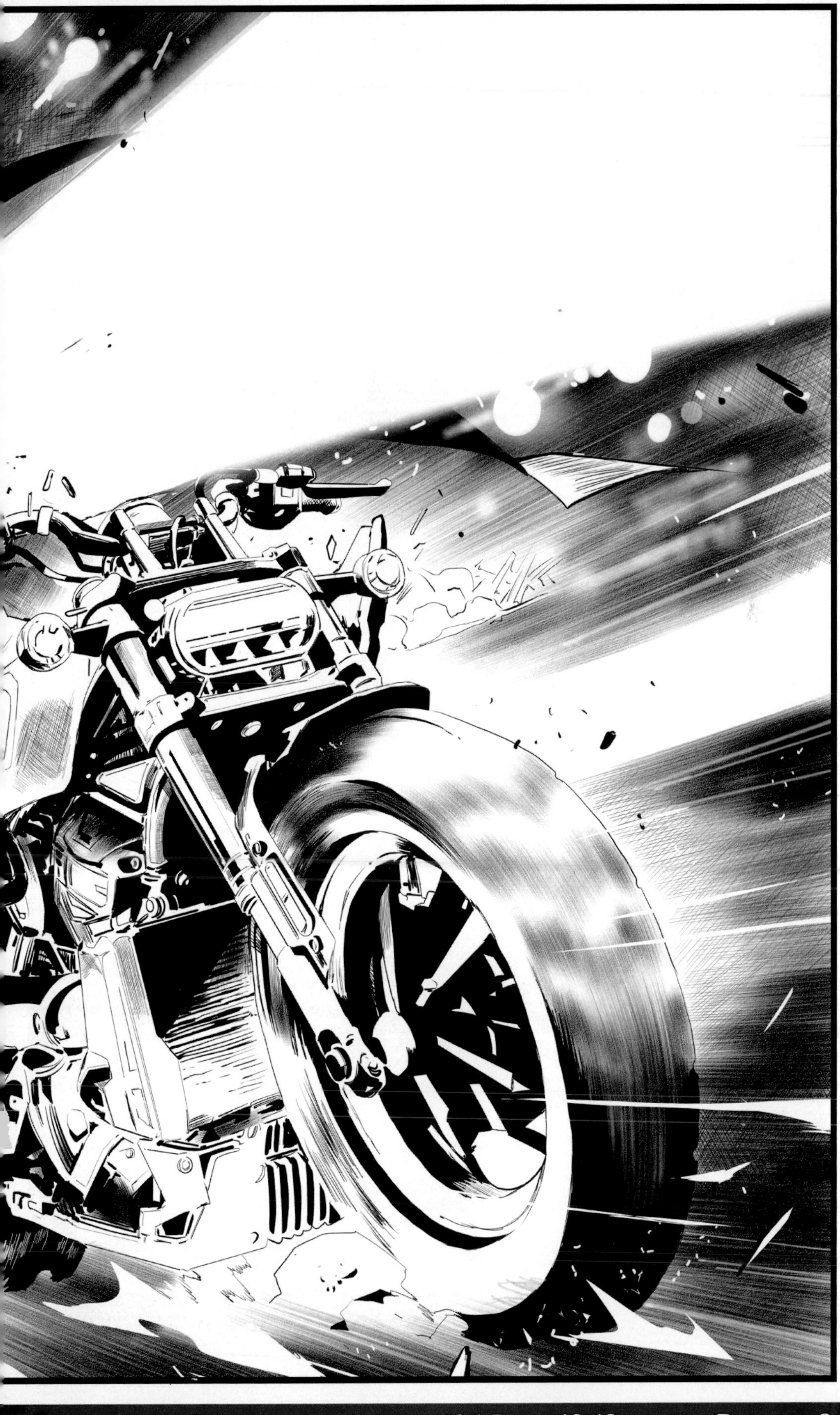

GUNSLINGER SPAWN #26 PAGE 18-19 ART BY DEXTER SOY

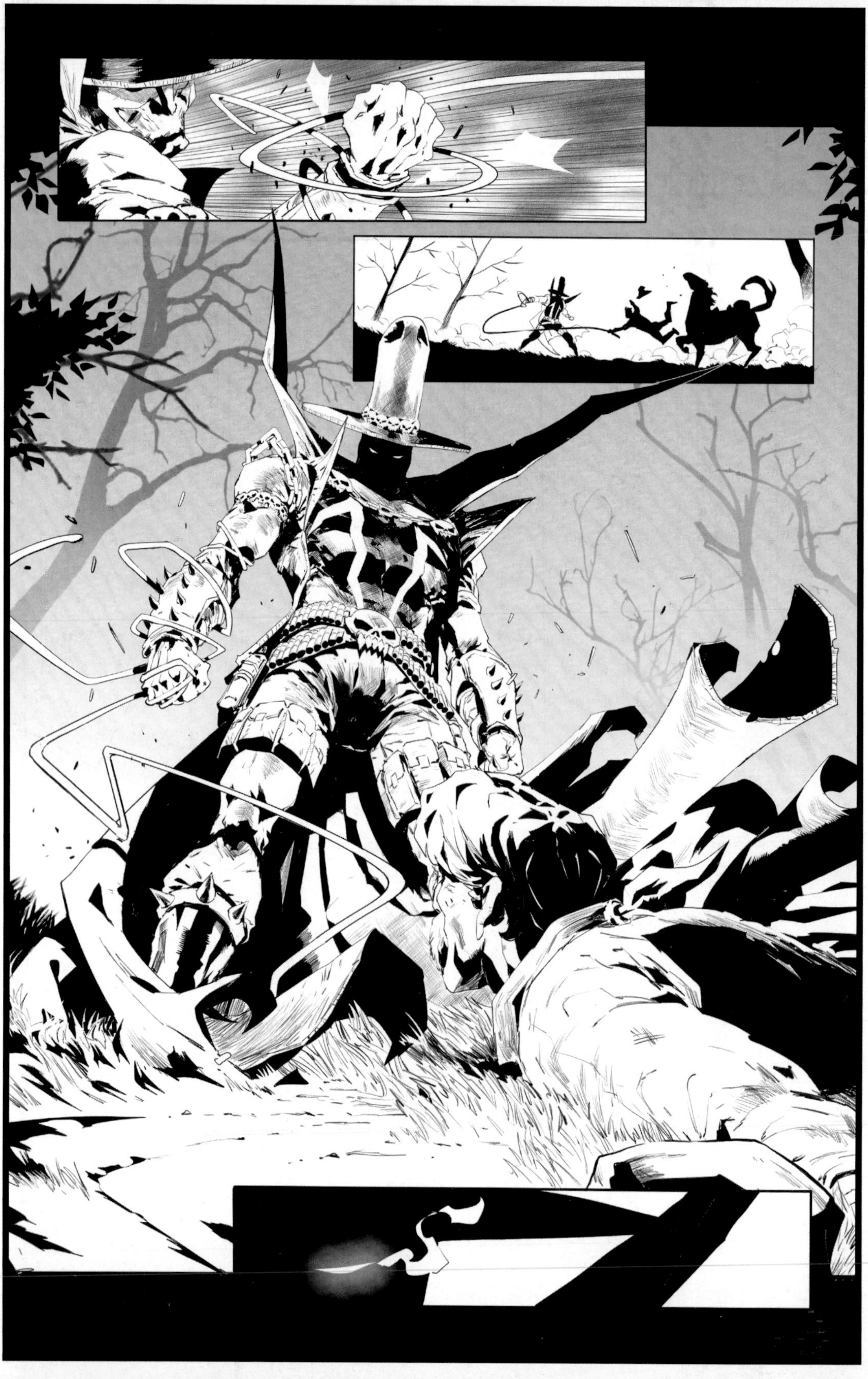

Gunslinger Spawn #27 Page 13 art by Dexter Soy